net.wars

net.wars

Wendy M. Grossman

NEW YORK UNIVERSITY PRESS
New York and London

NEW YORK UNIVERSITY PRESS
New York and London

© 1997 by Wendy M. Grossman

Library of Congress Cataloging-in-Publication Data
Grossman, Wendy, 1954–
Net.wars / Wendy M. Grossman.
p.   cm.
Includes bibliographical references and index.
ISBN 0-8147-3103-1 (cloth : acid-free paper)
1. Internet (Computer network)—Social aspects.   2. Electronic
discussion groups—Social aspects.   I. Title.   II. Title: Netwars.
III. Title: Net wars.
ZA4201.G74   1997
303.48'33—dc21   97-21214
                    CIP

New York University Press books are printed on acid-free paper,
and their binding materials are chosen for strength and durability.

Manufactured in the United States of America

10 9 8 7 6 5 4 3 2 1

Contents

Acknowledgments

I hate being edited, so I'm not going to suggest that Tim Bart-lett in any way improved the quality of this book with his care, attention, and comments, even though he did risk near-certain death to do it (edit this!). I would like to thank, though, the many editors at the *Guardian, PC Answers, Internet Today,* and *Personal Computer World,* who commissioned much of the work on which this book is based: Jack Schofied, Bill O'Neill, Azeem Azhar, Tom Standage, Ben Rooney, Steve Patience, Richard Baguley, and Ben Tisdall, who also began the whole business by loaning me a modem and some communications software to write a beginner's piece about BBSs. Dan ("hacks the media") O'Brien at the now defunct *Wired UK* was the person who first spotted that the debates we were watching on *alt.religion.scientology* were heating up into a story of some significance, and he saw the first version of that story through most of the editing process; more help came from John Browning, who edited the piece for *Wired UK,* and Martha Baer, who edited the second version for *Wired.*

The Net is a collaborative medium, and ideas flow so freely that after a while you can't always be sure whose they were; thanks, therefore, for many inspirations to all my unwitting collaborators, as well as the hard core who show up at the annual Computers, Freedom, and Privacy Conference. Thanks also go to Demon Internet and the WELL for facilitating my online presence, and especially to CIX, which bears the brunt of my weird online habits, as well as to the many people, such as Mike Rogers, Ron Newman, Rupert Goodwins, and David Morton, who have taken the time to explain technical details for me. Lucy Kewney deserves to be appreciated for checking URLs and sorting papers.

Thanks also go to my agent, Diana Finch, who seems to like grinding contracts into dust; to Bill Steele and Carol Hemsley for picking out what would have been embarrassing errors; and to my friends Barbara, David,

Alison, and Owen Long, who spent their Christmas vacation watching me work and trying to get on their own computer and phone line; and to the byline conference on the WELL for all the help and advice, and for providing the closest thing there is to a productive displacement activity.

Introduction

The idea for *net.wars* came from three things. The first was repeated exposure to theories that the Net would wipe away the world as
we know it (with the corollary that this would be a Good Thing). I think
this is far from certain, if only because I learned about inertia in high
school. The second was John Perry Barlow's declaration that cyberspace
should be its own sovereign state. It seems unlikely this will be allowed to
happen, but it's an interesting idea. The third was watching the Net's con-
vulsions over the years 1993 to 1996 as it tried to assimilate huge numbers of new users who didn't share the culture that had been developing
over the previous decade. Around the time that I finished writing up a
year's worth of observing folks duke it out on *alt.religion.scientology* for
Wired, I decided there was a book in the wars along the border between
cyberspace and real life, a metaphor that was inspired by discovering that
a few years after Ireland was partitioned in the early 1920s there were
riots along the border when an outfit called the Boundary Commission
proposed to change it slightly to bring more Protestants into the North
and more Catholics into the South.

Around the time the book was commissioned, in June 1996, I went to
Cornell University for a science workshop and found myself staying in
roughly the same area of North Campus I had lived in my first summer
there in 1970. Walking down the path through the empty landscape
around Clara Dickson Hall and its courtyard, I finally understood the
meaning of the word timeless: shorn of students and their changing fash-
ions it looked the same when I was forty-two as it had when I was sixteen. Doubtless it looked the same before I was born, and it's easy to
imagine that generations of alumni will help ensure that it will look the
same a century hence.

The Net is not like this. The oldest area I visit regularly didn't exist before 1985, and while it will probably exist ten years from now, I have no
idea whether it will look or behave the same. For a hundred years from

now all bets are off, although it's nice to think that future generations might not only tread in my path but relive my interactions in cyberspace. Reading what new friends said in old, stored topics and conferences is the nearest we come to time travel and the ability to see our friends and lovers as they were before we knew them and altered them subtly, as knowing people does.

I used to say that a key crossroads in an expatriate's life comes at five years after emigrating. Before then, going back is still easy: your friends' kids remember you, your career is retrievable, your life is still there. After five years, it gets hard: your friends move, your work contacts change jobs or even professions, and you lose touch with the common culture. I mean, you don't get the jokes. (After ten years, there is no longer any such thing as going back. There is only starting over in a new place that's partly familiar.)

Having now been online for more than five years, I note a similar watershed. It became clear to me around the same time as that Cornell trip, when I suddenly found it difficult to feel a sense of shared community with a large group of people, many of whom I knew, who shared some of my long-term interests. They were not on the Net, you see. These are people who make their lives with ideas, and yet their primary perception of the Net was negative: they didn't see it as a tool they could use to spread information or counter misinformation, or interact with like-minded others. Instead, they saw it as a new danger. And I reacted as any typical Nethead might—protective instincts to the fore, along with a sort of exasperated alienation: they didn't get the jokes.

This all leads up to saying that I'm not sure how objective any journalist is about the Net. Journalists who don't use the Net themselves routinely make such egregious technological and cultural errors that you can only compare the results to what would happen if they were assigned to write about the interstate highway system based on their experiences at sea. With that lack of context, if the police told you that prostitutes routinely and openly solicited truckers and other visitors to roadside rest areas and that therefore they were risky places for families to visit, you would probably believe them and write the story.

At the same time, after a while it's easy to lose perspective and forget that behavior which is common and tolerated on the Net seems shocking to newcomers. If you hang out, for example, in the newsgroup *alt. showbiz.gossip* for more than a week or two, you begin to realize that the participants are simultaneously gossiping about celebrities and making fun of celebrity gossip from their virtual "trailer park." This is a level of irony that completely by-passes the casual visitor; my own first thought on seeing that group was that it was a lawsuit waiting to happen. Now, months later, I think the *alt.showbiz.gossip* list of fifty ways to tell if a star is gay is one of the funniest things I've ever read on the Net and feel sorry for anyone so humorless as to think there oughtta be a law against it.

This warping is so common among the Net-savvy journalists I know that I've concluded that the best objectivity I can offer you is to declare my biases up front: I love the fact that in this age of polite political correctness there is a place in the world where people feel free to speak their minds, even offensively; I love the fact that others can tell them off for it and poke holes in their reasoning. I admire the courage of at least some of those who defend those rights, even though I don't always agree with their methods or their behavior. I would like to see the freedom of the old net.culture survive in the face of the many competing commercial and regulatory interests that might prefer to limit its reach and openness. I am less confident than others that such survival is ineluctable and that attempts at regulation will inevitably fail; they may indeed fail, but there will be lots of boundary disputes while we try to define the rules in the grey area where real life and cyberspace intersect. Either way, the stories should be told.

Wendy M. Grossman
wendyg@skeptic.demon.co.uk
March 1997

1

The Year September Never Ended

> The lore of the frontier is filled with contradictions that liken it to those great epics of the distant past populated by characters like Eric the Red and El Cid, who were uncertain of the differences between good and evil. For instance, western hospitality and kindness to strangers, especially to those in distress, is one of the most solid of American traditions. Yet at the same time, a common stereotype is the frontiersman's demonstrated contempt for a tenderfoot or newcomer. Let a tenderfoot fall into the hands of a western miner, cowboy, gambler, soldier, or whomever, and he is certain to be tricked and harassed, cheated of his money at cards, fired upon and made to dance, put into the saddle of the wildest bronco, and otherwise physically endangered or harmed.
>
> —Dee Brown, *Wondrous Times on the Frontier*

"What's the most amazing thing you've ever found?" Mac (Peter Riegert) asks Ben, the beachcomber (Fulton Mackay), in the 1983 film *Local Hero*.

"Impossible to say," Ben replies. "There's something amazing every two or three weeks."

Substitute minutes for weeks, and you have the Net. On a good day, something amazing washes up every two or three minutes. On a bad one, you irritably wonder why all these idiots are wasting your time with their stupid babble and wish they would go somewhere else. Then you remember: there's a simple solution, and it's to unplug your modem. Never works.

For one thing, once you get started using email it's almost impossible to do without it: cheaper and faster than fax, far more convenient than letters, more efficient and streamlined than phone calls, email makes it possible for an expatriate American like me to stay in touch daily with old friends and family and even, using online public discussion areas such as online forums or Usenet newsgroups, have a social life with them. You could stay in touch via letter, fax, or phone, but those are all private. Until bulletin board systems (BBSs), online services like CompuServe or America Online, and Usenet newsgroups became generally available, there was no way to enjoy your friends the way you do when you live in the same town or subculture in real life: in social contexts, with other people. No amount of personal updates makes up for that loss of shared experience.

These public discussion areas are a huge source of help and information because they are so widely read; these are places where people participate when they can and leave messages for you to find when you have time. The day I arrived at the 1994 Computers, Freedom, and Privacy Conference to find my palmtop computer's screen had gone black because the machine's settings were wrong for the new batteries, I posted a panicked message in CompuServe's Palmtop forum before collapsing for the night. The next morning, before the first session, I logged back in to find that someone with a manual had been on in the meantime and left instructions telling how to reset it. Every day for the last four years, when I wonder what happened around the professional tennis tours the previous day, I can find out by checking into *rec.sport.tennis*, where I'll find the match results, and often a live report from someone who was at the tournament and sometimes has more of interest to say about it than the official press stories.

Then there's hard information: maybe you want stock prices, more details on a story your local newspaper missed or covered in a single paragraph, the weather report for Hong Kong, background on the company where you've just landed a job interview, or a look at a painting you've just read about. All these things are on the Net right now in one form or another, some official, some simply the pooling of information that happens wherever humans congregate.

The Net is also a wonderful place if you love jokes and have a taste for the bizarre. Browse one way, and you find someone advertising, for $19.95, a lifetime certificate that will pay out $10 million if you're abducted by aliens—provided that you can produce a signature from an Authorized Onboard Alien on the claim form. Click another way, and you find yourself in Partenia, the virtual diocese defrocked French bishop Jacques Gaillot set up after he lost his standing in the church. Peruse the lovingly detailed coverage of the longest court case in British legal history, the McLibel trial, the story of two self-defended leaflet writers who in the process of defending themselves against allegations of libel have managed to bring out a whole lot of information McDonald's would probably rather they hadn't. The case, which has been written up in the British press with a kind of gleeful admiration, lacks only Court TV, a white Bronco, and a bloody glove to be Britain's answer to the O. J. Simpson trial. Or, more soberly, study the medical images of Chinese patient Zhu Ling, a twenty-one-year-old musician whose friends got permission in 1996 to post her medical records on the Net in the hope that someone, somewhere could identify what was wrong with her before she died in a coma. Eighty-four experts from around the world did: she had thallium poisoning, from which she is now slowly recovering with help and advice from doctors worldwide.[1]

Switch to text, and you might find a bunch of actors batting out Ham-Net, a version of Hamlet acted—or rather, typed—out on Internet Relay Chat (IRC), a sort of worldwide text-based CB radio where anyone can set up a channel at any time. Written in the local lingo of arcane computer commands and shortcuts and performed live on February 6, 1994, from the offices of London-based Demon Internet, HamNet rendered the famous monologue as "2b . . . . or not 2b. . . Hmmmmmm. . . :-(Bumm-errrr!!" I feel sure Shakespeare would have approved of the ASCII art stage decoration and felt flattered by the excited post–first night chatter.[2]

Or perhaps you like to weave your own fantasies in the collaborative text-based role-playing worlds called MUDs (for multi-user dungeons, after the role-playing games from which the idea came), where over time you become part of a community in which you can have adventures, build a house, and even get married. This sounds weird to people, but loosely it's the online equivalent of organizations like the Society for Creative Anachronism, which, while attempting to recreate the Middle Ages in the present as they should have been, joins people into fantasy marriages, households, and baronies and encourages the perpetuation of skilled crafts such as lace-making and calligraphy.

All these areas have one thing in common: a feeling of community. Those daily postings slowly and incrementally add up to human relationships. Like any bar or club, some people stand out, some people lead, some people irritate, and some people (actually, by best estimates, about 90 percent) just sit back and watch the ebb and flow.

What makes a community? One could argue that Net-based communities are so loosely bound that they barely seem to notice if one member, even a long-term regular, disappears. But the closeness and emotional support that's found in some online areas can be real and compelling, especially as your real-life friends join the services you use and intermingle with your online friends.

Howard Rheingold, in *The Virtual Community*, surmised, quoting Grateful Dead lyricist John Perry Barlow, that "You aren't a real community until you have a funeral."[3] I might have believed this if Rheingold had stuck to the WELL, the unusually close San Francisco–based electronic conferencing system of which he is a founding member. But when he moved on to the 1991 death of a regular on the London-based conferencing system CIX,[4] which I use every day, he lost me. While it was certainly true that a small portion of the CIX community grieved deeply over the loss of this particular motor-biking CIXen (as CIX users are often called), another group still describes the departed as "an odious little shit." What enraged this portion of the community was not just seeing people who had hated him the week before posting long eulogies, but that they went on to delete old messages evidencing the less pleasant side of this character's personality. Some of the disaffected got as far as planning a revenge prank: starting a conference named *dead_biker*, joining the mourners to it, and then removing themselves. It was a common trick of that era in CIX's history that has largely disappeared with the near universal use of offline reader software: an example of technology's influence on behavior.[5] By now, few outside his circle of friends remember him; people come and go from CIX all the time, most only scratching a tiny percentage of its surface.

I'd argue instead that what makes a community is a mark of difference between the community members and the rest of the world and, more importantly, an external threat, real or imagined. Who hasn't at some time felt a temporary sense of kinship with other members of the same minority, whether you're Americans abroad in a non–English-speaking country, VW Beetle owners, tennis fans, or folk musicians?

The Net started like that, as a loose group of people who all used computers but knew that other people were desperately bored by them. Older systems that prompt newcomers for information about themselves always ask what type of computer you use. A depressingly large number of people fill this in, even though any normal person would unplug his or her modem to avoid the folks who fill in the make, model, and serial numbers of their work, home, and portable computers. I'm sure in the days before we useless non-academics were allowed onto the Net, those who were wired had the heady sense of excitement that comes with having your own private, almost secret, playground.

That was then; this is now. Older online communities like the WELL and CIX have survived through years of fussy, unstable equipment and bad phone lines, through business challenges posed by dropping prices and Internet competition, to today, when the biggest perceived threats are coming from governments and other organizations seeking to regulate the Net. In between there have been enormous social changes as the size of the Internet population has shot from an estimated 30 million in early 1994 to as many as 60 million in early 1997.

What makes the Internet such a difficult beat to cover is that no two people experience cyberspace the same way, just as no two people ever quite experience real life the same way. What you find online very much depends on what you're looking for. This, along with the fact that with so much to choose from you simply stop seeing the parts that don't interest you, is one reason why the Net can look so innocent to those who have been online for years, but simultaneously so full of subversion and filth to outsiders whose only contact with it is through media coverage or police complaints. Such a wide disparity of views is a significant difficulty in determining whether and how the Net should be regulated or governed; the choice so far seems to be between people who understand the Net and insist it can't (and shouldn't) be controlled and people who don't understand the Net and are overeager to make bad laws in the hope that they will stick long enough to win a couple of elections. Coming to grips with how the Net works and disentangling issues for the Net from matters that are properly dealt with in the physical world are important steps in understanding what a digital future may be.

I was not one of the first settlers, although I thought about getting a modem as early as 1983. It was the summer of 1991 when I started out on online services—primarily CompuServe and the London-based conferencing system CIX, both of which now hook to the Net in the wider sense—after I bullied an editor into believing he really did need a feature about bulletin boards by a beginner for his beginners' computer magazine. Usenet came later, sometime in 1992, when I began sporadically reading a couple of newsgroups, primarily *rec.sport.tennis*, through CIX's read-only gateway. When the United Kingdom's first and still biggest domestic Internet service provider (ISP), Demon Internet, started up in mid-

1993, I had direct, two-way Internet access for the first time.[6] Life online wasn't as easy back then as it is now: a technically literate friend of mine, one of Demon's founding subscribers, remarked at the time that setting up his Demon account was "a bit like giving birth—so difficult that afterwards you can never quite remember how you did it." The help manual for that early software suite—or perhaps garage sale would be a better phrase—was incomprehensibly written for packet radio (a system for transmitting data via radio), and Demon's technical support guys helped you out over the phone by poring over the original program code.

It was just in time. Those of us who got onto the Internet in the summer of 1993 were the earliest fringes of what became massive waves of commercial immigration from 1994 onward. We were probably the last newcomers to glimpse the Net as it was before the boundary disputes between cyberspace and the real world began in earnest. Those of us whose real lives have become inextricably intertwined with cyberspace find these disputes difficult, like having the country you were born and raised in go to war with the country to which you've emigrated. But it is through these battles that the future in which our descendants will live is being defined.

It's easy to let nostalgia take over and imagine that the years leading up to 1993 were quiet, perhaps accompanied by the distant strains of Beethoven's Pastoral Symphony. But they weren't. When you track down the histories and memories of the early days of the Net that have been written and posted, you find that wherever and whenever there has been change on the Net there have always been net.wars. People complained, debated, and flamed—a Net word for sending angry, attacking messages —in 1986, a time mythologically dubbed The Great Renaming, when the structure of Usenet was reorganized into the present collection of hierarchies to make it easier for people to find the subjects they were interested in.[7] People complained, debated, and flamed some more about the cultural shift when Bitnet, an early network of electronic mailing lists started at the City University of New York, was made accessible via Usenet, the global collection of discussion groups available to Internet users (and many others).

And each year there was September.

To understand about September, you must consult the *alt.culture. usenet* FAQ, maintained by Tom Seidenberg. He defines September this way:

The time when college students return to school and start to post stupid questions, repost MAKE MONEY FAST, break rules of netiquette, and just generally make life on Usenet more difficult than at other times of the year. Unfortunately, it has been September since 1993. With the growing sensationalism surrounding the "Information-Superhighway" in the United States, the current September is likely to last into the next century.[8]

One habit the Net developed in its early days to suit its own needs is the practice of creating information files, at least one per newsgroup, lovingly maintained by volunteers. Known as FAQs, for "Frequently Asked Questions," these repositories of useful information are carefully documented lists of the answers to questions old-timers wish were asked less frequently. The newcomer arriving on *alt.fan.letterman* and asking for the millionth time that week how to get tickets for the Big Shew will be told in no uncertain terms to go read the FAQ. He will probably not be told how to do this: one of the less pleasant sides of old-time Net users is a lack of patience with newcomers' ignorance.

David DeLaney, in his four-part "Net.Legends FAQ," made the definition of September a rule ("There are no hard-and-fast Rules on Usenet, only Guidelines"):

> Rule #9: It's *always* September, *somewhere* on the Net.

> Dave Fischer's Extension: 1993 was The Year September Never Ended [so far, there doesn't seem to be much evidence he's wrong . . .][9]

Seidenberg gives some more detail, sourced from DeLaney:

> The first recorded outbreak of this was Warren Burstein saying "It's *always* September, *somewhere* on the net" in response to a particularly Clueless outburst from Delphi.com on alt.folklore.urban, in fall 1993.

September was a time when large numbers of newcomers had to be assimilated into the existing Net culture, much like a small college town each year has to put up with a huge influx of rowdy kids who keep stopping you on the street to ask where everything is and clogging all the bookstores. MAKE MONEY FAST postings (see chapter 2) are like those chain letters you probably remember from high school; seeing them pop up regularly once a year and having to explain why they're (a) illegal and (b) irritating is a repetitive experience easily understood by anyone who's had more than one child.

"Delphi.com" refers to Delphi, which in early 1993 became the first national commercial online service to open a gateway to the wider Internet through which its members could participate. At the time, Delphi, which would be bought up by international media mogul Rupert Murdoch toward the end of that year and sold back to its first owners in 1997, had about 100,000 subscribers, small compared to the annual intake of freshmen issued with accounts by their universities, and a drop in the bucket compared to the 1.2 million members CompuServe had at the time, or Prodigy's 2 million.

None of those, though, is the service most hated by the Net. That honor is reserved for America Online (AOL), which as the number-three service in 1994 unleashed its one million users onto the Net in what was then the largest single block of new users the Net had ever been asked to absorb. The service's reputation still bears the scars out on the wider Net, where sporting an email address ending in *aol.com* is an instant sign that you're probably too stupid to be taken seriously (or you'd find a better service provider).

But saying that raises a different problem: it makes the Net sound like one seamless organism that's just Out There somehow—like television or radio—that you tap into all at once, like the first time you hook up a CB radio and discover that all those cars around you have been talking to each other. In fact, "the Net" is no more a cohesive whole than what we call "real life," with its streets and libraries, bars and clubs, companies and subcultures. For one thing, the Internet itself, technologically speaking, is not a single entity; it is the network that interlinks other networks, large and small. Cornell University's campus network, CompuServe, San Francisco's 10,000-member conferencing system the WELL,[10] the 16,000-member conferencing system CIX, AOL, and the White House all use the Internet to connect to each other, even though internally their own systems are only open to their own members. Similarly, each of the many ways—Usenet, IRC, the World-Wide Web—of using the Internet as a communications medium is a separate entity with its own cultural norms and in-jokes. The newest of these, the Web, is the most immediately understandable to commercial interests looking to exploit the Net. Like the media that businesses understand, such as TV, radio, or publishing, the Web offers companies a way of displaying information about themselves and their products in a controlled way. It is also appealing to consumers because it's a simple way of tying together old Internet facilities, such as FTP (for file transfer protocol, a facility that allows you to retrieve files from the Net equivalent, known as FTP sites, of public libraries), and new ones, such as live audio and video, into a single interface.

But the Web, appealing and convenient though it is, is not the reason the Net is spoken of with such great reverence by old-time Netheads.

"There is such a thing as net.culture," said John Perry Barlow earnestly in the spring of 1996. "There is such a thing as net.religion."[11] Barlow is voicing a deep-seated belief, echoed by many others, that the Net's two-way, many-to-many communication has brought us something so new and special that it's almost sacred.

Barlow, whose business card styles him a "cognitive dissident," became one of cyberspace's few net.prophets in 1990, when he circulated on the Net a long article called "Crime and Puzzlement," part of which recounts a visit from an FBI agent who thought Barlow might be a hacker. Describing the scene as "Kafka in a clown suit," Barlow was dumbfounded by the agent's lack of technical knowledge, calling it an "immigrant's fear of a strange, new land." Barlow concluded that this ignorance was both disastrous and important. He had a point: 1990 was the year of the Operation Sun Devil raids, in which a lot of innocent computer users were caught in the undertow of an attempt to crack down on hacking. Barlow's account of his strange encounter got him a prompt visit from Lotus founder and fellow WELL user Mitch Kapor; jointly they decided to found the Electronic Frontier Foundation (EFF) to lobby for the extension of our traditional civil liberties into cyberspace. For Barlow, who hates writing ("I'd rather pump out septic tanks"),[12] it established his credentials as someone with broad experience, a way with words, and a particular point of view that many in cyberspace shared, but that hadn't yet found a voice.

Barlow was that voice, and he followed up with other articles that codified most of the important issues facing the Net in the early 1990s. He analyzed the battles over the "guerrilla cryptography" program PGP in "Decrypting the Puzzle Palace" (1992). In "Jackboots on the Infobahn" (1994), he argued against Clipper, the U.S. government's proposals for retaining its control over the use of strong cryptography, considered a key technology necessary to support commercial activity over the Net. In "Selling Wine without Bottles: The Economy of Mind on the Global Net" (1994), he attacked attempts to redefine intellectual property laws, saying no amount of revision could possibly make them work in a digital era.[13] Barlow's own career followed the pattern outlined in that last article, as the wide circulation of his writings (for free) turned him into both an advocate for the Net and someone with the credibility to explain how it worked to business and legal folk. At a conference in Amsterdam in early 1996, Barlow compared this process to the career of the Grateful Dead, whose massive popularity and cult following was built on the band's habit of allowing free taping at all concerts.

One of the beliefs Barlow began propagating in early 1995 to anyone who would listen was the idea that cyberspace was by nature its own sovereign state that could not be governed by traditional means. Again his timing was exquisite: 1995 and 1996 were two years of intense pressure on the Net from all sides. In addition to the continuing battle over the legal status of cryptography, all kinds of governments from the United States to Singapore began attempting to impose controls on what kind of information could flow, and even the telephone companies began carping about the amount of time users tied up their phone lines (while frantically trying to launch their own Internet services).

Censorship was a hot-button issue on the Net long before the passage by the U.S. Congress of the Communications Decency Act as a rider to the Telecommunications Bill on February 7, 1996. The received wisdom is that it's just not possible. For once, the famous aphorism isn't Barlow's. Instead, it was coined by the Electronic Frontier Foundation's third co-founder, John Gilmore, who said, "The Net interprets censorship as damage, and routes around it."[14] This famous (at least on the Net) line makes the Net sound like a force of technology that can't be stopped. What it really reflects is the fact that once the technology exists and enough people are aware of it, circumvention of censorship will happen, and that the Net as a collection of human beings perceives censorship as a threat and bonds together against it.

Gilmore should know: he was one of the founders of the *alt* hierarchy in May 1987, as a reaction to the formal voting and creation procedures of Usenet's so-called Big Seven hierarchies: *rec, comp, talk, misc, soc, sci*, and *news*. The problem, as Henry Hardy writes in his "History of the Net,"[15] was that although a proposed *rec.drugs* had passed its vote, the group then known as the "Backbone Cabal" (because they controlled all the backbone sites on the Net, and so could control what newsgroups were created and propagated) had refused to create it. Hardy quotes a message from Digital Equipment Corporation (DEC) researcher Brian Reid as to what happened. Reid, who was unhappy at plans to name his newsgroup *rec.food.recipes*, Gilmore, and Amdahl employee Gorden Moffett agreed to create an "alternative" network by linking Gilmore's and Reid's home computers to Amdahl and circulate the newsgroups so created that way.

By the end of May 1987, *alt.test*, *alt.config*, *alt.drugs*, and *alt.gourmand* were active, and Reid, who was in charge of DEC's Usenet feed at the time, added the *alt* groups to the list of those DEC carried. When, a year later, *soc.sex* passed its vote but was also blocked from creation (by Gene Spafford, according to Reid's note), Reid created *alt.sex* and also, feeling it was "artistically necessary," *alt.rock-n-roll.* The result is that anyone can set up a newsgroup on any topic, at will (though of course, no amount of appearances in newsgroup lists can make people actually post anything even vaguely relevant to the newsgroup's title), and that these newsgroups can never be killed, only slowly abandoned. There are, as you might guess, newsgroups that were probably never intended to be used other than to spread the joke in the title—things like *alt. fan.tonya-harding.whack.whack.whack* or (we hope, anyway) *alt.sex. bestiality.hamster.duct-tape.*

Given that the day-to-day reality of the Net is so bizarre and often so completely useless (do you really need to spend time picking up a program to reword the beginning of Genesis to read, "In zee begeenning Gud creeted zee heefee und zee iert. Bork Bork Bork!"—a process known as encheferation after its inventor, a poster signing himself the Swedish Chef after the Muppet character?), it may be hard to understand why its workings are regarded with such reverence by so many. Barlow, for example, has spoken many times of the "life forms" that are created in the space between people when they interact. Rheingold writes of the "groupmind" on the WELL and the way it offers emotional support to members caught up in their children's hospitalization and almost magically produces an answer to almost any question you post within hours. Even a more skeptical writer like the *New Yorker*'s John Seabrook can thoughtfully analyze the effect that filling in the subject line on an email message has on his thought process and personality.[16] I don't know if I'm just too New Yorkishly impatient and practical or just haven't taken enough drugs, but it seems to me a fairly commonplace prediction that if you pull together large numbers of people using any reasonably flexible means of communication you are going to find that knowledge is pooled and that relationships form between the participants.

And yet, a lot of people don't get either what's genuinely new about the Net or what looks like it's new but isn't. In September 1995, BBC's Radio Five service put out an edition of its Sunday morning program about computers, *The Big Byte*, that the producers enthusiastically claimed was the first radio show ever produced by the audience (exclamation point on the press release). The array of technical facilities was indeed impressive: they were set up in the studio to take live questions via email and IRC. Wow. So at the end of the first segment, the producer looks at his watch and says, "That ended exactly on time." Folks, the audience did not produce that show, however many suggestions they sent in by email in the weeks before it was broadcast. The producer produced that show and got it to time out right. What that show did was little different from any phone-in show that encourages listeners to write in and suggest topics. Only the speed and reach were changed; when a question about German prices for ISDN, a kind of digital telephone service, came up, a correspondent in Munich emailed in the answer and we were able to read it out.

What is new is the promiscuous pooling of knowledge that previously existed only in tiny, discrete pockets, and the force that comes when disparate individuals are able to discover their common interests and work together. The best example of this is the story of Scientology versus the Net (see chapter 6), where threaded through in-fighting, viciousness, and some sheer stupidity is a serious attempt to build, piece by piece, a multinational knowledge base about a large, multinational, well-funded, and relatively secretive organization that some people believe to be truly dangerous. Whether the Net's activities, which the Church of Scientology claims violate its intellectual property rights, are legal or not will be settled by courts of law. In the meantime, for better or worse, the Net in this case has empowered individuals who in a previous era would not have known of each other's existence.

The increased reach and scope that the Net can give an individual is one reason why some people think that what is happening there is so important that it's worth battling over the laws being created to control it. "The Internet changes the economies of scale in favor of the little guy," Electronic Frontier Foundation chair Esther Dyson says in *Digerati*, a 1996 collection of profiles of leaders of the digital revolution.[17] "It used to be only big guys could send stuff, only big guys could advertise, only big guys could have newspapers. Suddenly, everybody can reach the audiences they deserve, more or less for free. They won't necessarily get mass audiences, because they may not be worth listening to, but everybody can distribute their information pretty much as widely as they want, almost without cost."

Dyson may be a little over-enthusiastic on that "almost without cost." True, the costs are decreasing almost weekly, and starting up an electronic newsletter is far cheaper than starting a full-fledged newspaper, even a local one, but "almost without cost" is only true if you already have a computer, a modem, an Internet connection, and a telephone line. These are not "no cost" if you live the kind of life where you have to walk four miles to get water.

The belief in the Net is also being challenged as fancier effects that are harder (and therefore more expensive) to produce become commonplace. As Seabrook points out in his book *Deeper*,

> In an information society such as the Web, all the members have to have their nuggets of information, and the poorest had only charcoal to set in front of their corrugated-tin huts, while the richest had glittering and irresistible palaces of mind candy. . . . The superior graphics and other bells and whistles effectively wiped out the democratizing potential of a distributed network. And since no one had yet figured out any way of making much money from Web sites, only corporations with large promotion and marketing budgets could afford to build expensive ones.[18]

That was true in early 1996, when Seabrook was writing. But things were already beginning to change again. Democracy has to some extent reasserted itself via the search engines, high-speed computer systems that search the millions of pages of information on the Web and tell you where to look for what you want. Several of the best of these, such as Altavista, only became available at the end of 1995. The big guy with the known brand name has the advantage if you get your Web addresses from TV ads and go straight to those addresses (correctly known as URLs, for Uniform Resource Locators). But computers searching through their indexes of Web pages for the keywords you've entered know nothing about fancy graphics or jazzy animations. They see only hits and misses, and it's not until you go clicking through the pages of hits that you find out whether an individual site is fancy or not; if it has the information you need you may not care. So far, attempts to force specific pages to appear at the top of the list have been defeated by changes to the search engines.

There is one advantage, though, that no one can take away from the "little guy": net.culture has no mercy on the humorless. Large corporations are not known for being able to take a joke. Microsoft's Web-based publication, *Slate*, was followed almost immediately onto the Net by a word-perfect and hilarious parody called *Stale*, just as *Wired* is shadowed by *ReWired: The Journal of a Strained Net* and the Net itself is told not to take itself so seriously on the sardonic Web site *Suck* ("A fish, a barrel, and a smoking gun").[19]

It is not clear that what we now know as net.culture will survive. Besides the blows of attempted censorship, sudden growth, legal battles, and other types of legislation that have bonded the Net together as a community, the Net is under siege from the many commercial interests who want to exploit what they perceive as a virgin medium. It is fashionable to claim that the Net has the greatest democratizing potential of any medium ever invented; but as writer Todd Lappin pointed out in *Wired,* that's what they said about the medium we now know as commercial radio.[20]

2

Make.Money.Fast

Your signature can be a TrueType font! Make $50,000 at home in just two weeks auditing Web sites! FREE Internet access by calling THIS 1-800 Number!!! You MUST read this message all the way to the end and send 200 copies to all your friends!

—Personal email, 1996

Once upon a time the Internet had no advertising. . . .

The Internet's origins as a largely academic research network included prohibitions against its use for private or personal business, much like ham radio still does. (In fact, a lot of the technology underpinning the Internet was invented by radio hams, and those who have been part of both say the two cultures are extremely similar.) These restrictions began to lift in 1992, opening the way for all kinds of commercial traffic, from businesses exchanging email and other data to Web-based retailing and advertising-sponsored content.[1]

This is not to say there was no commerce in cyberspace before the liberalization of the Internet: commerce happens wherever humans gather. On closed systems such as CompuServe and the WELL and even on some smaller BBSs, special sections were set aside for classified ads so members could buy or sell new or secondhand equipment. On London's electronic conferencing system CIX, small online vendors have been operating almost since the system's founding in 1987, selling modems, hard drives, computers, and peripherals. In general, it's not an easy way to make a living: online users tend to expect sharply cut prices and responsive service. The feeling of daily close community on such systems meant that these trades seemed—and in general were—less risky than dealing by mail order with strangers. After all, buyers who didn't pay up or sellers who supplied faulty goods risked being outed in front of people they argued with every day and having their reputations ruined in front of several thousand computer buyers, some of them from major companies.

The one thing you didn't do was march into any old forum or conference and set up shop by posting advertisements. If you did want to market yourself or your services online, you did it subtly, by getting to know people and letting them know what you did when asked, or offering help or information when they needed it in the hope that you would stick in their minds as a knowledgeable source. Computer networking, like real-life networking, was all about making contacts, not about barraging people with pitches. On Usenet in the early 1990s the same culture prevailed. Call it snobbish if you will, but there were and are practical reasons for keeping newsgroups and other online forums streamlined and free of off-topic material; those strictures are what make those areas useful as resources.

If you're paying money to check into a Novell forum to pick up the latest technical tips, arguably what you get should have some relation to what you think you're paying for, just as you'd be annoyed if you paid to take a class in psychology at a nearby university and the instructor decided instead to teach you math or spend all the lecture sessions reading you advertisements for his radio show. Similarly, if you're looking online for help with your Macintosh computer you don't want to read some guy's comments on Pete Sampras's backhand, and if you're looking for information on Pete Sampras's backhand you don't want to read an ad for a Web site full of "Chewbacca ate my balls" cartoons. This notion that the Net should be structured so that users have maximum control over what material they choose to look at is the bedrock on which all online culture has been built.

According to their own testimony, the two people who brought this consensually organized culture to an abrupt halt must have known this. Arizona-based Laurence Canter and Martha Siegel say in their book *How to Make a Fortune on the Information Superhighway* that they were among the earliest users of CompuServe and had been online for more than ten years.[2] However infectious Barlow believes net.culture to be, they apparently didn't catch the bug. On April 12, 1994, they posted a message about the so-called "Green Card Lottery" to every newsgroup they could find.[3] This posting coupled a threat—that the 1994 lottery would be the last ever (it wasn't)—with an offer of their services (for a fee, of course).

The green card lottery is a U.S. government effort to bring an element of hope to the miserable, bureaucratic, and lengthy process of applying for U.S. residence visas. Essentially, would-be immigrants from most foreign countries are eligible to fill out a form and enter; lucky winners, chosen according to quotas, by-pass the normal procedures and get green cards. When I lived in Ireland, I knew quite a few people who had entered just on the off-chance of winning, even if they weren't sure they'd ever want to live in the United States. A few had won. The service is free, wherein lay the first objection to Canter and Siegel's message: they were proposing to charge people.

A couple of technical points may help make sense of the fury that followed Canter and Siegel's mass posting. One is that when they posted their "Green Card" message to every newsgroup they did it in such a way as to cause the maximum disruption: they ran a computer program that posted it separately to each newsgroup rather than using a method known as cross-posting. Cross-posting would have treated the message as a single news article while making it available to all the newsgroups in Canter and Siegel's very long list. Instead, their method created 10,000 copies of the message, one per newsgroup.

First, this meant that each news-storing computer (technically, a news server)[4] around the world had to find space for 10,000 copies of the message instead of just one. Second, it disabled the facility within most newsreader software[5] to mark a post as read if it's been seen in one newsgroup, so that you don't have to keep rereading the same post in newsgroup after newsgroup. Most users probably didn't notice the first point until they did some math, but they sure noticed the second one when the message kept popping up.

The "Green Card" posting was not the only mass-posted message of the period, but it was the first advertising an off-Net commercial service so widely. It vied for attention with "MAKE.MONEY.FAST" postings (usually abbreviated MMF), which go back some months before Canter and Siegel and still (unfortunately) circulate widely.[6] These postings, and the thousands of imitations that have followed since, are variations on the chain letters most people remember from high school. They all claim there are huge sums of money to be made legally from following the instructions to repost or email them to 200 more users and send one dollar or five dollars (depending on the version you get) to the five or ten names and addresses listed at the end. In fact, as many on the Net have pointed out, this kind of pyramid, or "Ponzi," scheme is illegal and something the Post Office has been stomping on in court for years. Not much is known about the original MMF poster, Dave Rhodes; according to the

"Net.Legends FAQ,"[7] he was a student at Columbia Union College in Takoma Park, Maryland, when he sent out the first ones and has been "voted number one on list of people *every* UseNetter would like to see die an excruciatingly slow and painful death."[8] Just as late-night comedians pick up oft-repeated TV ads (like the Energizer bunny), anything that circulates widely enough on the Internet becomes part of the shared culture and therefore fodder for in-jokes. A number of MMF parodies have circulated, such as one detailing the miserable jail time served by the poster after his arrest for circulating illegal pyramid schemes.

The "Green Card" message was quickly followed by a posting known as "Skinny Dip," which advertised a thigh cream by that name that was supposed to have slimming properties and that interested readers could order from a Miami address.[9] These few postings stood out because they were first; since then, so many ads have been posted widely to Usenet that they just blur into useless noise, called "spam" after a well-known *Monty Python* sketch in which a waitress offers customers a long list of varying combinations of breakfast foods, always including Spam.[10]

The immediate response to the "Green Card" posting was sheer fury on the part of Netheads, who set off a kind of giant, Net-wide immune reaction to the thing, flooding every newsgroup with complaining follow-up postings. The volume of complaining email—estimated at 100Mb, roughly the equivalent of two hundred copies of this book[11]—to Canter and Siegel themselves and to the system administrators at Internet Direct, their small Arizona ISP, crashed the provider's servers repeatedly. By April 16, a posting was circulating that listed better places to complain to, most of them offline: Canter's and Siegel's other email addresses, their business street address, the state bar associations in Arizona and Tennessee (where Canter and Siegel were licensed), their local newspapers, and their congressman. Other proposals included faxing them a continuous loop of black paper in the hope of burning out their fax machine.

In their book, Canter and Siegel say of these reactions which included email flames, mail bombs (a mail bomb is a bombardment with massive amounts of email or huge files), and phone calls, "We were absolutely amazed that there were people who could become so distraught by the appearance of a simple message on their computer screens." Further, "Certain individuals, mainly university students, cared little who they hurt or how they lied. They wanted things their own way and would trample over anyone to achieve that goal."[12]

They didn't like the instructions offered in Netiquette (which they list fairly accurately), either—things like not advertising on the Net, reading a newsgroup for a couple of weeks before posting, and reading the newsgroup FAQs, all standard advice given to newbies, as the Net calls newcomers. "If you had to worry about that much every time you opened your mouth in the real world, you would probably never say anything at all," they complain. "It is equally true that if everyone to whom you spoke criticized your behavior for failing to follow all these rules, there would be more fist fights than conversations. The arrogant tone here is not hard to perceive."[13]

But this is not just a social problem. Do some arithmetic. If you save the Green Card posting in a text file, it takes up approximately 1.5Kb of disk space. Multiply that by 10,000 for the estimated number of newsgroups to which it was posted, and you get something like 15Mb of data coursing around the arteries of the Internet and washing up onto servers worldwide like a large, fatty deposit. At the time, a typical home computer was considered well endowed if it had 100Mb of disk space, and all of Usenet was estimated at roughly 40Mb daily after more than a decade of phenomenal growth—in 1988 it was running at only about 4Mb per day.[14]

Canter and Siegel appear not to regard this as a valid argument. They complain, "What we did find difficult to grasp was why these people were wasting everybody's time trying to inject themselves into matters that didn't concern them."[15] In a chapter on crime on the Net they paint themselves as net.saviors: "we'd like to offer you a not-so-practical reason for seeking your fortune on the I-way: Cyberspace needs you. . . . Like the Old West with which analogies are often drawn, Cyberspace is going to take some taming before it is a completely fit place for people like you and me to spend time," they tell all those nice, normal people they want to help get rich, concluding, "The only thing that remained with us and does so until this day is the unshakable conviction that the Net community is the last bunch on earth who have the right to tell anyone else how to behave."[16]

It was the social disruption that really got people mad. The message simply had no relevance to most newsgroups, and the overall effect was as if you were at a party and someone broke in to interrupt each conversation and shout at the participants to buy his used car. You can throw the bozo out, but the party doesn't easily recover afterwards.

The point is not that there's no way to advertise one's services on the Net, even if you're a lawyer. Bearing in mind that it's not so long since lawyers weren't allowed to advertise at all by their bar associations, there are plenty of lawyers online offering information about green cards and how to get them. One immigration specialist has even posted on his Web site the one hundred questions from which citizenship tests are thought to be drawn, along with the correct answers to help would-be immigrants. You can get to know a lot of potential customers in a non-controversial way by being helpful about answering questions on newsgroups like *alt.visa.us*. Canter and Siegel could easily have adopted this kind of long-term, awareness-building approach and met no resistance. But, to quote their book, "We didn't want to lose a golden opportunity to get rich."[17]

The point is that none of this is what the Net had ever been for. The Net was, the argument ran (conveniently overlooking flaming, the practice of expressing angry hostility that seems to be endemic to electronic communication), a sacred place where minds could meet and merge into a non-corporeal whole. If, as Canter and Siegel said, "Cyberselling is the future of marketing,"[18] the Net was going to fight back. A newsgroup was quickly set up to discuss and coordinate responses to the incident in the *alt.current-events* hierarchy, a newsgroup classification for short-lived, quick-response newsgroups. For many months *alt.current-events.net-abuse* seethed with anger, and although it was replaced with the permanent *news.admin.net-abuse.misc* in early 1995, it has never died. Some discussion focused on whether the commercial *biz.** hierarchy was an area advertisers could use and others could access if they were interested. While some older Netheads didn't like the idea of giving advertising a home on the Internet, it was generally seen as a fair compromise, since it worked in the tradition of the Net: user choice and user control. You didn't have to go there if you didn't want to, which most people didn't. However, the *biz.** hierarchy, while it allows some types of commercial postings, does not want spam either.

This was the moment when cancelers became a feature of life on Usenet in the form of the Cancelmoose (usually written Cancelmoose[tm] on the Net) and other, less anonymous agents. Most newsreaders have a built-in cancellation facility, as there are many times when someone might need to cancel a message after hitting the send button—second thoughts about an angry flame, a message sent out publicly that should have been private, or accidental duplication. The cancel message the user generates goes into a special newsgroup called *control* and propagates around Usenet by the same means as any other message. The cancel instructs the system not to distribute the posting, which is identified by the unique ID assigned to every Usenet post when it's written.[19] News servers are constructed so that the cancel message will work whether it arrives before or after the original message.

Canceling spam requires an added twist, because the person doing the canceling is not the person who wrote the original message. This means forgery: the canceler has to fool the news server into thinking the message came from the original poster. It's actually not that hard to do, and instructions are readily available on the Net.[20] It is, however, a controversial practice, and one that gets discussed to death in the relevant newsgroups. Most people generally accept third-party cancels if they are not content-based (that would be censorship) and there are extenuating circumstances: if someone publicly posted your private email; if the message is spam or spew; if it's a binary file[21] posted to a text-based newsgroup; or if it's part of attempted newsgroup voting fraud.[22]

This system of canceling messages mostly works to keep the spam levels down. People post complaints to *news.admin.net-abuse*, and if they are upheld on investigation the offending messages get deleted. The precise definition of spam varies slightly, but in general a message will be considered spam if it goes out to more than twenty newsgroups on unrelated topics or if many copies are posted to the same newsgroup within a short period of time ("spew"). After havoc was created when a number of people independently set up anti-spamming robots to get rid of the "Skinny Dip" posting, the cancelers developed systems to make sure they don't duplicate each other's efforts.[23]

At the same time, the cancelers are aware that the difference between providing a useful service and exercising censorship can be slim. Accordingly, they operate with checks and balances and a trail of accountability. Check into any of the *news.admin.net-abuse.**[24] newsgroups and you'll see careful logs explaining what's been canceled and why; in addition, each cancel message clearly identifies who the canceler was, although some cancelers protect their real-world identities.

Any reasonable person would have to conclude, however, that all the fears that the "Green Card" posting raised have pretty much come true. There are very few areas of Usenet these days where you don't have to pick your way through piles of spam. And most of them follow precisely the patterns set by the MMF, "Green Card," and "Skinny Dip" postings: they offer questionable services or products, or get-rich-quick schemes better described as rip-offs. It is exceptionally unpleasant and wasteful.

Nonetheless, even though cancellation activities identified roughly

275,000 spams in October 1996 up from about 100,000 in October 1995,[25] they are still controversial on the Net among what appears to be a small but vocal minority of Usenet posters who don't like censorship in any form. An alternative has been proposed by Cancelmoose itself, now retired, a system called NoCeM (pronounced "no-see-um"), which instead of canceling messages distributes authenticated cancels, leaving it up to each individual site to decide whether to honor all or some of these. As of early 1997, this system looks to be gaining some acceptance.

Canter and Siegel remain two of the most hated people who ever posted a Usenet article. Their book was panned on the Net[26] as well as offline by Net-loving reviewers who rubbed their hands at the prospect of trashing it, while *Wired* refused to accept ads for it. (In 1996, when the magazine ran a profile of "Spam King" Jeff Slaton, who said he'd taken his cue from the lawyers, Siegel wrote a letter to the editor accusing the magazine of hypocrisy.)[27] The book itself not only did well enough to warrant a second edition in 1997, but spawned a plethora of imitators, most of which advise at least some restraint. The electronic "mall" Cybersell, which they announced in 1994 to market products across the Net, seems to have disappeared, although there are others, such as Barclays Bank's Barclaysquare.

As of this writing, it looks like the old net.culture is fighting a losing battle. An endless number of chain letters, pyramid schemes, envelope-stuffing scams, and "promotional opportunities" are circulating, and no amount of education in Netiquette will make the perpetrators care about contributing to a useful environment. At the same time, some of the old controls that might have curbed some of this abuse are gone. Internet service providers (ISPs), anxious to grab as many new users as they can, make it fast and easy to sign up online. By the time the credit card number gets checked, the spammer has posted and moved on, not caring about either the Net or the ISP, which is left to cope with the complaints. Serious responses are directed to the spammer's own email address on another ISP somewhere else, or to a phone number or address offline. Britain's Internet Watch Foundation, considering strategies to control the availability of illegal material on the Net, identified users of free trials as "probably the most significant source of anonymity which is abused."[28]

On the Net you can never be sure, but probably no one thinks that if Canter and Siegel had never lived the Net would never have been spammed. The technology was there, and computers were made to be programmed to do boring, repetitive tasks such as post the same message

10,000 times. Canter and Siegel were simply the messengers who arrived to tell us that the Net had reached a critical mass and was attracting people who neither knew nor cared about all those sacred values of net. culture and net.religion. Evidence that there are probably more such people on the Net than there are dedicated Netizens mounts daily. The best efforts of the Cancelmoose and others notwithstanding, very few Usenet newsgroups escape without at least some garbage. At least people have caught on to the notion that replying and complaining is worse than the original disease, so these messages are less disruptive than they were at first. People, sadly, have to some extent gotten used to the junk, just as Canter and Siegel insisted they should. But there is still a loss, in that those who really want to get away move to electronic mailing lists. This is a shame, because although mailing lists are also public, they're less convenient to use and not as easily found by newcomers.

One commonly proposed solution is moderation, that is, putting the newsgroup into the hands of someone whose job it is to make sure that irrelevant material doesn't get posted. Although this works, it means someone has to devote a great deal of time to managing the newsgroup (or mailing list), and it also undercuts the public, accessible nature of Usenet and makes it more difficult to get quick answers to questions when you need them. While moderated electronic conferences have a place—systems like CompuServe have built their entire business model on them —there is a value in the existence of open, public cyberspaces. In the real-world analogy, you don't have wardens patrolling the public conversations in bars and coffeehouses, even though a host will control the flow of questions and discussion after a lecture.

That was 1994 and 1995. But 1996 brought a new scourge: junk email. Somewhere along the line the spammers figured out that a whole lot of people didn't read Usenet and began sending spam directly as email. In the last week of November 1996, I got ten or fifteen of these things, advertising "adult" Web sites, investment schemes, online newsletters, a cookbook (three copies in less than an hour), "Free Stuff!" and three different varieties of bulk emailing software.

I get much less junk email than many long-time Net users do, because I post to relatively few newsgroups (apparently posting to the Novell NetWare newsgroups will get you a ton of advertisements), read only a few mailing lists (and generally don't post to those), and until early 1997 didn't have a personal Web page (even though I wrote an article on how to do it as early as 1995). One of the most sinister and upsetting episodes of junk email I ever heard about occurred on one of the commercial on-line services, where a group in one of the support areas received a mailing clearly derived from their participation there.

What's especially galling is that the emailer always pretends to care about your time. "Reply to this message and type REMOVE in the Subject field," they all say, promising if you do this you will never hear from them again. The problem is that on a lot of text-based systems (Delphi, to name one) there's no way to edit the subject field of emailed replies; you have to start a whole new message. In addition, most people suspect that sending a remove message in fact validates your address as a working address, and that while this particular advertiser may never write to you again, all the others will. (It's more likely that the remove messages are just discarded.) Quite often, by the time you send the remove message the emailer's account has already been terminated and the mail bounces.

Once, in the many junk email messages I've received, I got an apologetic, obviously personal reply when I wrote requesting that the advertiser cease and desist. He had, he said, bought my address as part of a list that had been represented to him as consisting of people who were interested in receiving this type of material. He would be taking it up with his supplier, Mailstar, whose Web address he helpfully enclosed. There must be many more like him, who paid for a service in good faith out of ignorance of the Net and its ways, and who were simply taken in by people who figured out that the best way to Get Rich Quick was to get others to pay them up front.

Mailstar turned out to be small fry; the big fish in the polluted pond was Philadelphia-based Cyber Promotions, which in September 1996 went into court after America Online (AOL) began blocking all email sent from any of its known domains.[29] Cyber Promotions won a temporary restraining order requiring AOL to lift the block, but by early October this ruling was lifted and AOL instituted user-controllable blocking facilities that users could disable if they wanted to receive junk email. Sanford Wallace, the president of Cyber Promotions, made a brief foray onto *news.admin.net-abuse.misc* in late September, "Just to talk." His discussions with the assembled system administrators, spam cancelers, and irate Netheads made an entertaining spectacle—if you're the kind of person who likes to read Usenet wearing an asbestos vest.[30]

On the newsgroup, as on the company's Web site,[31] Wallace reiterated that many users wanted to receive his company's material and argued that blocking his mailings was censorship and an issue of freedom of speech.

The Web site also boasted a collection of email messages (since removed) from AOL users dissatisfied with the company's new policy of mail controls on just those grounds. But there is another freedom of speech issue that Wallace doesn't mention, namely, the fact that a growing number of Net users are deterred from posting to public areas for fear that their email addresses will be snaffled up by the bulk emailers and added to the lists. (To protect themselves from automated address collection software, in early 1997 Usenet posters began editing the reply email addresses on their postings; by August junk email was advertising software to remove the most common edits.)

There is also the small point that most of the junk emailers—though not necessarily the businesses, many of them not Net-literate, whose ads they get paid to send out—know that what they're doing is contrary to acceptable practice. For one thing, whatever they claim in the ads they send out for their own services, their lists are not targeted at all, as far as I can tell, beyond rejecting academic addresses (identifiable by the ending *.edu*). It's routine for messages advertising U.S.-only services to arrive in large numbers of mailboxes at *.co.uk* addresses. You would think that the simplest targeting software would check for country identifiers.

And yet, when an email message lands in your mailbox with a note "You have been chosen to receive this because your name appears on a list of those interested in such material," people's first reaction is to believe there really is such a list and that their names really are on it. In October 1996, a message saying just that hit perhaps a couple of million spooked users worldwide. It advertised child pornography—videos, customized audiotapes, pictures—for sale. It was almost certainly a hoax designed to cause lots of trouble for the guy whose name and address appeared at the bottom. In countries such as Britain, where possession of any type of child pornography is illegal and police may search without a warrant under some circumstances, it terrified people.

For another thing, ads for bulk email software all promise systems for filtering out flame and other angry responses. If their lists were so carefully targeted, why would they need to do this? More than that, many offer to do the emailing for you to protect your own Internet account from cancellation. Shortly after AOL restarted its blocking policy, Cyber Promotions got hauled into court by CompuServe and Concentric Network, a San Jose–based ISP, for forging its message headers to make it appear that its bulk email was coming from those systems. In early October, Cyber Promotions agreed to desist. When people take the trouble to implement this amount of falsification to get around the rules, they must know they're doing something wrong even if it's not illegal.

These guys are only the scouts; the real pack will follow them onto the Net sometime in late 1997 if the Direct Marketing Association has its way; it spent six months writing a report to consider the question of how to make junk email respectable. The plan, as of early 1997, is to set up an Email Preference Service, which, like the telephone and postal Preference Services, would allow consumers to add their names to a list of those who don't want to get such mailings. Privacy campaigners such as the organization Privacy International believe the opposite approach—you opt in if you want the mailings but are left untroubled otherwise—would be more appropriate. Since on the Net, like at the fax machine, the user pays, this is a legitimate argument. Meanwhile, some of the early sales sites on the Web are doing their best to choke off electronic commerce at the start by pursuing hapless shoppers with unwanted "newsletters." One of the worst offenders was the British publisher Penguin, whose marketing department in 1996 anti-publicized a new Web novel by clobbering the Net with millions of copies of a hoax virus message that claimed that reading the message would delete all the files on your computer. Penguin called it "Irina," but this hoax first circulated under the name "Good Times" and has since turned up as "Penpal Greetings" and "Deeyenda." The message is harmless, in that a text message can't contain a virus, which has to be embedded in a program file; the "virus" is merely the fact that everyone who sees the message for the first time thinks the warning is real and, meaning to be helpful, sends out copies to all their friends.

Businesses with reputations to protect might bother checking their lists against the one from a Preference Service, but it's a fair guess that most of today's spammers wouldn't, given their current track record. One thing the larger service providers could do is supply their users with better tools. One reason AOL and CompuServe have such a problem with junk email is that their built in email software is poor; it lacks the filtering and killfiling[32] abilities Internet users have enjoyed for years. Blocking whole sites is unreliable if the spammer is forging headers, and for some larger services it could be too much of a blunt-instrument approach. I could block *aol.com*, but in doing that I'd also be blocking email from my agent and several of my oldest friends.

It would also be nice if the major services implemented controls to stop junk email from being *sent* from their own sites. One of the ironies of AOL's ban on Cyber Promotions and other junk email sites is that a lot of junk email comes from its own service. You rarely see junk email from CompuServe because its design discourages it.

All these real costs—including the expense of staffing an email complaints desk—eventually must be borne by the consumer. Some commercial services have limits on how many messages a user's mailbox can hold at a time, and junk email can block out wanted email for those users. The cost of building better and more flexible tools eventually gets paid for by the consumers who buy and use the software or service. Since most kill-files and filters work by downloading the messages and then discarding them, the user still pays for the downloads—and it's not safe to assume that everyone is paying flat rates to their ISPs and gets free local phone calls. Users outside North America and rural users inside North America all have to pay per-minute phone charges. There is also the cost of users' time in wading through the crap and deleting it or sending complaints. It sounds so reasonable when the message says "Just hit delete" or "Just type remove" if you don't want the message. But it doesn't seem like it when you have to do it forty-two times a day or when the instructions are impossible to follow on your system.

This battle is unique, because it's the only one where a substantial number of people on the Net are beginning to think regulation, rather than self-regulation, might be the answer. Junk faxes are illegal because the user pays. Why not junk email? Rumors that flew around the Net at the end of October 1996 that Cyber Promotions was on the verge of bankruptcy turned out to be just wishful thinking. In early 1997, Cyber Promotions' Web site advertised the usual services plus address collection software for the World-Wide Web ($495) and domain redirection ($300 a year). However, in July 1997 the word came that Canter had been disbarred by the Tennessee Bar Association, in part because of the Green Card spam.

3

The Making of an Underclass
AOL

Why are AOLers so clueless?   —Technology correspondent of
                                      a major daily newspaper,
                                      in conversation, 1995

Here's one of the secrets they don't tell you when you first whip that modem out of its plastic wrapper and fight your way through arcane commands to log on: cyberspace is full of cliques.

One of the more famous examples of this was the 1994 invasion of the newsgroup *rec.pets.cats* by a disruptive gang from *alt.tasteless*, a perfect clash between a group to whom nothing is sacred and one to whom cats, in their ineffable fluffiness, are. The way the story got told in *Wired*, the *alt.tasteless* crew had a fine old time posting messages about nailing cats to breadboards, cooking them, electrocuting them, and spraying them with acid while the *rec.pets.cats* regulars writhed in agony. Eventually, the *rec.pets.cats* people were taught how to use killfiles so they'd never see the invaders' messages, and *alt.tasteless* gave up after complaints to their system administrators nearly cost them their Net accounts.[1]

Other examples abound. On systems that allow such things, small groups will set up their own closed conferences where they can snigger at other, less with-it users in private. On systems that don't, the same kind of behind-the-scenes, backbiting discussions go on by email or live chat; if you're very clever about such things you might be able to pick up hints of hidden alliances by watching which users regularly back each other up in arguments or fights. Closer to the *rec.pets.cats* invasion is the kind of trolling and baiting that goes on when a group of, essentially, playground bullies hound some other user for offenses real or imagined—he might be a fundamentalist Christian, say, or have no sense of humor, or just be generally annoying. Or he might simply come from the wrong domain—the Internet word for a system's name.

This last seems to be the situation of 8 million (and counting fast) America Online (AOL) users, many of whom may even believe that AOL is the greatest thing since television. That the system had problems became known at the end of 1996, when AOL switched from hourly to flat-rate pricing and immediately found its system swamped with users who got on and wouldn't get off. In early 1997, several state district attorneys began studying the company's new pricing scheme, and AOL announced a $350 million upgrade over six months to its network to handle the volume. Although the service was still adding users, the effort to acquire them was expensive; as a result of a change in how AOL amortized those users, at the end of 1996 it declared a loss bigger than all the profits it had ever declared put together. Nonetheless, if you have 8 million users you'll have no trouble finding business partners.

AOL was a lot smaller—only a million users—and far from the market leader in March 1994, when it set up its "Usenet feature," which allowed a seemingly endless stream of people to tap nervously on their newsreaders, type out, one after another, "Hey, is this working?" and then hit the SEND button to relay this world-shaking message to all of Usenet.

The problem was where they said it. There is a newsgroup called *test*, and its purpose in life is to provide a place for people to take their newsreaders once around the dealership parking lot to make sure they understand the controls. Various things, some of them people, monitor the *test* newsgroup and send replies to people who post messages there.[2] And there's no doubt: it is a thrill the first time you see the message you wrote on your computer come back from Deep Cyberspace with replies attached to it. But that's not where they said it. A lot of them picked *alt.best.of.internet*. However anarchic Usenet seems, particularly the *alt* groups, there is often a kind of internal logic to the way newsgroups are named. This particular newsgroup was intended to counteract the generally low signal-to-noise ratio of Usenet postings and serve as a place where people could repost their favorite messages from other newsgroups so everyone could see the gems without having to do their own strip mining. So the rule was and still is: no comments, no original messages, repostings only. Very strict. And this setup worked remarkably well as long as the number of new users popping up with comments stayed at a manageable level. Unfortunately, the arrival of AOL changed all that.

Within a couple of months *alt.best.of.internet* had turned into a battleground. AOLers would post hello messages, old-timers would follow up with vituperative diatribes about reading the FAQ without telling them how to get it, and other old-timers would pile in and take up more bandwidth and create worse useless noise than the AOLers' messages did in the first place. Tempers got short. Repostings got lost.

If that had been AOLers' only sin, they might eventually have been forgiven, especially by the many who do not read *alt.best.of.internet*, "due to the collective memory of the Net being about one week, maximum," as David DeLaney observes in the "Net.Legends FAQ."[3] But several factors ensured that AOLers' transgressions would not be forgotten. First was the sheer volume of new users; if only a small percentage of a million people causes trouble, that's still a lot of people. Second was the fact that, unlike each year's arriving freshman class, all AOLers came from a single domain: *aol.com*. Every message, every crude sexual come-on, every misplaced question reinforced the initial impression of that particular domain as populated with willfully stupid people—or, as the Net would put it, clueless. In the collaborative effort of one newsgroup, AOLers "couldn't get a clue if they stood in a clue field in clue mating season, dressed as a clue, and drenched with clue pheromones."

The final factor was one of instinctive resentment of any hint of commercializing the Internet. Where traditionally, Internet users shared their resources for the public good, the perception was that AOL neither knew nor cared about net.traditions but was only interested in sticking a meter on a free resource and billing its users extortionately.

"AOL's philosophy borders on net-abuse," wrote David Cassel, the maintainer of the *alt.aol-sucks* FAQ,[4] saying that the earliest version of AOL's Usenet newsreader was buggy and wasted resources by reposting articles multiple, unnecessary times, and complaining that AOL had failed to consider adequately the impact of its users' demands on FTP sites[5] and made no such facilities available on its own servers for the rest of the Net. "This gets into an ideological war," noted Cassel. "Technology now allows people to freely exchange information at an amazing rate. AOL attaches a meter to that process. In addition, aggressively pursuing new users, AOL exploits the lack of awareness of existing technological capabilities, and establishes a model that follows the traditional role of pre-packaged entertainment designed for a mass audience."

At the time, a thoughtful and intelligent user named Edward Reid did some research and came to an interesting conclusion: AOLers weren't (necessarily) stupid; they were software-disadvantaged. In a carefully written and thoughtful article (reposted to *alt.best.of.internet* by Ron Newman, an old-time user with widely respected technical knowledge), Reid analyzed the interface AOL had given its users and concluded that it was the source of much of their disruptive behavior.

One problem was that the software AOLers used to access Usenet offered no offline reading or editing facilities. Therefore, AOLers, who were then paying $3.50 an hour for their access, were under pressure to read and write as quickly as possible, encouraging them to skimp on what Reid called "think time." Reid noted that many AOLers were complaining about this in the system's internal newsgroups. Reid couldn't figure out why AOL, which even then provided offline facilities for email, didn't provide similar facilities for Usenet.[6] (The answer may be that AOL doesn't supply offline facilities for its own rather rudimentary message boards.) AOL, others have commented since, is geared toward instant messages, online chat, and real-time interaction, creating a culture where a hasty "Me, too!" is acceptable comment—another culture clash, since Usenet norms consider such messages a waste of bandwidth.

A second problem, in Reid's opinion, was that AOL's software interface confused mailed replies (private) with posted follow-ups (public), encouraging AOLers to post publicly messages which to old-timers seemed more appropriate for mail. Quoting, a staple on Usenet because follow-up messages may arrive before the originals, was not available. Reid also complained that AOL's threading—the facility that shows how a series of messages on the same topic relate to one another—was weak, and that features built into Usenet to allow newer postings to supersede old ones (used with regularly updated messages such as FAQs) were not enabled. There was no search facility (common in Usenet newsreaders), and limits on the number of articles in a single newsgroup the AOL software could show further restricted users' ability to find, and therefore read, FAQs.

The biggest problem for the embattled *alt.best.of.internet* specifically had to do with AOL's suggested list of newsgroups for its members to try out to get acquainted. It's understandable that the service would want to put *alt.best.of.internet* at the top—it was a great showcase for Usenet. But the result was that as all those AOLers trooped to the edge of their world and stepped off (I imagine this as one of those long parades of goofy, green-haired aliens dropping through a trapdoor in the game *Lemmings*), they exhibited normal, human behavior—that is, they hit the first newsgroup they came to and said, Hello, world. And they got flamed.

As one AOLer complained to *alt.best.of.internet* in May 1994, in response to the presumption that all AOLers were bozos, "Is this any kind of behavior for people in an electronic community? Just because AOL subscribers PAY for their Internet access, not have it provided free through a university, some other users are assuming that they are uneducated morons."

Some of these things have been fixed since 1994. But the deeper problem had to do with AOL's decision to make the "Usenet feature" look as much as possible like the colorful graphical world of the rest of AOL. Consequently, many AOLers may not have understood that they were not on just another part of AOL, and so they couldn't possibly have registered that the standards of behavior were different. In any case, there is a natural tendency to assume that whatever service you first use is the way online *should* be, and that anything that deviates from that is wrong. Many people started with online services like AOL, CompuServe, or Prodigy partly because these came bundled with new computers, but also because for a novice these services were substantially easier to set up than a direct Internet access account. This balance began to shift in about 1995, when Internet service providers like Netcom and Pipeline began marketing their services nationwide, including software packages that were designed to be easy to set up and use. The advent of the World-Wide Web as the most important unifying interface to the Internet helped a great deal.

Further resentment was created on the Net side by AOL's habit of advertising itself as "the Internet, and a whole lot more," further confusing where the boundary, if any, might lie. AOL also took it upon itself to improve upon certain Usenet conventions: some newsgroups are listed on AOL by descriptions supplied by the service rather than their actual names. For example, *alt.aol-sucks* is listed as "Flames and complaints about AOL."

It's fair to say that AOL as a company can't have understood how many problems its interface was going to cause for its members and for the Net at large. Although it was slow to change, it did correct most of the mistakes Reid listed over the next two years. However, it made errors again when it launched its Web browser, which irritated Webmasters (the people who maintain Web sites), who were left to field AOLers' complaints when the company's browser didn't support some common Web features correctly or failed to update pages regularly enough on its proxy server.[7] (Ironically, the company that benefited most from AOL's Usenet debut was probably its nearest competitor, CompuServe, then nearly double AOL's size, which observed the situation and determined to construct a gateway that would cause less trouble. CompuServe has never suffered from anything like the same image problem on the Net, although it, too, is resented as too expensive. However, in early 1997 WebTV users were joining AOLers in the "clueless" ranks.)

Whatever the Net thinks about it, within its own modem ports AOL has been a roaring success. Between 1994 and 1997 AOL's claimed user base grew from 1 million to 8 million; the company launched a public stock offering; and it became the number one domestic U.S. service, estimating its daily contribution to Usenet at 300,000 postings. Plastering the world with free disks and free trial accounts helped create for AOL a throwaway accounts culture whose flame-and-run tactics were in general more destructive to the Net in encouraging spamming and other types of abuse than the far more controversial anonymous remailers that allow users to interact on the Net over a long period of time without revealing their real-world identity. But the strategy netted AOL a ton of subscribers (and supplied a generation of computer users with free backup disks).

It only added to the Net's contempt that there were several significant Internet services that AOL didn't offer, notably outbound Telnet, the function that allows you to log on to remote computers as if you were directly connected to them. The buzz may be all about the Web, but Telnet is a vital service and one the other major providers were supplying by 1995. More than that, it seemed that no matter what you did on AOL you ended up twiddling your thumbs while AOL downloaded "artwork"—all those colored graphics that give the service a large part of its character. And on top of that, the ability that old Netheads take for granted to multitask—like being able to download a file in the background while browsing the Web in one bit of foreground and hanging out on multiple channels on Internet Relay Chat in another—just couldn't be had. AOL, like all dial-up services of the era before the widespread use of Internet standards, only let you do one thing at a time. AOL did have the capability of running Internet sessions like those offered by flat-rate ISPs for those with the knowledge to seek out their own software, but it was an expensive—and, people complained, slow—way to get your Internet service.

AOL's chat rooms[8] were another sore point. Chat is one of those functions that most systems offer to let groups of users type messages to each other in real time, emulating a live meeting or conference. Internet Relay Chat (IRC) is far more flexible than AOL's setup, which limits users to one chat room at a time, with a maximum of twenty-three users. That relatively small objection was easily trumped by the activities of AOL's Guides, volunteers detailed to keep the service "clean."

AOL Guides act as monitors. If someone starts abusing other people in a public chat room, using sexually explicit words, or trying to trade illegally copied commercial software, any of the users can complain to a Guide, who will join the conversation and monitor the situation, warning the miscreant if it seems appropriate. If unacceptable behavior persists, the Guide can eject the person from the chat room and even the service—*alt.aol-sucks* posters call this getting "TOSsed," a word derived from "Terms of Service." AOL has also faced complaints about censorship from other users, such as the Creative Coalition, a group formed to protest the disappearance of members' poetry from the AOL message boards.[9]

If you think of AOL as a privately owned commercial service aimed at the family market, these policies make some sense even if they fail. And they have failed on a few occasions: some of the most frightening stories about the Internet and pornography or contacts between children and pedophiles did not happen on the Internet but within the supposedly safe confines of AOL. Their being reported as Internet stories is yet another source of resentment on the Net at large.

In a long article on the service in *Rolling Stone*, writer Jeff Goodell called sex AOL's "bedrock," estimating that sexually explicit real-time chat was contributing at least $7 million a month to AOL's free-disk fund.[10] Goodell's story of one AOL user—a schoolteacher who discovered sexual freedom online and then incorporated it into her real life— would be enough to horrify many in the religious right even though it combines the best qualities of experimentation with those of safe sex. Her experiences were possible because, besides the closely monitored public chat rooms, members may set up unmonitored private ones at will. These are used for anything from private conversation between real-life friends to the jointly created one-handed online typing fantasy sessions known as cybersex.

In the Net world, this monitoring puts AOL on the wrong side of one of the Net's major continuing flame wars: censorship. A significant portion of Net users hold freedom of speech to be sacred. The answer there, of course, is simple: if you don't like having your speech controlled, don't subscribe to AOL. There are plenty of ISPs out there to choose from that have adopted no-censorship policies. But on the Net, you don't just disagree with somebody and go away quietly. (Well, you may, but if you do, no one will know you did it unless you post a large, public announcement). It's much more satisfying to make fun of them as publicly as possible in *alt.aol-sucks*, the newsgroup for people who love to hate AOL. Many of the inhabitants are themselves former AOLers, and their relationship to the service is not unlike the attitude of zealously reformed smokers. Others just hate corporate America on principle.

It may have been this kind of thinking that inspired the writing of AOLHell, a free program that adds a slew of functions deemed to be missing from AOL's client software (besides a few facilities that are illegal); a Web site with a test to take to determine if you're ready to leave AOL for the wider Net; a site designed to show up the failings of the AOL Web browser; and a site listing what are claimed to be the words that will get you TOSsed.[11] Those assembled on *alt.aol-sucks* therefore cheered when, in 1995, several AOLers brought a class action suit against the service challenging some of its billing practices, specifically alleging that various built-in connection delays inflated users' bills. AOL denied the claims but settled the case, which included all AOL customers between July 14, 1991, and March 31, 1996, by giving the affected customers free time according to their service use.[12] The group cheered again at the end of 1996, when AOL declared its overall corporate loss.

I know what you're thinking. You're thinking these people need to get a life—to share, if they can't afford one each. You're thinking they have *way* too much time on their hands. You may even be wondering why Steve Case, the CEO of AOL, doesn't sue the pants off of all of them instead of continuing to be their chief provider of (free) floppy disks. And if it weren't for bisk poetry I might agree with you.

"Bisk" is the *alt.aol-sucks* subcultural name for one of those free trial disks that show up everywhere from magazine inserts to airline lunches. Anything that ubiquitous has to be a source of jokes, so posters have come up with all sorts of imaginative uses for these: props for wobbly tables, toys for the cat, even bathroom tiles. You figure this out after reading the newsgroup for a few days or by reading the FAQ (or by posting to ask, if your address isn't on AOL or your computer happens to be coated with asbestos). Bisk poetry is doggerel written in the same deliberately semi-literate style that produced the word "bisk," and late at night, when the peanut butter sticks to the roof of your mouth, it can be hilariously funny. Here is the official, earliest known sample:

Subject: Aol is sucks!!!!!what you can do with their cd rom bisk
From: xxxxxxxx@xxx.com (xxxxxxx)
Date: 1996/04/27 alt.aol.sucks
cost to mutch
it suck
no good
send to many disk.
Me and my friends took a bisk and lit it on fire and froze it slamed
it angaisnt the boor.[13]

At this point, prejudice against AOL and all those who click in her is probably not going to go away, even though it did join the coalition against the Communications Decency Act (see chapter 4). It's sort of appropriate, though, that evidence to support this comes from the WELL, the system whose users arguably believe they run cyberspace in the same unrealistic way some tiny secret conferences I'm in believe they run the systems they're on.

The WELL is sort of the other end of the coolth spectrum from AOL, even down to its austere, text-based interface, which is about as far from AOL's whizzy graphics and cute trivia quizzes as you can get and still be on the end of the same modem. The WELL's cachet comes from the fact that most of the Netizens of any fame as net.activists have at one time or another hung out there: Electronic Frontier Foundation founders, *Wired* editors, and technology wizards jostle with journalists from the major national media and the organizers of the annual Computers, Freedom, and Privacy Conference to argue about the most vital issues affecting cyberspace. The result is that the WELL, with 10,000 users, is the most written about online system and probably the most influential, at least in its own estimation.

In late 1995, a user on the WELL decided to test her perception that AOLers were unfairly discriminated against on the Net. She posted a blank message to an unfamiliar newsgroup from an address on a "plain vanilla" ISP. She got mailed offers of help and advice, plus a couple of jokes about her "profound" message. A week later, she posted another blank message to the same newsgroup from an AOL address. She got flames and abuse—from the same people. Reporting on this afterwards on the WELL, she said, "Seeing *aol.com* in the domain and making assumptions about them, reading their posts with a filter that says they are all jerks, is really not far removed from your basic garden-variety bigotries."

Viewed from a distance, these petty prejudices must seem only amusing. Many AOL users are completely unaware that their address is on the wrong side of the telephone lines and will never find out. It's more serious in terms of the sharing of resources the Net was designed to facilitate if valuable sources of information decide that AOLers are just too stupid to talk to (or they'd choose a better service provider), or if, conversely, vital information is discounted simply because it comes from AOL. Unlike real-world identifying factors such as gender, skin color, and accent, AOLishness can't be hidden—although it can be changed at will. However much we would like to believe that humans are universally goodhearted, kindly creatures, we have a built-in tendency to divide ourselves into "them" and "us" and to create and maintain prejudices against classes of people, presumably to convince ourselves that we are OK folks. This is the dark side of the network of trust that will come up in later chapters, but it is not limited to the Net itself.

There are two other important lessons. First, as more and more of our communications are mediated by computer, AOL's online hazing experience shows how vital it is that the influence of system design on human behavior be examined and understood. Different cultures develop in cyberspace in part because of the technology that supports them. The WELL has a system design that fosters highly structured discourse by allowing no threading within a topic, forcing a would-be participant to read through to the end of the discussion before adding his or her thoughts. Repetition is therefore rare. On Usenet or CIX, with built-in threading, the interface encourages responses to specific points; while this allows discussions to branch into other topics without confusion, repetition abounds because many posters answer without reading to the end of the thread to find out that their point has already been made. This is especially a problem with the widespread use of offline readers.

Second, it's easy to lose perspective on the Net. The embedded sorting of the Net into topics is an efficient way to sort computerized discussions. But a consequence of that structure is that people tend to focus only on topics that interest them, and because those topics fill their computer screens they tend to imagine that those topics are the most important ones, not only on the Net, but possibly in the world. This kind of intensity is vital in some professions (including writing, researching, and programming, some of the earliest classes of Net user). But it leads to skewed fantasies in which people whose interests are different from yours cease to exist or may be discounted: out of sight, out of mind. Any group that thinks it runs cyberspace must remember that the real in-group with the real power are the bastard operators from hell (BOFHs).[14] And they don't let any of us read their newsgroups.

4

Guerrilla Cryptographers

Oh Squidgy. Kiss me, please. [Sound of kissing.] Do you know what
I'm going to be imagining I'm doing tonight, at about 12 o'clock?
Just holding you so close to me. It'll have to be delayed action for
48 hours.   —Man talking to Princess Diana over
an unencrypted cellular phone, 1992

Privacy was one of the big concerns on the Net even before
junk email and spam. Because the Internet was designed to enable the free
flow of data, it's not particularly good at protecting anyone's secrets, as
several well-publicized computer hacking (read: breaking and entering
with a modem) cases have showed. When, for example, the world's most
demonized hacker, Kevin Mitnick, was arrested in early 1995, he was ac-
cused of having stolen a copy of a list of leading domestic Internet service
provider Netcom's customer credit card numbers, 20,000 of them in all,
and posted it on the WELL in a file directory from where anyone could
retrieve a copy. As far as anyone knows, none of those numbers were ever
used fraudulently, but that's not the point: the point is that the data
needed to be protected properly and wasn't.

San Francisco software developer Bruce Koball, a key organizer of the
annual Computers, Freedom, and Privacy Conference, took advantage of
his brief moment in the arc lights as the discoverer of the copied files to
point out that there was and is a simple solution to such theft: encrypt the
files, garbling them so they can only be read by the authorized owner. The
one problem: the lack of well-designed, easy-to-use cryptography products. The reason: governmental distrust of what citizens can hide by such
means.

Cryptography is not the only possibility; a second school of thought
holds that legislation is needed to control what information may be col-

lected and how it may be used. In most European countries, for example, privacy laws enjoin corporations from collecting user data for one purpose (say, building a customer database for internal marketing purposes) and using it for another (say, selling it to another company as a bulk mailing list) or exporting it to another country without such protections. There are arguments that such laws primarily protect the rich and powerful; however, one problem as Europe unifies is that the United States's lack of privacy legislation may make it illegal for subsidiary companies abroad to send certain types of data to their U.S. headquarters.

The problem is that laws move slowly and data moves quickly. Cypherpunks, as the heavy-metal fans of cryptography are known, tend to believe it's better to protect the data directly. Unlike privacy advocates who favor legislative solutions, cypherpunks can vote with their computers to write, use, and deploy their own technology.

Or at least, they can *now*. Although codes and ciphers are thought to go back to 1900 B.C.,[1] if you want something uncrackable these days you need a computer. For that reason, for the last few decades strong cryptography was largely the province of governments. Amateurs simply didn't have access to the necessary hardware. That was why the dream that gripped Phil Zimmermann in the 1970s of writing a microcomputer implementation of a new kind of cryptographic system was so unattainable at the time.

Like a lot of kids, Zimmermann was fascinated with codes and ciphers. He says he was only in about fourth grade when he read Herbert Zim's *Codes and Secret Writing*[2] and thought it was "so cool."[3] In seventh grade, a schoolmate challenged Zimmerman to crack a message written in a code of the schoolmate's own devising, an alphabet that looked something like the runes in *Lord of the Rings*. Zimmermann took it home and attacked it by comparing the frequencies with which individual symbols recurred with the frequencies with which the letters in the English language are known to be used. Shades of Sherlock Holmes in "The Dancing Men": who could ever forget Holmes's well-known listing of those frequencies, ETAOIN SHRDLU (also famous as the copyeditor of the *Computer Underground Digest*)? Zimmermann brought the message back decoded the next day.

The story illustrates more than the insecurity of simple substitution ciphers. A truism you hear uttered frequently by the cryptographic community is that if you want to write a good cryptographic system, you must first have learned to break such systems. Understanding what methods are used to break the locks is important in understanding what weaknesses to avoid in constructing them. Zimmermann's schoolmate could have added a layer of difficulty by, for example, first translating his message into another language, or possibly by using multiple symbols for each letter of the alphabet and choosing randomly which to use at any given point. Those possibilities lead to a corollary: cryptanalysis, the science of cracking codes and ciphers, is much harder and more time-consuming than encrypting messages once you have the code designed because you may have to try multiple methods of attack.

Zimmermann was studying computer science at Florida Atlantic University in Boca Raton when he discovered the usefulness of computers in encryption. The basis remains the same: garbling the message so it can't be read by anyone except the intended recipient. But computers make it possible to implement systems that are much more difficult to crack than anything a human could do unaided.

The basis of any encryption system is an algorithm, a mathematical term for a procedure—in this case, a procedure by which data can be encrypted. Letter substitution is a very simple example of an algorithm. A key specifies exactly how you use the algorithm to code the text, just as a single type of lock can be designed to use many individual keys, none of them interchangeable. In general, the longer and more complex the key, the more difficult and time-consuming the encryption is to crack. Someone with enough time and money to buy the most powerful hardware may be able to mount what's called a "brute-force" attack, where every possible key is tried until one works. In designing or choosing a cryptographic system, you have to assess how long that would take and how much effort (both yours and the cracker's) and cost it's worth to defend the information you're protecting. Like securing your house against burglars, you may not be able to keep out someone who's truly determined, but if you slow the intruders down enough they may move on to someplace easier to penetrate.

Until the mid-1970s encryption schemes relied on the key's being kept secret and out of the hands of all but the sender and recipient of the message. If the two parties, by cryptographic convention known as Alice and Bob, were geographically separated or unknown to each other, arrangements had to be made—say, sending a courier with the briefcase handcuffed to his wrist—to transmit the key securely from one to the other and verify identities before any exchange of encrypted data could usefully take place. This type of system had other risks, notably to the courier. For public data networks such as the Internet, such a system is too unwieldy to allow the kind of seamless exchange of protected data that everyone wants; it simply can't facilitate unplanned, secure communications between strangers.

But in 1976 two researchers at Stanford University, Whitfield Diffie and Martin Hellman, came up with a radically new approach, which they dubbed *public-key cryptography*, that eliminated this first step. In Diffie's and Hellman's original description, known as the Diffie-Hellman key exchange, each user had a secret key, and when two users wanted to talk securely in real time, the two keys would provide information from which a private single-session key could be generated to encrypt the conversation in both directions. It's a bit as if you spoke one secret language and your correspondent spoke another, and a computer could from these concoct a unique mix for transmission that, since it would only be used once, would be difficult for anyone else to learn quickly enough to understand what you were saying.

The better known implementation of public-key cryptography, the RSA algorithm formulated in 1977 by Massachusetts Institute of Technology researchers Ronald L. Rivest, Adi Shamir, and Leonard M. Adleman, is a bit different. The idea is simple and elegant: a mathematical system generates a complementary pair of keys. One of the keys is public. This key you distribute as widely as you like, getting as many third parties such as trusted friends or organizations as you can to "sign" it to verify that it's yours. In another imperfect analogy, think of the wax seals once used to verify the security and authenticity of written letters; a person's seal had value because it was recognized as his.

The other key you keep secret. Messages encrypted with either one of those keys can only be decrypted with the other, so that anything you encrypt with your private key is authenticated as coming from you, and anything encrypted with your public key can only be read by you. Now if the sender, who we'll perversely call Nancy, encrypts her message with both her private key *and* the public key of the recipient (William), the message is both authenticated as coming from her and readable only by William. Nancy gets William's public key from him by email, from a mutual friend, or even from a public key server. William can do the same to check the authenticity of Nancy's key.

Because this scheme makes it possible to add security and privacy to the kind of spontaneous and promiscuous use of communications that the Internet is good at, it's considered to be one of the fundamental pieces of technology needed to enable all kinds of uses of the Net: shipping confidential patient data between general practitioners and hospitals, business documents between lawyers, bank statements, checking account balances, credit card numbers, and so on. Importantly, it also handles both of the most important functions of cryptography: authentication (the message can only have come from Nancy) and confidentiality (the message can only be read by William). Authentication is important: you want your stockbroker to be sure that order to buy or sell really comes from you and not some hoaxer; you want your business associates' electronic documents to be legally binding; and if political systems start to use electronic voting systems, you want them to be as fraud-proof as possible.

Diffie and Hellman published their proposed public-key cryptography in a paper called "New Directions in Cryptography" in November 1976; Rivest, Shamir, and Adleman followed with their version in February 1978.[4] Zimmermann, reading of these new discoveries, was inspired: he dreamed of writing an implementation for microcomputers that anyone could use. The fact that the computers available then were too weak to handle the demands of such a program was only one of several problems standing in his way. The mathematical basis of the RSA algorithm requires a lot of arithmetic with very large (three-hundred digit) numbers. Even a computer can't handle this without shortcuts. It wasn't until 1986 that Zimmermann learned enough about how these shortcuts work to write them into a program in the C programming language.[5]

Even then, nothing happened right away. Zimmermann was busy working as a software engineer specializing in cryptography. Because RSA was patented, any program he wrote couldn't be sold, so it made more sense to concentrate on making a living.

Then, in 1991 the U.S. government introduced Senate Bill 266, an anti-terrorism measure that contained a clause to prohibit communications and file security via systems without a backdoor that would "permit the government to obtain the plain text contents of voice, data, and other communications."[6] Such a rule would effectively outlaw encryption. The clause was later removed (making a brief reappearance that summer in an omnibus anti-crime bill, from which it was also removed) after lobbying by the Electronic Frontier Foundation and other organizations, but in the meantime the threat that strong encryption would be outlawed seemed very real.

To many early Net users it seemed plain that this was a crisis: because of the way the Internet is constructed it is not possible to guarantee that communications can't or won't be read as they flow from one place to another. Even within a single system, email and other stored files are accessible by the system's administrators, if no one else. In general, system administrators have better things to do than read those files. But the fact remains that on most systems they *can*, and if policemen were to show up with a court order, they probably would turn over copies.[7]

Facing the possibility that legal access to encryption might soon be lost, Zimmermann put together the first version of his encryption program, PGP (for Pretty Good Privacy), and gave it to a friend, who proceeded to upload it to as many bulletin board systems as he could find. Zimmermann, who speaks passionately on the right of ordinary citizens to protect their privacy, said for a long time that his whole concern was domestic: he wanted to secure access to strong cryptography for American citizens. "I figured other countries could solve their own problems." However, Zimmerman has since modified this, telling a London conference in 1997, "I did it for human rights."

Unfortunately for Zimmermann's immediate future, the program very quickly headed out into cyberspace at large, and it didn't take long before copies were available all over the world—even at a time when relatively few individuals outside of the academic and government community had access to the Internet. For example, PGP's availability on the WELL was announced to the *eff* conference there on June 7, 1991.[8]

It may well have made its way out of the United States much sooner, but it was definitely posted to the *crypto* conference on CIX, in London, on June 29, 1991.[9] Today it all happens even faster: by the time Zimmermann demonstrated a new version of PGP that offered military-grade security for phone connections made across the Internet, PGPfone, at the 1996 Computers, Freedom, and Privacy Conference, rumors were that it was already available on an Italian site on the Net, from where it could be readily downloaded by non-U.S. citizens.

In February 1993, Zimmermann was informed by the U.S. Department of Justice that he was being investigated to determine whether he had illegally exported strong cryptography, which is actually classed as a munition under the International Traffic in Arms Regulations (ITAR). It was three years before the investigation was dropped without charge. It was a very shaky time for Zimmermann, who seriously believed he might wind up bankrupt and on the receiving end of a trial and possibly a jail sentence.

During that time, however, PGP became solidly established on the Net as a standard; at the same time, as cryptanalysts examined it and failed to crack it, its reputation grew. It also went truly international, with teams outside the United States working to develop the program further. Even if Zimmermann had been arrested, charged, and jailed, the program would have gone on being developed, distributed, and used. With development teams working in countries such as England and Australia, the export question was somewhat moot: if a British citizen picked up a copy of the British version of the program from an FTP server at Britain's Demon Internet, this was not a situation covered by ITAR.

PGP would have taken off even faster if it hadn't had a second legal problem: it used technology that was patented, and Zimmermann and his company, Phil's Pretty Good Software, did not have a license from the patent-holder. Rivest, Shamir, and Adleman's work developing RSA at MIT was done with funding from the Navy and the National Science Foundation. As is the way with these things, although the government retained the rights to use the technology itself, the ideas were patented by MIT and the rights were handed over to a new company, Public Key Partners, for commercial exploitation. This outfit also had the rights to the patent for the Diffie-Hellman key exchange scheme and two other key patents in this area, giving it exclusive licensing rights to what seemed in 1992 to be all of public-key cryptography. The sole licensee for RSA at the time was the California-based company RSA Data Security. In a document dated December 4, 1992, covering legal issues with respect to PGP, Zimmermann stated that he had obtained the opinion of a patent lawyer before proceeding with PGP, and that he was therefore "convinced that publishing PGP the way I did does not violate patent law." He did not, he argued, steal any source code: "I wrote my PGP software from scratch, with my own implementation of the RSA algorithm."

Nonetheless, a complaint from Jim Bidzos, president of both Public Key Partners and RSA Data Security, speedily followed PGP onto the WELL. Within four days of its original June 7, 1991, posting, the original poster removed PGP from the WELL's libraries after a request from the system's management, who felt this was a legal dispute the WELL could afford to miss. The legality of using PGP within the United States was a hotly debated topic on the Net for the next couple of years. Endless megabytes were churned out in cryptography-related newsgroups like the scientifically oriented *sci.crypt*, with one side arguing that it was important to respect intellectual property rights and the law, and the other side insisting that a mathematical algorithm should not be patentable.

This is not just sophistry and rationalization: the question of what constitutes intellectual property is constantly being revisited. In general, copyright law has covered the *expression* of ideas and facts, not the ideas or facts themselves. New designs for machines or drugs can be patented; but the sequence of words describing what those machines and drugs do and how they do it can only be copyrighted. Software, however, raised a new problem: was it a literary work or a new type of infinitely copyable machine? The European Community considered this question and decided to class it as a literary work. In the United States, however, the use of patents to protect software—even such basic routines as drawing a cursor on a computer screen—began proliferating in the 1980s. The difference is profound. Copyright protects the precise arrangement of words and letters on the page. Patents protect functionality, that is, what the program actually does. You can copyright a book's text; but if the book itself were invented today someone would patent it.

Because patenting was such a profound change from the early days of the industry, when software was generally free, in 1983 MIT researcher Richard Stallman set up the Free Software Foundation with the goal of creating a full suite of free software designed to run on the computer operating system UNIX.[10] UNIX itself was free, as it was written at AT&T at a time when the company was enjoined from selling such non-telecommunications products. At least one company, Cygnus Support, has been set up with the idea that software should be free and companies should derive their incomes from selling services and support for that free software, following the same kind of argument circulated by John Perry Barlow. Not surprisingly, one of Cygnus Support's founders was also one of Barlow's EFF co-founders and the man who invented the *alt* hierarchy, John Gilmore.

Stallman, Gilmore, and many other industry leaders argue that the widespread use of software patents can chill technological development.[11] They have a point: technology develops incrementally, as each new developer tries to improve on what others have done. The entire computer industry is built on the practice of reverse engineering: taking a product apart to work out what it does and then building a different product that does the same thing by different means. Companies as large and diverse as Compaq, Borland, and Microsoft have all created products by this means (respectively, Compaq PCs, Borland's Quattro Pro spreadsheet, and Microsoft Windows, which is still trying to catch up to the Macintosh interface pioneered in 1984). Then leading software companies

Lotus (since bought by IBM) and Borland (then as now struggling) fought a long and bitter legal battle over just this question after Borland copied the ordering of certain program commands for Quattro Pro from Lotus's classic 1-2-3 spreadsheet. Borland eventually won a ruling on appeal that this was not a violation of Lotus's intellectual property rights.

Software is just one area where the extension of intellectual property rights is being hotly debated. Biotechnology companies are claiming rights over natural substances they discover and even human genes they've mapped. On December 2–20, 1996, the World Intellectual Property Organization met to consider a database treaty which would create new rights in databases that might, some specialists warned,[12] bring certain types of facts, such as sports statistics, stock prices, and even weather reports, into private ownership from the public domain, where they've always been thought to belong.

So when Net users argued that a mathematical algorithm is a discovery rather than an invention, they had more in mind than rationalizing their own use of PGP. And there was an odd twist to the patent situation: the RSA patent is not valid outside the United States. The reason has to do with its publication in print. In Europe generally, if print publication precedes the patent application, as it did in this case, the patent isn't granted. This created a weird situation in which PGP, developed in Colorado using technology dreamed up in California and Massachusetts, was illegal to use in the United States, illegal to export, and yet legal for non-Americans to use abroad once it got there. This is probably not something any of the lawmakers would have thought desirable.

The odd thing about the ferocity of these discussions and the passion of PGP supporters is that there were competing products, even then, built to conform to the Internet RFCs on privacy-enhanced mail.[13] RSA Data Security had a $200 product called Mailsafe, and other programs such as RiPEM were also available. In his December 1992 document on the legal issues surrounding PGP, Zimmerman stated that he thought the patent controversy had given PGP the air of forbidden fruit, and he may be right. Its being free didn't hurt either. In any case, it acquired a cachet no other encryption program has had, enhanced by Net users' habit of appending their public keys to their Usenet postings as a show of solidarity. The Justice Department's investigation of Zimmerman probably added an air of authenticity to the program, since it's logical to think the government would hardly bother investigating the deployment of a program that didn't work.

Even odder is the fact that the program was not all that easy to use. In the years since, people have written add-ons that help ease the process of getting started with PGP and Windows front ends that make it more intuitive. But even as late as 1995, one of the program's own international developers admitted in private conversation that the development team preferred to send unencrypted email because it was so much more convenient.

But PGP was a cause célèbre, even though for a long time many people who had downloaded the software and were keeping copies "just in case" refused to use it because of the patent issues. These were resolved in 1993, when Zimmermann made a deal with a Phoenix, Arizona, company called Lemcom which had obtained a license from RSA Data Security to sell software based on the RSA algorithm. Lemcom got the rights to sell a commercial version of PGP called Viacrypt; Zimmermann and the PGP development teams got the legal right to distribute the freeware version. The Net got legal PGP: in 1994, the download rate of PGP from just the single, export-controlled FTP site at MIT was 500 to 1,000 copies a day.[14] This opened the way for use of the software by businesses, who were never going to rely on a product whose legality was in doubt.

Zimmermann himself may be in the best position to exploit this new legality: three years of government investigation probably have made him the most trusted cryptographer on the Net. In March 1996, a month after the government investigation was dropped, Zimmermann formed PGP Inc. to further develop software and other privacy and networking products with Seybold Seminars founder Jonathan Seybold and Dan Lynch, founder of Interop and chairman of CyberCash. In July 1996, PGP Inc. bought Viacrypt and its parent company, and in November it followed up by acquiring the leading company for privacy on the World-Wide Web, North Carolina–based Privnet.[15]

Once the patent issues were resolved, support for the idea that PGP should be distributed as widely as possible among the Net community was phenomenal. Spreading PGP, even in defiance of the government regulations, was seen as a way of ensuring that encryption would have to remain legal. The more people have and use PGP, the argument went, the more difficult it will be for the government to outlaw it. This argument gained greater urgency after the 1994 passage of the Digital Telephony Act, which requires telecommunications providers to design their equipment to assure the government a backdoor for access. Besides, the pervasive culture of the Net combines a kind of permanent rebelliousness with a slightly malicious enjoyment of successfully defying authority. Making the government look silly felt good to a lot of people, especially because those who came to adulthood in the era of Viet Nam and Watergate felt they had right and prudence on their side. Today's government may be friendly; tomorrow's may not be.

One enterprising British Net user encoded the entire RSA algorithm into four lines of code in a programming language known as PERL, with a one-line "user manual" listing in order all the software switches[16] you could use to configure the program when you ran it. This was small enough to fit into the generally accepted size limits for *.sigs*,[17] and the author encouraged others to copy the lines and distribute them further. Since you can never tell exactly what route a Usenet posting will take, at one point this algorithm was probably being illegally exported from the United States tens of thousands of times a day.

That wasn't all. The short version got printed and bar-coded on a T-shirt, which a few daring souls wore through customs on their way out of the country, and even onto small labels you could stick to the side of your laptop (or anywhere else). One of these was passed to me at the 1995 Computers, Freedom, and Privacy Conference by a lawyer; on the top it read, "This label is a munition," with a warning that handing the label to foreigners constituted export under the ITAR. People who believed that the program's continued availability was a vital plank in defending our traditional national freedoms handed out disks by the dozens at conferences, parties, and other gatherings.

The importance of the PGP story in terms of governing the Net isn't limited to the encryption facilities it gives Netizens, although those have already proven important in circumstances where keeping data confidential is important, such as dissident groups in repressive regimes. Equally important is the fact that powerful national and intellectual property laws were overridden by the Net community when that community felt strongly enough that it was important to do so. The patent questions kept newsgroups like *alt.security.pgp* buzzing and buzzing with violent arguments between people who argued that PGP violated RSA's patent, was illegal, and shouldn't be used by any responsible human and cypherpunks who said that to keep cryptography legal everyone should use it. But they didn't stop a large number of Netizens from signing their Usenet messages with their public keys (which just look like four or five lines of gibberish), partly as a badge of honor, and partly as a means of authenticating messages, important in a contentious group like *alt.religion.scientology*, where forgeries and personal attacks have created an atmosphere of suspicion. By now, the program is a de facto standard even though its first release was greeted with suspicion because so few home-built encryption systems had ever been any good.[18] Grady Ward's announcement on *alt.religion.scientology* that the program, used to encrypt his hard disk, had withstood a month's worth of cracking attempts by the court-appointed special master has also served to help its reputation.[19] (Ward, sued in 1996 by the Church of Scientology, was subpoenaed in September 1993, as part of the Zimmermann investigation, over a product he wrote called Moby Crypto, a 9Mb compilation of source code for a wide variety of cryptographic algorithms.)

Like the Internet itself, PGP flourished because its supporters understood that if the program were distributed widely enough there would be no central point at which its availability could be knocked out. As always on the Net, the owners and operators of the Internet service providers were the pressure points. But that is already a community large enough to make it difficult to secure universal cooperation. Systems like CompuServe, America Online, and even the WELL were successfully pressured to remove PGP from their systems at various times. But those are of minor importance compared to the number of public FTP sites around the world on university and other systems where both PGP and PGPfone remain accessible. There is no calling these programs back. If the government wants widespread use of encryption that has a backdoor by which it can gain access, its one chance is to hope that the program never becomes so easy to use that it attracts mainstream consumers. With Zimmermann poised to build a large, serious, and successful company around just such a product, that seems unlikely even though the patent issue was revived in early 1997 when Bidzos filed suit, alleging that Lemcom's license was not transferable to PGP Inc.

As they say on the Net, when the going gets weird, the weird turn pro.

5

Stuffing the Genie Back in the Can of Worms

> In common with sacred writings everywhere, omen records were couched in deliberately obscure wording. Because omens affected national security and required specialized knowledge, omen work was restricted to small teams of scholars who were more like academics than magicians or priests, men of high rank whose office was hereditary and who reported directly to the king.
>
> —Geoffrey Dean, explaining the origins of astrology in Gordon Stein's *An Encyclopedia of the Paranormal*

Spreading PGP across the world is only a partial solution if the desired result is the ready availability of strong cryptography. Individuals may take the risk of using software whose legality is uncertain (although most would rather not), but businesses can't—and a lot of our most private communications are with businesses such as banks, lawyers, doctors, and government departments. For encryption to become standard practice, it has to be clearly legal. More than that, it has to be standardized the way the Net itself is. Otherwise, the first time you wanted to send anyone an encrypted message you'd first have to contact them to find out what products they were using. PGP may yet become that standard. But in April 1993, the National Institute of Standards and Technology (NIST) approved a different standard, the Clipper chip, for government use.

Clipper, which the government imagined would be built into all kinds of telephony devices from modems to mobile phones, was a bit of hardware that was supposed to garble data just as effectively as PGP. To cypherpunks, there was a significant difference: Clipper had a special built-in function that would store, or escrow, a copy of your private key with a government agency so that in case of need law enforcement could retrieve the key and decrypt your communications. Only with a court order, of course.

Clipper was one of several results of ten years of research and development authorized by the Computer Security Act of 1987 and carried out by NIST and the National Security Agency (NSA), the super-secret agency no one was supposed to know existed until the publication in 1982 of John Bamford's comprehensive history, *The Puzzle Palace*.[1] Investment on this level would have been considered necessary even without the Net. As hardware gets ever more powerful, yesterday's uncrackable encryption systems become tomorrow's easy targets. The previous standard, DES (for Data Encryption Standard), developed at IBM in the 1970s, was certified in 1977 as a government standard, and was reviewed in 1993 and certified until 1998. But the NSA could look ahead to the day when replacement was essential if the security agencies were to remain confident that their encryption could not be broken by other countries in a war, as the United States did to the Germans in World War II when it cracked their Enigma cipher. At the Crypto93 conference, Michael Wiener, a cryptographic advisor at Bell-Northern Research, published a paper containing a design (complete with circuit diagrams) of a $1 million machine that could crack DES in seven hours. Triple DES—a new technique that involves encrypting data with one key, decrypting it with a second, and re-encrypting it with a third—is thought to have substantially extended DES's useful life.

At the 1994 Computers, Freedom, and Privacy Conference (CFP'94), an NSA staffer in a Boyzz T-shirt adorned with a conference badge sporting a sticker saying, "We are everywhere" explained that the memory of Enigma still dominates NSA thinking from two viewpoints: (1) we should be able to crack other people's encryption systems; (2) no one should be able to crack ours. In a world where PGP and the Net didn't exist, those views must have seemed reasonable, and planning ahead must have made sense.

To create Clipper, the NSA came up with a proprietary algorithm called Skipjack, which uses a form of public-key cryptography. This algorithm was implemented in a chip (Clipper) that was intended to be tamper-proof, so that any attempt to get into the chip to extract its program code (and deconstruct the algorithm) would destroy the hardware. The controversial bit was the built-in function that allowed law enforcement access to each user's secret key.

Roughly, the scheme worked like this: each chip contains a unique serial number, a unique encryption key, and a family key that is the same across all Clipper chips but is known—or supposed to be known—only to authorized law enforcement personnel. Private keys are eighty bits in length (in general, the longer the key the greater the security), and in the original proposal were to be split into two pieces to be escrowed with two government agencies, NIST (in the Department of Commerce) and the Treasury Department.

The bit of code that unlocks Clipper for interested police officers, though, is the Law Enforcement Access Field (LEAF), which is exchanged when two Clipper-Inside devices negotiate at the start of a session (or the chips won't work). The LEAF is derived by first using the chip's unique key to encrypt the session key that's been generated and then appending the chip's unique serial number and a checksum (a number generated for verification) and re-encrypting the entire mess with the family key.

At least that was the plan when Clipper was announced, in early 1993. The objections were immediate and so broad-based that the NSA representatives who showed up to debate the issue at CFP'94 seemed stunned. After all, the argument went, what we're offering people is much stronger and safer than the nothing everyone uses even now, three years later.

The political objections were obvious: why should the government have the ability to read people's private electronic communication? The Post Office doesn't keep an escrowed copy of every letter we write, and no little chip tracks our daily movements in case law enforcement later needs to find out what we were doing on February 23, 1973 (even if video cameras go up daily). Opposition came from all sorts of places: the Electronic Frontier Foundation, Computer Professionals for Social Responsibility, the American Civil Liberties Union, and software industry giants like Microsoft and IBM's Lotus subsidiary (whose product Notes is made to handle complex, confidential, business-wide databases). The software companies figured (correctly) that the continued ban on exporting strong cryptography and the key escrow requirement would not make it easier for them to sell their products in foreign markets. Less predictably, opposition to Clipper also came from Christian fundamentalists, and even Rush Limbaugh.

Nonetheless, then NSA general counsel Stewart Baker dismissed the protests this way at CFP'94 and later in print in *Wired*: "The opposition to Clipper is coming from people who weren't allowed to go to Woodstock because they had to finish their math homework."[2] This was received with about as much enthusiasm as (though less hilarity than) White House science spokesman Mike Nelson's comment at CFP'96 that key escrow in fact would be acceptable to non-U.S. citizens because they'd trust our government sooner than their own, and that "we do not help countries that oppress their own people."

Nonetheless, Baker's comment had an element of truth to it: a lot of the protest *was* coming from the forty- and fiftysomethings who came of age in the era of distrust engendered by Viet Nam and Watergate and reinforced by Oliver North. It's hard not to think of your government as potentially hostile when you remember that four college students just like you were shot at Kent State during anti-war protests, or when your first exposure to Senate hearings was to those that wound up with the resignation of a president. American tradition is, in any case, on the side of limiting the powers of government and always paying healthy attention to the possibility that today's benevolent government may be replaced, someday down the line, with one that's not so friendly. As Phil Zimmermann has often put it, "If you're looking at technology policy, you should ask yourself what kind of technological infrastructure would strengthen the hand of a police state, and then don't deploy that technology. That's a matter of good civic hygiene."

There are, of course, good reasons for giving someone a copy of your key. It's too easy to look ahead and imagine the day when Aunt Minnie dies, leaving all her assets locked up in electronic cash on her laptop, and no one in her family can guess the passphrase that unlocks access to the money because no one knows about the illicit lover whose name she used. Making sure a copy of the key is safely stowed somewhere is just as logical as giving a friend the keys to your house in case you lock yourself out. On the other hand, if you were being prosecuted by the government and were using email to communicate with your lawyer, knowing the government couldn't get a copy of your key might be awfully important. That's why privacy campaigners feel so strongly that escrow should be voluntary, not mandatory—an argument that gains some force from the fact that encryption software spreads across the Net faster than politicians can argue.

The other big issue, the International Traffic in Arms Regulations (ITAR) that restrict exports of strong encryption, can't be argued fast enough for American software companies, all of whom would love to be able to build encryption into their business-oriented products. It's a measure of the general air of official provincialism that, when the two spokesmen the White House threw to the CFP'94 wolves were asked by re-porters about this, their answer was, "Well, the domestic market is pretty big." Two years later, Nelson followed this up by saying that the compa-nies' complaints showed that the export controls were having precisely the effect they were intended to have: "Keeping cryptography from where we don't want it to go."

Did these guys really not know that even in 1993, 40 percent of the revenues of a company the size and dominance of Lotus (at the time Microsoft's chief competitor) came from Europe? Lotus, then two years away from big losses and acquisition by IBM, was betting its future on the groupware product Notes, which uses encryption to protect the con-fidentiality of the company-wide databases it helps generate. Encryption has a place in business in everything from fileservers to databases and word processors as well as email, and European companies are if any-thing more security-minded and suspicious than American companies. Does the U.S. government really think Europeans will tamely settle for whatever encryption it decides is weak enough to export, especially when they have access to top-notch cryptographers like the Israelis (including Adi Shamir, co-formulator of the RSA algorithm) and respected algo-rithms like IDEA being developed in places like Switzerland?

These export controls arguably have given companies in the rest of the world the chance to compete in and even dominate a market that other-wise might have gone to American companies by default. If they haven't succeeded, it's because U.S. dominance of office software makes integrat-ing cryptography a problem. A May 1996 government report, "Cryptog-raphy's Role in Securing the Information Society" (CRISIS),[3] ended up agreeing with the things the Net had been saying for years: "Export con-trols also have had the effect of reducing the domestic availability of products with strong encryption capabilities. The need for US vendors (especially software vendors) to market their products to an international audience leads many of them to weaken the encryption capabilities of products available to the domestic market, even though no statutory re-strictions are imposed on that market." The reason: it's too expensive to support two versions of every product. Nonetheless, the report recom-mended that export controls should not be eliminated, only that they should be "progressively relaxed."[4] Interestingly enough, by late October 1996, European companies were equally unhappy about the American restrictions, and the European Electronic Messaging Association began lobbying the European Commission in Brussels to improve matters both by harmonizing European legislation and by negotiating with the United States to lift restrictions on access to the software developer kits that allow third parties to integrate encryption into the market-leading business office software such as that produced by Microsoft.

Encryption is just as controversial outside the United States, though not as publicly debated. France, the most often cited example of a repressive regime, cryptographically speaking, requires anyone using cryptography to obtain a license. Japan tightened its export regulations in September 1996 to require businesses to get prior government approval for any overseas order of encryption products worth more than 50,000 yen (about $450), way down from 10 million yen (about $91,000). However, RSA announced earlier that summer that its Japanese affiliate would shortly begin selling a triple-DES chip stronger than U.S. companies were allowed to export, a move critics felt vindicated their stance against the U.S. government's regulations. The Organization for Economic Cooperation and Development (OECD), too, spent much of 1996 talking about developing a network of trusted third parties to hold keys in escrow; however, its draft guidelines of December 1996 speak of "key management" only as a "possible solution" and come down heavily on the side of international interoperability and the removal of controls that might hinder cross-border electronic commerce. In early 1997, the U.K. government introduced proposals for a government licensing requirement for trusted third parties.

The technical objections to Clipper were equally strong. For one thing, the whole system was going to be based on a secret algorithm. While even "guerrilla cryptographers" like Phil Zimmermann have said that the NSA really is as good at cryptography as it thinks it is,[5] it's generally not considered a good sign for a security system to rely on secrecy. In the case of cryptography, what proves an algorithm's soundness is the failure of informed attempts at cracking it.[6] The respect PGP has won for itself on the Net doesn't come from its status as "outlaw software," but rather because five years of widespread availability and analysis from the cryptographic community have failed to expose weaknesses.

So the cryptographic community reacted with general discomfort when the NSA said the algorithm was classified. On top of that, there were objections about the encryption system's implementation in hardware instead of software (more flexible and cheaper) and cost (estimated at $30, a price level probably higher than current demand for anyone except celebrities who have already been caught telling their innermost secrets over analog cellular phones).

The Clipper version of the encryption battle was rendered moot, however, in early 1994, when the NSA actually let a few sample chips out for inspection by members of the cryptographic community. One of them went to Bell Labs researcher Matt Blaze, who that February had established a reputation of fairness for himself by posting a report to the Internet on a demonstration of Clipper the NSA had carried out while visiting Bell Labs.

As Blaze told it at the 1995 Computers, Freedom, and Privacy conference,[7] he came back to home base with his Clipper chip, and his Clipper chip reader, and his NSA mug (nice to know where our tax dollars go), and started by looking at the law enforcement field to see what the mechanism was for reading traffic through it. "As I expected," he said, "the obvious ways of circumventing it don't work. But very much to my surprise, only very slightly less obvious ways worked." What Blaze found was a way to falsify the field so that no amount of applying your escrowed key to the garbled data would produce plaintext. The scheme, he said, requires some technical literacy, but not enough to defeat the determined terrorists and child pornographers the law enforcement agencies were insisting were too dangerous to trust with a non-escrowed system like PGP. Blaze wrote up his discovery and sent a copy of his findings to the NSA, and then published them as a research paper. What he didn't expect was to land on the front page of the *New York Times*.[8]

Clipper pretty much died there, although some products were released that use the chip. But the idea behind it—that law enforcement needs assured access to the communications systems of the future—didn't. It continues in proposals (quickly dubbed "Clipper II") for a key escrow infrastructure, called variously a network of trusted third parties (Europe) or public-key infrastructure (PKI; United States). "Key recovery" is beginning to appear as the government's (inaccurate) euphemism of preference. As of early 1997 it's clear that the debate is going to continue for some time, as late 1996 proposals from the Clinton administration are for the appointment of a crypto-ambassador to promote international acceptance of the government's desired escrow infrastructure, along with the conditional lifting of export controls.

This is even more mediocre than it sounds, since the plan is to raise the key length allowable for export to 56 bits (from 40 bits) for two years, but in return companies selling encryption products must have ready a key-escrow system by the end of that time. This is nearly a year after seven leading cryptographers, including Blaze, wrote a January 1996 report for the Business Software Alliance advising that DES with 56-bit keys was "increasingly inadequate" and that since there is little extra expense involved, current implementations should use a minimum of 75-bit keys. Assuming that Moore's Law holds and computing power continues to double every eighteen months (product cycles are, if anything, speeding up), to protect data adequately for the next twenty years the team recommended 90-bit keys.[9]

In addition, control over the export regulations and their implementation passes from the State Department to the Department of Commerce.

The Net's significance in all this may not be immediately obvious, since Clipper's first defeat didn't come from the Net but from a well-funded corporate research lab that was, as Blaze put it, "very adult" about the whole matter even though it could reasonably have expected to make a lot of money selling Clipper-based products. When it comes to government policy, successful lobbying of administrators must still come from off the Net; a box of letters still looks more impressive than a megabyte file full of email.

Privacy International director Simon Davies pointed this out at CFP'94, at a time when Net-based campaigners had collected 50,000 electronic signatures. Davies argued that 50,000 handwritten signatures collected in supermarket parking lots would have had far more meaning for members of Congress. This sort of prejudice is changing quickly. What hasn't changed as quickly is the arrogance and elitism rife on both sides of the argument—from NSA types who insist that their classified arguments would be persuasive if anyone knew what they were[10] to cypherpunks who sometimes seem to believe that the public is too stupid to understand cryptography. It's true that cryptography is an exceptionally difficult mathematical cross-discipline, but you don't have to understand the intricacies of how RSA uses 300-digit prime numbers to grasp that handing over your private key might mean that the government had access not only to today's communications session but to every transmission you have ever stored. Both sides were in for a shock. Once the Clipper debate became public, opposition was widespread and cut across some surprising boundaries. A 1994 *Time*/CNN poll found that 80 percent of their sample of a thousand people were against Clipper when it was explained to them.

Where the Net has made a big difference is in making available information that two decades ago would have been too hard and time-consuming for any but the most highly connected researchers to track down. It has, in other words, worked as a communications medium in precisely the way that was intended when its earliest precursor was set up: it allowed file-sharing and access to experts worldwide on an unprecedented basis. You can track the entire Clipper argument across the Net, starting with the earliest proposals for key escrow, posted to *sci.crypt* and other newsgroups in the summer of 1994 by Georgetown University computer science professor Dorothy Denning, another of the experts who was allowed to examine Clipper up close and personally. She has consistently argued in the face of Net fury that law enforcement needs key escrow, and her views have been received with the kind of warm Net welcome normally reserved for Laurence Canter, Martha Siegel, and that "Spamford" Wallace guy.[11] The Net was gleeful when, in July 1997, Denning published research casting doubt on her own contentions.

Everything from Denning's proposals to the current set of reports and white papers is there on the Net for examination, together with analyses from legal specialists like University of Miami associate professor A. Michael Froomkin,[12] practical cryptographers like Blaze and Zimmermann, and academic specialists like Britain's Ross Anderson, a professor at Cambridge University. His Web site in particular is full of important perspective for anyone inclined to assume that the government can deliver the security it's promising: you'll find papers on techniques for attacking tamper-resistant hardware and cracking RSA and DES, along with a paper on "Why Cryptosystems Fail," which should be required reading for all those seeking to set government policy in this area.[13]

Also on the Net in thorough detail is the full record of two court cases that are exerting another kind of pressure on the government to change its thinking by challenging the constitutionality of the export laws. One centers on the distinction made in the export regulations between printed and machine-readable versions of the same source code for encryption algorithms. This suit was brought by Phil Karn, a software engineer at Qualcomm, a developer and manufacturer of digital cellular and personal communications systems and the widely used email program Eudora. Karn is challenging a ruling by the State Department under ITAR that allows him to export copies of Bruce Schneier's classic book *Applied Cryptography*, which contains in printed form the source code for many of the world's most popular cryptographic algorithms including triple DES, but not to export floppy disks holding electronic versions of those same algorithms.[14] As Karn said in his June 26, 1996, testimony to the Senate Subcommittee on Science, Technology, and Space, "I guess only Americans can type."

The other case was brought by Daniel J. Bernstein, then a graduate student at the University of California at Berkeley and now a professor at the University of Illinois at Chicago. Bernstein wanted to publish the results of his research on the Internet and in scientific journals for examination and peer review by the cryptographic community. This meant making available a paper about his work, an algorithm he called Snuffle, and a program using that algorithm. Snuffle uses a technique called a hash function[15] to allow interactive encryption in real time, which would allow secure live communications. On June 30, 1992, he asked the State Department for permission to publish. Within a couple of months, he was advised that he first had to apply for and receive a license as an arms dealer; then he would have to get approval for each recipient of the software or the paper about the software. After failed attempts to clarify this ruling, he appealed in 1993 but never received a response. Accordingly, he filed suit on February 21, 1995, seeking declaratory and injunctive relief on the grounds that his freedom of speech rights are being violated.

The two cases met with opposite fates in their lower court decisions, both of which came in April 1996. First, in Karn's case, Washington, D.C., district court judge Charles Richey granted the government's motion to dismiss the complaint. The ruling was a bad one for opponents of export controls, as it essentially held that the courts did not have the right to review what items were included on the munitions list. Karn appealed. In the meantime, in Bernstein's case, Judge Marilyn Patel of the Northern District of California ruled that Bernstein's source code was indeed speech for the purposes of the First Amendment. Bernstein's legal team, from the San Francisco–based firm McGlashan and Serrail, argued its motion for summary judgment in September. The motion was granted just before Christmas, 1996.[16] The ruling was reviewed and upheld after responsibility was shifted to the Department of Commerce; however, the government immediately requested and won a stay, pending appeal.

Pressure on the government to change the laws is also coming from within Congress: in the spring of 1996, Senator Conrad Burns (R-MT) and Senator Patrick Leahy (D-VT) both introduced bills seeking to lift export controls; Burns's bill (known as "Pro-CODE," for Promotion of Electronic Commerce in the Digital Era) would also prohibit the government from promoting its own standards for encryption.[17] A similar bill introduced in 1994 in the House by Representative Maria Cantwell (D-WA) failed; 1994 instead saw the passage of the Communications Assistance for Law Enforcement Act (often referred to as "Digital Telephony" on the Net, after the failed 1991 rider). This bill, like the language that scared Zimmermann into releasing PGP in 1991, requires that new communications systems be designed to allow law enforcement secret access to specific electronic communications. The government has promised funding of $500 million to help pay for these changes.

Karn, testifying in support of Pro-CODE, highlighted the delays faced by his company in complying with the ITAR while trying to sell digital phones in Hong Kong in competition with European companies that have no such regulations to worry about. That bill failed, although it attracted a lot of support. Burns followed up with a new version on February 27, 1997, while a second, called SAFE, for Security and Freedom through Encryption, is also under consideration.

A less formal test of the workings of the ITAR was carried out in 1995 by Matt Blaze, who decided to donate some of his time to following the full set of legal procedures for exporting temporarily a cellular phone with built-in encryption that he wanted to use to communicate with his head office back home. His eventual conclusion: "Anyone who is aware of and who tries to follow the regulations is made to jump through pointless hoops that are so obscure that even the people charged with enforcing don't know quite what to make of them."[18]

What becomes obvious as you study the massive amounts of material available on the Net on this subject is just how radically the science of cryptography and its uses are changing, and how slowly the government and law enforcement areas are adapting to the new encrypted order. For privacy advocates, these new developments in encryption offer as big a chance to create a new world order as the Net itself: they represent a chance to claw back a large chunk of the privacy that has been lost over the years of increasing computerization since the 1950s. Technology today can track you everywhere you go; but encryption could cover your tracks, giving each site or agency you interact with only the single piece of information it needs to know.

Cypherpunks and promoters of electronic cash such as David Chaum, the American former technical director of Digicash, talk of systems where the amount of information any one official can get about you is limited.[19] Given a smart card using the right sort of encryption, a police officer stopping you by the roadside might be limited to checking that your license was valid, rather than being handed by default your name and address. Similarly, a doctor might be limited to retrieving your medical records and the validity of your insurance (but not your social security number), and the social security people might be limited to checking your eligibility for benefits. Limiting departments' and officials' access to more than a small subset of your personal information might go a long way toward preventing a future that until recently seemed inevitable, in which so many marketing and governmental databases were linked and cross-referenced that a complete dossier on each of our lives would be readily available. Similar coding might make it possible to screen correspondents for a variety of personal characteristics; the many women-only online forums is just one example of a group who might want to take advantage of such technology.

Encryption is also the key technology in creating electronic cash, since such systems won't work unless the digital "money" can't be counterfeited, falsified, or easily stolen.[20] Electronic cash is a necessary component of many of the grand plans for electronic commerce, because so many of those plans depend on the availability of a method of payment that will work even for tiny amounts. Visa and MasterCard aren't going to be thrilled by your running up hundreds of five-cent charges (for, say, reading individual articles or playing music files from Web sites) every month because their current transaction costs are much higher than that. Besides, credit cards leave an electronic trail in all those databases. With privacy in mind, Chaum designed a system that blinds the issuing bank to the serial numbers of the money you get and blinds the vendor to the identity of the purchaser. All the bank needs to know is that the digital money is properly issued and paid for; all the vendor needs to know is that the money accepted in payment for goods or services is valid. If the goods are in a form that can be delivered over the Net to an email address, possibly an anonymized one, the vendor doesn't even need a real-world street address for delivery. The bank doesn't need to know which serial numbers were spent where, as long as the transactions can be properly authenticated. After all, in the real world we use cash and it can't be traced. Why not on the Net?

Uses like these open up a whole new world of possibilities, and also a whole new world of threats to traditional government structures. It may seem unlikely now that you would buy services such as consultancy expertise or software development from someone whose name and credentials you haven't checked out personally, but someone may function on the Net in an anonymous—or, more correctly, a pseudonymous—form, and establish a reputation by consistently posting useful and accurate information or writing workable programs over a period of time. However, in which country would that consultant or programmer be taxed, and how would a national revenue service be able to verify his or her income? If the income is used only to purchase more intellectual property that can be transmitted across the Net, this might be difficult. The point where it becomes easy to follow the money is when it leaves the Net and is either translated into traditional bank account holdings or physical goods for which good tracking systems exist. We've heard of tax exiles; in such a world it might be possible to set up a business in a foreign country and operate it without leaving home.

These are distant problems and are unlikely to affect more than a small group of people for the near future. But they are the kind of thing that key escrow theoretically might deter if you believe that people would be less likely to cheat on their taxes if they knew they could be caught. These are not, however, the issues we hear about. Instead, the specters most commonly invoked to argue against the ready availability of non-escrowed strong encryption for the masses are what Timothy C. May called the "Four Horsemen of the Infocalypse": terrorists, pedophiles, drug traffickers, and spies. These people undoubtedly exist, but in what numbers compared to the vast majority of innocent citizens who want something more to stand between them and government attention than a court order? As Bruce Sterling put it at CFP'94, "Are we to allow our entire information infrastructure to be dictated by the existence of pedophiles? Are they that important and precious to us? . . . If you're that concerned for children, go down to the projects and rescue some real ones."

That's not to say that there will never be serious dangers or crimes where encryption isn't a problem for the security forces. But Net technology is going to have to add an awful lot of functions before someone can digitize drugs. These crimes are physical events that take place largely off the Net and are most likely to be proven by physical, not digital, evidence. Which would you believe first: a decrypted email message from a drug trafficker to a supplier, or a pound of cocaine found in his house?

There are some serious questions being raised about the government's most recent set of proposals. How, for example, will a public-key infrastructure work? No one has ever tried to manage what is likely to run into millions of keys before. (In fact, the CRISIS report recommends the government begin doing its own key escrow to get a handle on how such a system can work.) What will be the liability for key holders? If all those millions of keys are held in one location, what kind of a target will that location be, and how can the nation's keys be protected? How will authenticating those keys and tying them to their owners be handled? Will other forms of encryption be criminalized? If not, what's the point of escrow? What other penalties might be imposed for using non-approved cryptography? (Already one government report could be interpreted as proposing that those using non-escrowed keys or encryption might be locked out of tomorrow's electronic commerce markets and in early 1997 news circulated that draft legislation to this effect had been proposed.)[21] What will happen if the approved encryption system is cracked unexpectedly? Security systems have so many bases to cover that it's not unusual for weaknesses to be found only after they've been deployed. In early 1996, Netscape's built-in secure sockets layer, the facility that sends sensitive information such as credit card details and passwords between browser and Web site, was cracked by two French students. It was only the 40-bit export version, but the problem was traced to a flaw in the random number generator, which was supposed to ensure that patterns didn't develop to make the encryption easier to crack. Such tiny errors can reduce the security of cryptosystems in unexpectedly important ways—another argument against introducing the security risk of key escrow without fully understanding the mathematical implications behind it.

"The design and implementation of even the simplest encryption systems is an extraordinarily difficult and delicate process. Very small changes frequently introduce fatal security flaws," notes Matt Blaze in his draft December 1996 paper "Cryptography Policy and the Information Economy."[22] "It is possible, even likely, that lurking in any key recovery system are one or more design weaknesses that allow recovery of data by unauthorized parties. The commercial and academic world simply does not have the tools to analyze or design the complex systems that arise from key recovery." Blaze names one additional serious problem: the "enormous expense" of building and operating such an infrastructure. One thing Blaze doesn't ask, as anyone with a minimum of experience with computers might, is why the government thinks that this extremely important, very large, never-before-tried computer system is going to work first time. Can you think of a single product that wasn't a buggy mess in release 1.0?

None of the above questions will be easy to answer, and the very nature of a single authority for key escrow is in conflict with the nature of the Net as we know it: distributed, decentralized, robust. It would be more logical and more in keeping with the character of the Net, to allow the structures that are already beginning to form organically around the world, in the form of public key servers, to continue to grow, multiply, and add functions. Governments may trust banks and large corporations to manage keys; the rest of us are more likely to trust individuals or organizations we have chosen ourselves, be they friends with well-secured computer systems, relatives who live in another country, our own local lawyers or accountants, a safe deposit box under our personal control, or in some cases even the Internet service providers we use, who can verify our attached identity as they're already billing us and providing our email addresses.

But as Sterling noted at CFP'94, "Encryption is mathematics. It is not our friend." Assuming export controls do get lifted and encryption applications become widespread, there will certainly be new twists on old challenges for law enforcement: new types of fraud, money laundering (a potential problem if electronic cash really is fully anonymous), tax evasion, theft, deception, electronic impersonation, and anonymous smear campaigns. It's easy to imagine that the combination of untraceable electronic cash, Internet-assisted searching, and encryption-based anonymous remailers could create a very lucrative business for a blackmailer. Cypherpunk and physicist Timothy C. May created a stir in 1994 when he sent a couple of friends a sample advertisement for an information black market operator he called BlackNet (the document caused much furor when it was copied and posted to Usenet by others). It asked correspondents to use public newsgroups, PGP, and encrypted anonymous remailers to create "a secure, two-way, untraceable, and fully anonymous channel" through which information such as trade secrets and business and national intelligence could be bought or sold.[23] May's point was that cryptography really will pose a "mortal threat" to governments: "National borders are just speed bumps on the information superhighway," he concluded in a response to critics on the cypherpunks emailing list in February 1994.[24]

In the short term, spreading cryptography may pose a technical problem: what happens to the interoperability we have now, where everything depends on standards? Typically, every aspect of the computer industry goes through a period where competing products are wholly incompatible. Before IBM developed the PC in 1984, there were all sorts of weird machines floating around, none of which could read each other's floppy disks. Before the widespread adoption of Internet standards in the early 1990s, members on closed systems such as CompuServe couldn't email anyone outside their own service. If this pattern gets repeated now, we could be facing a period when you have to know what email software, network, or hardware your correspondent is using before you can use secure communications. This was, in fact, another objection to Clipper.

One solution, being attempted by the ever-active John Gilmore, is to secure the Internet against wiretapping by installing PC-based boxes running a specially tailored version of the free operating system software Linux to sit between the Internet and local-area networks and encrypt traffic going to other sites using the same system. His goal for 1996 was to secure 5 percent of the Internet; by early December he was admitting this was "too ambitious" but was continuing the attempt.[25] His request for more volunteers to help install boxes and train administrators in their set-up and use was accompanied by a note that he wanted to hear from those who could write cryptographic software—and lived outside the United States. In the early days of the Net, that sort of community spirit seemed to be hard-wired into each computer running the Internet protocols, TCP/IP, but in today's gold rush era it may be harder to find. If Gilmore's scheme can be implemented, given the speed with which the Internet can reinvent itself, by the time the governments are through negotiating they may find that their treaties are already out of date. As John Perry Barlow said in a different context (copyright law) at a February 1996 forum in Amsterdam: "Any time you have large numbers of people scoffing systematically at the law, it's usually the law that changes."[26]

There seems to be no chance that even all the world's governments put together will be able to stop the use of non-escrowed encryption entirely, even if they can get the public to agree to the rules they want to pass. The programs and algorithms are too widely available, and there are too many competent people who can and do put them to use. The consensus on the Net is strongly in favor of access to strong encryption. In any event, you could escrow one key for mundane Net-based transactions like buying groceries and use a different system for private email, or hide vital data using a technique called steganography, which essentially buries the real data in the background noise of a picture or sound file. That won't help legitimate businesses, who are the least able to afford to deliberately flout the law—although they are also in the best position to lobby for changes. Non-legitimate businesses, who might be the most dangerous potential users of the Net, are hardly likely to balk at a spot of illegal encryption. The bottom line is that the people who will be most readily controlled by restricting access to encryption are the ones we least need to control.

6

Copyright Terrorists

> We of the Church believe.... That all men have inalienable rights
> to think freely, to talk freely, to write freely their own opinions and
> to counter or utter or write upon the opinions of others.
>
> —L. Ron Hubbard, from "The Creed
> of the Church of Scientology"

What will happen to the traditional notions of intellectual
property and copyright in the face of a technology that can create infinite
numbers of copies and spray them freely across the world in seconds?
This question has already been raised, and it worries many people, from
small-time freelance writers to major publishers and software companies,
all of whom make their living by selling the intangible products of the
human mind.

You might have thought that when the laws defining the boundaries
between free speech and copyright infringements, or fair use and trade-
mark violation, were finally tested in the courts against the existence of
cyberspace, it would be by a large software company. Instead, the pro-
tagonist was the controversial organization known as the Church of Scientology (CoS).[1] The story is important for two reasons. First, there had
never been a case like it, where the boundaries between real life and cyberspace had been stress-tested so fiercely and for so long. Second, it
began to define exactly how far intellectual property laws can be made to
apply in cyberspace.

Scientology is the brainchild of the pulp science fiction writer L. Ron
Hubbard and grew out of the theories about human psychology that
Hubbard first published in the form of a long article in *Astounding Science Fiction* and then in a best-selling book, *Dianetics*, originally published in 1950 and still in print. I first heard of it at Cornell in the early

1970s, when Scientology, like many other belief organizations such as TM and est, recruited on college campuses; the science fiction fans from whom I heard about it had quite a skeptical view, as does much of the SF world even now. That fact and the heavy presence of science fiction fandom on the Net was what made it seem obvious, when I first saw *alt.religion.scientology* on the list of newsgroups in early 1994, that this was not going to be a quiet, orderly place. In fact, *alt.religion.scientology* is one of the most contentious, roisterous, fiery, and vicious newsgroups ever, and the story of what's come to be known as Scientology versus the Net is the most extraordinary and bitter of any online hazing experience a newly wired organization has ever had.

We're talking police raids and lawsuits here, in places as far-flung as Finland (Julf Helsingius and his *anon.penet.fi* anonymous remailer), Sweden (Zenon Panoussis), the Netherlands (the service provider xs4all and the writer Karin Spaink), Virginia (Arnaldo Lerma), Colorado (Bob Penny and Lawrence Wollersheim), and California (Dennis Erlich, Tom Klemesrud, Grady Ward, and Keith Henson). One observer on the WELL called it "a flame war with real guns."

We're also talking about the mass distribution of documents previously kept as closely guarded by the CoS as the inner workings of classified encryption algorithms have been by the National Security Agency (see chapter 5). They are, in fact, the heart of Scientology's teachings, written by L. Ron Hubbard and reserved for those who have passed through the requisite lower levels and many hours of "auditing," which from the sounds of it is a sort of confessional therapy session aided by an "E-meter," a device that is claimed to register emotional and psychological blockages much the way a polygraph detects lies. Hubbard claimed that exposure to these secrets could harm or even kill those who were unprepared. A separate organization, the Religious Technology Center (RTC), was created in May 1982 to guard the intellectual property rights in these documents, along with the many registered Scientology trademarks.[2] Critics allege that the secrecy has more to do with financial gain; the CoS admits on its home pages that this is also a consideration, but stresses that it's a minor one.[3]

The mass media coverage of the case has stressed the distribution of these documents and the CoS's attempts to get them back, or at least taken out of circulation. What many people don't realize is that the hostilities between the Net and the CoS go beyond just those documents and started much earlier than the day the first suit was filed. It's also important to understand that most people on both sides of the dispute believe they are acting in the public good.

The action centers on a single Usenet newsgroup: *alt.religion. scientology*. It also includes Web sites, Internet Relay Chat (IRC) discussions, and even court cases, but it was in this newsgroup that all the important connections began. By all accounts, *alt.religion.scientology* was never exactly a quiet newsgroup, or even intended to be so. It was created on July 17, 1991, by Scott Goehring, whose former wife was a Scientologist. Goehring says he started the newsgroup half as a joke and half as a place to discuss the truth about the organization. Many *alt* groups start with a forged message,[4] and this one was no exception: Goehring forged the signature "miscaviage@flag.sea.org" on the "newgroup" message.[5] The signature is itself a joke: "miscaviage" is a misspelling for CoS leader David Miscavige, and the Flag and Sea "Orgs" (for organizations) are two of the most important Scientology branches.

From the beginning, the group attracted both skeptics and believers. While the two groups never came close to agreement, they managed to coexist in the sort of tense balance the Net seems to specialize in. They argued rabidly about the scientific underpinnings of the E-meter and the medical validity, or lack thereof, of a Scientology treatment for new recruits and drug addicts called the "Purif" (short for "Purification rundown"), which involves large doses of niacin and long sojourns in steam baths, thought by Hubbard to detoxify the body. Between arguments they hammered out a more or less stable agreement to have multiple FAQs to introduce newcomers to both sides of the hot tub. While each side has criticized the other's writings, there have been no serious attempts to interfere with these FAQs, which persist to this day.

People who frequent *alt.religion.scientology* generally fall into one of four types. The first two are obvious: critics and CoS supporters. In early 1994, these were a high percentage of the group's membership, but their relatively reasoned debates have largely been drowned out in the increasingly polarized and contentious years since. Third is the Free Zone, former Scientologists who hate the CoS but love Hubbard's teachings, known as "the tech" (for technology), and want to continue using them independently. Fourth is the group of net.defenders who started arriving in mid-1994 in response to reports of what was happening on the newsgroup; they represent the Net's immune response.

In an ordinary newsgroup, this sort of mix works. You can have, for example, Microsoft customers, employees, former staffers, and critics all in one newsgroup without anyone's getting raided for posting the copy-righted source code to Windows, while others cheer them on (although there is an I-hate-Microsoft spirit in the land). The trouble is that when you mix current and former Scientologists with strident critics, someone is bound to mention that portions of Hubbard's writings that have been made public by former Scientologists allege that those who leave Scien-tology or who criticize it may be dubbed "Suppressive Persons" (SPs) and become fair game for all types of harassment.

Sometime around 1992, the newsgroup began attracting posters from the Free Zone. One of the best known, Homer Wilson Smith,[6] inter-viewed in early 1995 by email, said initially he was too scared to post any-thing himself. He was inspired to start posting by anonymous Usenet articles signed only "Electra," which went into great detail about "the tech" and contained the kind of productive material he'd been hoping to find. Electra disappeared from the Net by the end of 1992, but shortly afterwards Smith received through the mail two floppy disks full of her articles, from which he went on publishing excerpts. Smith, however, was unhappy about the overall content of *alt.religion.scientology* and wanted a newsgroup where he and others could seriously discuss the tech. Ac-cordingly, he created a second newsgroup, *alt.clearing.technology*, where relatively reasoned discussion continues today.[7]

(Occasionally, in older guides to the Internet, you'll see a note to the effect that *alt.clearing.technology* is for discussing acne cures. This was another Usenet joke—Chris Schafmeister, a graduate student in molecu-lar biology at the University of California at San Francisco, sent out a newgroup message to this effect. Because there was a mistake in one of the fields, the message failed. Smith's version, the real one, went through a day or two later, although some system administrators objected that the group's name was badly chosen and should have conformed better to the existing hierarchy.)

When I first began reading *alt.religion.scientology* in early 1994, it was the unexpected existence of the Free Zone that most intrigued me, since I had only ever read about two types of Scientologists: dedicated and disaffected. My initial impression that the Net had enabled these people to discover each other's existence was wrong, however: Smith said he first heard the term in 1982, and the Free Zone publishes print news-letters, holds conventions, and schedules face-to-face meetings much like any other subculture.

Schafmeister was well known on *alt.religion.scientology* as one of the earliest strident critics on the newsgroup, inspired by posters on the walls of the UC San Francisco medical school. He was, he said, "really, really upset"[8] at the way these posters targeted the sick, the sad, and the bereaved to get them into $60 Scientology courses. Accordingly, he took to spending his study breaks arguing against the organization on Usenet.

It was, he said, a Scientologist he'd befriended on the Net who on May 6, 1994, gave him a copy of a letter from a staffer in the CoS's Office of Special Affairs (OSA) named Elaine Siegel. (According to former insiders, the OSA is the CoS's security branch.) Appalled by its content, he posted it to *alt.religion.scientology* the following day.

Addressed to "Scientologists on the Net," it reads, in part: "If you imagine 40–50 Scientologists posting on the Internet every few days, we'll just run the SPs [Suppressive Persons] right off the system. It will be quite simple, actually." She continued by describing Smith as "a squirrel and declared SP" and closed with, "I would like to hear from you on your ideas to make the Internet a safe space for Scientology to expand into."[9]

A safe space. Few of the non-Scientologists attacking the CoS and its belief systems troubled to ask themselves what it would be like to be a Scientologist in such a milieu. Even granted that in the long run it's been the critics who have wound up raided or in court, for unsuspecting believers, happening upon the newsgroup thinking it would be a home on the Net must have been a singularly unpleasant experience. Several messages making precisely that point appeared in 1994.

One Scientologist willing to talk about what it was like is Jack Farmer, who started reading the newsgroup sometime in 1993. He describes himself as a "book auditor," that is, someone who practices Scientology with the help of books but has no standing in the CoS; his Usenet *.sig* read "Scientologist since 1974." Farmer also runs a Bulletin Board System (BBS) at home and does some computer consulting on the side. Farmer largely disappeared from the newsgroup by 1996, but in a spring 1995 interview he talked about how he tried to "straighten out some of the miscomprehension in the newsgroup."[10]

It wasn't easy. "I went in there to answer people's legitimate questions, and from the time I went in there I was fucking attacked—as soon as I said I was a Scientologist." He went on, "What gets me—and I'm trying to be objective on this—is I've been a Scientologist for about twenty years, and the only thing I've seen is people going out and trying to help people and people's problems. So what is all this hate about?"

Another Scientologist interviewed around the same time who didn't want to be named—in an example of the way people often think the Net has nothing to do with real life, she uses her real name on the Net, but didn't want her offline friends and colleagues to find out about her affiliation with Scientology—said her postings on the Net brought her abusive email, for which she wasn't prepared. "To see all that ill-will is dismaying. It makes you sad. You can't understand it, because you know what Scientology really is, and then to see all this rabid anti-religious [feeling]—not everybody is like this, but some people are." She is, as she says, soft-spoken, friendly, and polite by nature, but the postings on the newsgroup brought out a vein of anger she didn't know she had. The timing of her arrival didn't help: she showed up in August 1994, about the same time as Dennis Erlich, who was attracted to the newsgroup in part by the Net-wide anger over Siegel's letter, which was widely copied and distributed.

Farmer told me, "When Dennis Erlich came in, it started turning nasty." Erlich does not have a sense of humor about Scientology. He was in the CoS for fifteen years, in which time, he told me, he was assigned personally by Hubbard to the position of Chief Cramming Officer: "It's like the quality control engineer in the skull-fucking factory." He left in 1982 after what he describes as a failed attempt to reform the CoS from within. "That made me persona non grata, and they couldn't work with me because I wouldn't follow their orders any more." He was declared an SP, and has since devoted himself to debunking the CoS at every opportunity.

Given the strength of Erlich's convictions that CoS is a dangerous organization, it's hard to imagine a situation in which he could come to any sort of amicable agreement with Scientologists—especially the CoS staff who started showing up on the newsgroup—or they with him.

In December 1994, messages started disappearing from *alt.religion.scientology*. The contents of all such messages are not known, for obvious reasons. Even without detailed information, though, many people believed they knew who was responsible. Gathering evidence and understanding what was happening, however, were altogether different matters.

Unlike postings canceled by the more or less official cancellers, such as the Cancelmoose, these messages were not spam (usually defined as any message posted to more than twenty newsgroups of widely varying character). Further, no one claimed responsibility, whereas the spam cancellers post regular reports of their actions to the *net-abuse.** newsgroups and openly take responsibility.[11] The Net hates a technology vacuum, so a program called Lazarus was quickly developed to get a look at what was being canceled.

Lazarus was another of Schafmeister's ideas. It takes advantage of the fact that along with a unique message ID every Usenet posting has a header containing the date, subject, sender's name and email address, and a mess of other identifying information, and that those headers are recorded in a general header log on Usenet servers, while every Cancel message lands in a special newsgroup called *control*. Schafmeister's notion was that at a site where Cancel is disabled (some system administrators abhor even the merest hint of censorship), a program could scan the thousands of Cancels posted to *control* each day and compare them to the log of headers, looking specifically for the ones pertaining to messages destined for *alt.religion.scientology*. A match would mean that a message to the newsgroup had been canceled.

Smith took the idea and turned it into a working script in the programming language PERL, which is available to anyone on the Net though it takes some skill to use. Smith said he could have designed Lazarus to reinstate the canceled postings, but because cancellations are sometimes intentional, he decided to configure Lazarus so it just put up a note to the newsgroup saying the message had been canceled and including all the available information about the message, including any comments entered by the cancellers.

"At least we can see when messages have been canceled," Schafmeister said. He believed the cancellations had "too much intelligence" behind them to have been automatic. Those on the newsgroup took to calling the canceling agent—whatever it was—the "CancelBunny" or "CancelPoodle," terms intended to disparage the unidentified flying cancelers. In the absence of evidence, when Lazarus began reporting that some messages had been "cancelled because of copyright infringement," most of the newsgroup felt justified in assuming that the CancelBunny was one or more CoS representatives.

What Lazarus showed, according to frequent poster William C. Barwell, who signs himself "Pope Charles" and is one of the satirical Church of the SubGenius, Praise Bob! crowd,[12] was that "just about everybody got hit." Barwell's discovery that two of his postings had been canceled was quickly followed by another: USC Title 18, Part I, Chapter 121, "Unlawful access to stored communications." At the beginning of March 1995, he wrote a letter to the FBI asking it to enforce the code, with copies to his own Internet service provider (ISP), Neosoft, and to Netcom, the service the forgeries were coming from. "Two days later, Netcom FINALLY announced after nearly two weeks that they finally disabled the accounts through which the forgeries were occurring," Barwell wrote by email a few months later.

Another set of cancellation attempts surfaced not long afterward using the southern California provider Deltanet; the two accounts involved were terminated after only two days. After that, the forging cancellers got more sophisticated: starting in early April 1995, they were anonymized by using public-access newsreaders and falsifying the name of the machine the postings came from.[13] The many cancellations that spring that appeared to come from Britain's Demon Internet, for example, were eventually traced to a public-access news site in Dublin.

No one has ever owned up to the cancellations. When asked about them in April 1995, CoS in-house attorney Helena Kobrin replied in an email message, "In an effort to protect its rights, the Church has contacted several Computer Bulletin Board operators in recent months who, when apprised of the illegal and offensive nature of the postings, agreed to remove the infringing materials from the Net."

When the cancellations continued through July and August 1995, a team including representatives from the United States, Canada, and Germany and calling itself the Rabbit Hunters or, more formally, the Ad-Hoc Committee Against Internet Censorship, began some fancy technical detective work. By comparing system logs and monitoring news servers, the group believed it had finally traced the source of the trouble to the account of a Scientologist who had posted prolifically early that spring. Asked to comment on their claims, Kobrin did not reply.

In the meantime, more drastic action was being suggested: on January 12, 1995, Kobrin posted the following message in *alt.config*:

> We have requested that the alt.religion.scientology newsgroup be removed from all sites. The reasons for requesting its removal are: (1) it was started with a forged message; (2) not discussed on alt.config; (3) it has the name "scientology" in its title which is a trademark and is misleading, as a.r.s. is mainly used for flamers to attack the Scientology religion; (4) it has been and continues to be heavily abused with copyright and trade secret violations and serves no purpose other than condoning these illegal practices.[14]

The assembled system administrators' collective reply, essentially, was, "Forget it." Even if they had agreed, *alt* is enough of an anarchy that the newsgroup probably would have survived anyway, as most sites are set up to automatically honor all group creation ("newgroup") requests but ignore all group deletion ("rmgroup") requests. The reason is that there is a substantial school of thought that holds that no *alt* newsgroup should ever be removed, even if it's clearly past its use-by date, like the jokingly named *alt.fan.tonya-harding.whack.whack.whack.*[15] Many *alt* groups were not discussed on *alt.config*; many were also created with forged messages, just as many include company or other names without authorization. This is business as usual, however much it sounds like lawlessness to outsiders.

By email, Kobrin commented, "As the newsgroup involved were [*sic*] only a very small number out of the total newsgroups, it was considered that it might be preferable to do it that way than to take legal action. This did not turn out to be the case and the matter is a dead issue now." This was probably the moment when any chance that the Net and the CoS would find some way to reach conciliatory terms was lost.

At the same time, the CoS began heading to the courts. On January 3, 1995, Julf Helsingius, the operator of the best-known anonymous remailer, *anon.penet.fi*, posted a copy of a letter he had received from Kobrin on behalf of Thomas M. Small, counsel for the RTC and Bridge Publications (publisher of Hubbard's work), requesting that he block access to *alt.religion.scientology* and *alt.clearing.technology*. Copies had also been sent to four other anonymous remailers. The grounds given were that the remailers were being used as conduits for stolen copyrighted materials. On January 9, Helsingius posted a copy of his reply, which said that monitoring postings is impossible and that he didn't feel blocking the groups was appropriate. Felipe Rodriguez, who runs a similar remailer at the Dutch ISP xs4all, which he owns, says he made a similar reply.

Anonymous remailers get used a lot on *alt.religion.scientology*. What they do is simple: they strip the headers and identifying information off messages and then forward them to the email box or newsgroup specified by the sender. The services vary in sophistication. The most complex and secure keep no logs, support the use of strong encryption, and bundle messages together to defeat the kind of traffic analysis that might match incoming and outgoing messages and thereby identify posters. Helsingius's popular service was simpler than this: it could assign you an anonymous ID on the fly, rather than demanding pre-arrangement, and it handled replies. It would, in fact, be more accurate to call his service a *pseudonymous* remailer, since over time an individual poster could interact on the Net and build up a persona and reputation without revealing a real-world identity.

The reason for using such anonymizing services varies: discussing personal histories of child abuse or addiction, seeking technical information in contexts where your company would object to its name being revealed, or fear of the political regime in which you live. On *alt.religion. scientology*, fear of the CoS is common enough to make people feel they are in a similar position. Anonymous remailers allow them to feel freer to criticize the CoS or ask for information without fear of reprisal against themselves or friends or relatives who may still be members. (As an example of the prevailing paranoia level, when, in late 1996, one of *alt. religion.scientology*'s most persistent and strident Canadian critics disappeared suddenly, taking with him all his posted messages and his Web site, many were convinced he must have been strong-armed into silence, a fear that dispersed only when he repeatedly insisted it was his own decision.)

Anonymizing services can undeniably be abused to smear or defame without accountability, just like anonymous letters or phone calls can in the offline world. The anonymous poster who surfaced in early 1995 calling him- or herself Scamizdat and sending out collections of Scientology documents was an example of the way the most secure anonymous remailers can be used to help a mocking individual or individuals evade legal control. For the most part, though, the general feeling on the Net is that the positive uses for these remailers outweigh the potential for abuse.

Meanwhile, back at the newsgroup, the name-calling was growing vicious. Bashers posted affidavits from former Scientologists alleging corruption; Scientologists posted critiques of those affidavits alleging that the authors were known criminals, along with affidavits of their own. One such affidavit was signed by Erlich's wife, Rosa, and alleged he had abused their daughter. This didn't deter Erlich, who denied the allegations and went on posting quotations from CoS materials and his critiques of them.

Erlich's Usenet feed comes from a small BBS in the Los Angeles area called *support.com*, which in turn gets its Usenet feed from Netcom, one of the largest U.S. Internet providers. The sysop (system operator) of *support.com*, Tom Klemesrud, says that in early January 1995 Kobrin requested that he delete Erlich's Internet account, which he refused to do. In mid-January, Klemesrud followed up by reporting an *Outer Limits*–type incident in which his apartment was smeared with blood by a young woman he had met in a bar—although it's unlikely that exactly how and why will ever be adequately proven. Klemesrud believes this attack was meant to frighten him into removing Erlich's account.

On January 23, a poster signing himself "-AB-" from the address *an144108@anon.penet.fi*,[16] an account on Helsingius's anonymous re-mailer in Finland, put up an opposing account, allegedly an interview with the woman in question, that claimed that Klemesrud was the at-tacker rather than the victim (a claim Klemesrud vehemently denies). On February 2, Helsingius was contacted by an American CoS representative saying that information from a closed, private CoS system had been made public through *anon.penet.fi* and that the CoS had reported a burglary to the Los Angeles Police Department and the FBI. The representative wanted the identity of the individual who had posted that material. Helsingius refused, and he was told a request was on its way to the Finnish police through Interpol. The police arrived on February 8, with a warrant. Helsingius negotiated his way into giving up only the single ID that the CoS wanted instead of his entire database of 200,000.[17] He says that within an hour he was told the information had been passed on to the CoS. Helsingius later confirmed that the ID the CoS wanted was *an144108@anon.penet.fi*.

In an email message, Kobrin said of the *anon.penet.fi* raid: "The ma-terial that was stolen happened to relate to an investigation being con-ducted by the Church's lawyers into false allegations about the Church that had been posted on the Internet by Mr Erlich and Mr Klemesrud. These allegations centered on an incident involving a woman whom Mr Klemesrud had met in a bar, which the investigation proved were com-pletely unfounded." Asked if further action was being taken against the anon-poster whose ID was handed over, she said, "The matter is under investigation. I cannot comment." The CoS, when asked who was un-dertaking the investigation, did not reply.

Also on February 8, the RTC, the CoS arm that holds the copyright for Hubbard's works, filed a complaint in San Jose, California, against Erlich and his service providers. On February 10, Federal District Judge Ronald M. Whyte issued a temporary restraining order against Erlich, Klemes-rud, and Klemesrud's ISP, Netcom. The complaint said Erlich had been posting CoS materials in violation of copyright and, in the case of the upper-level materials the CoS calls "Advanced Technology," posting ma-terials that were unpublished and confidential. The CoS has called the lat-ter trade secrets, saying that the issue is one of theft, not of free speech.[18]

Erlich maintained that all his postings were merely fair use. "The most effective way I can discredit the cult is to use their own documents to show what they're about." Further, he said, "If quoting their internal documents that were legally obtained doesn't constitute fair use, then nothing does."[19] The CoS disagrees vehemently with this assessment of things. In a 1995 prepared statement about the Erlich suit, Leisa Goodman, media relations director for the Church of Scientology International, wrote, "Numerous attempts had been made by the Church's lawyers to persuade Erlich to halt his unauthorized, wholesale postings of the Church's religious scriptures, which went way beyond the concept of 'fair use' and constituted violation of copyright law." Later in the same statement, she wrote, "Freedom of speech does not mean freedom to steal. Erlich's attempts to misdirect and misinform the media are intended solely to divert attention from his own unlawful actions. He has spread polemic and sometimes obscene messages about the Church over the Internet—also a 'smokescreen' to divert attention away from his illegal activities."

Scientologists added that the only way Erlich could have obtained these materials in the first place would have been by signing an agreement that they be kept permanently confidential (in Scientology terms, a billion-year contract). Erlich says that's not true: "I never signed anything." This is repeated in his statements to the court, which are available on the Net, as are many other court documents from both sides.[20]

On February 13, 1995, Erlich's residence in Glendale, California, was raided. Erlich claimed afterwards that his constitutional rights were violated by the raid, in which he said floppy disks, books, and papers were seized, files were deleted from his hard drive, and his house was comprehensively searched and photographed. Afterward, two of his computers would not boot properly, and he was left with no back-ups from which to restore his system. He was not given an inventory of the materials that were taken.

A flurry of legal documents and court hearings followed. The temporary restraining order against Klemesrud and Netcom was quickly dissolved. The CoS filed a request to have it reinstated, and a motion was then filed to hold Erlich in contempt of court for reposting one of the articles the CoS objected to in the first place. Klemesrud's and Netcom's position is that no service provider can police all of its Internet traffic and stay on the air, especially considering the international connections—a U.S. federal judge can have no jurisdiction over what people post in the rest of the world. They would, says Klemesrud, have had to shut down.

"Netcom is the largest provider in the US," says Klemesrud. "It would have crippled the entire country's telecomms, and there'd have been a backlash throughout the entire world. The judge didn't even know that—which was kind of strange, because he's a federal judge in Silicon Valley" (telephone interview, 1995). He characterizes the raid on Erlich's house as the kind that's reserved for someone running off illegal copies of *Jurassic Park* by the thousands.

The Electronic Frontier Foundation found Erlich pro bono defense attorneys: the high-profile California law firm of Morrison Foerster. An electronic newsletter, *Biased Journalism*, started up to publish eyewitness reports from all the court hearings.[21]

Court time is geological eras on the Net. In November 1995, Judge Whyte ruled that Klemesrud could not be found liable for direct infringement. It wasn't until early August 1996, however, that Netcom, in a move widely criticized on *alt.religion.scientology*, announced it was settling out of court with the CoS, with both parties constrained from discussing the terms. Netcom simultaneously announced a protocol for handling future intellectual property disputes that involves restricting access to the disputed material pending investigation; the concern on the newsgroup was that this protocol would open the company up to the possibility of constant requests for investigation.

A settlement between Klemesrud and the CoS followed soon after, on August 22, 1996, when attorneys for the RTC agreed to dismiss Klemesrud from the Erlich lawsuit. Klemesrud wasn't entirely happy—he believed his case had the potential to set the precedent for all service providers and establish the principle that ISPs are not liable for contributory infringement. The settlement was, he said, mandated by his general liability insurance company, which agreed to pay the RTC $50,000. He did not, however, sign any agreement enjoining him from talking about the case, something neither he nor his lawyer would have agreed to.[22]

"The insurance company has the right to settle as long as they don't trample on Klemesrud's rights," said Dan Leipold, Klemesrud's attorney, noting that he had defended about forty lawsuits brought by the Church of Scientology in the previous five years. Leipold added that copyright must be revised for the digital world, but that "it should not be on an ad hoc basis by the courts. It should be revised by Congress" (telephone interview, 1996).

Said Klemesrud, "I would have liked to stay in there and participate in total exoneration." The settlement means that the question of whether ISPs can be held liable for contributory infringement has still not been tested in court. In early 1997 Erlich's case was still awaiting trial, although he hoped for a ruling from Judge Whyte that the general public availability of the secret documents invalidated the CoS's claim that they were trade secrets.

There were more raids to come, all grouped around a Net-based anticult information service called FACTnet. Based in Boulder, Colorado, FACTnet is run by a former Scientologist named Lawrence Wollersheim, who in 1986 won a judgment of $2.5 million against the CoS for damages relating to his days as a member. In 1994, the U.S. Federal Court upheld this judgment and ordered the CoS to pay the ordered sum plus interest for a total estimated at approximately $6 million. In May 1996, the California Supreme Court upheld it again. In early 1997 he was still trying to collect on the debt.

The second wave of raids began on Saturday, August 12, 1995, and were announced to the Net by a widely distributed emergency email message that a raid was in progress at the Arlington, Virginia, home of Arnaldo Lerma, Usenet poster, FACTnet director, and former Scientologist. The raiding party was said to consist of ten people, among them two federal marshals, two computer technicians, one of whom was former FBI agent James Settle,[23] and several CoS attorneys. One of the attorneys was Kobrin, by this time well-known to many on *alt.religion.scientology* for her many email messages demanding that files allegedly containing copyrighted material be deleted. Another was Earle C. Cooley, who is also the chairman of the board of Boston University. They took Lerma's computer, backups, disks, modem, and scanner. Like many of us, he keeps everything, both business and personal, on his home computer. They promised he'd have them back by Monday, but months later he was still waiting.

Two more raids followed on Wednesday, August 23, 1995. One was on Wollersheim. The other targeted nearby Bob Penny, who because of his advanced muscular dystrophy had been replaced on the board of FACTnet by Lerma at the beginning of July. FACTnet was prepared: it had been expecting a raid since early that spring, and had long ago told Internet users to download as much of its file archives as possible. There are now FACTnet anti-Scientology kits on Web sites all over the world. It would take a lot of international cooperation and a lot of police power to get them all, and even then, some of those countries have not signed the Berne copyright convention.

Like Erlich, Lerma, whose three-hour raid was videotaped by both sides, has been described by the CoS as a "copyright terrorist." In the familiar pattern, his service provider, Digital Gateway Systems, was included in the suit. He was defended by ACLU attorney David Lane. In Lerma's case, the bone of contention was a set of August 2, 1995, postings that contained the complete set of court documents from the Los Angeles case *Church of Scientology v. Fishman and Geertz.* Copies of these documents could be obtained from the court by anyone with $36.50 to spare for the copying fees, but the key to their interest is that portions of the top-secret "Operating Thetan" materials, usually only available to initiated Scientologists, were read into the record. The CoS maintains the materials are still copyrighted, even if they're in the public record; skeptics say there are no legal precedents to support this. Either way, by now there are thousands, if not tens of thousands, of copies of these documents around the world. Shortly after the raids, the judge granted a CoS request to seal the records. Digital Gateway Systems eventually settled out of court on undisclosed terms.

Lerma, however, lost in court in January 1996, when Virginia U.S. District Court Judge Leonie M. Brinkema issued a summary judgment that Lerma had violated the CoS's copyright. The CoS welcomed the ruling, but not the terms: Brinkema awarded the CoS only $2,500 in costs, dismissing in December 1996 a motion by the CoS demanding $500,000 in attorneys' fees. Earlier, in November 1995, Brinkema had thrown out a third suit, brought by the CoS against the *Washington Post*, which had quoted a few lines from the documents in its coverage of the story.

Wollersheim had better luck: in September 1995, Colorado Judge John L. Kane ruled in FACTnet's favor.

Around the time of the FACTnet raids, rumors began to fly that there would soon be another raid. The popularly predicted target was California-based critic and well-known net.activist Grady Ward, who had already told the group his seventy-four-year-old mother had been visited by a Scientology investigator, and who said publicly the CoS would find nothing if it did show up. The masses on *alt.religion.scientology* started a pool to guess how many people would hit Ward.

That spring, there were complaints about three users who posted large quantities—ten to twelve per few minutes—of single-paragraph postings in a practice eventually labeled "vertical spam." One of these users, Andrew Milne, who in an email message described himself as a "Church staff member," defends this on the grounds of stimulating discussion of specific points, but admits that after those postings, "A lot of complaints were made to Delphi [his service provider] to try to get my account canceled. In fact, it was suspended briefly but the suspension was lifted after I contacted Delphi and explained the situation."[24]

Milne, one of the three most prolific posters to *alt.religion.scientology*, eventually adopted more standard practice, but it didn't improve his image much—one regular gleefully posted a "killfile count" (sample: 534 of Milne's messages killed in one week). Milne criticized this: "What the killfilers are showing is that they can't tolerate a point of view other than their own—the exact allegation they level against the Church." He has, he says, also received hate email, including the statement "Scientologists should be hunted and shot like dogs."

Also in late March, Daniel Davidson, a student at San Francisco State University, found himself called on the carpet by his system administrator after Kobrin complained that he had posted copyrighted and confidential information to the Net. Davidson said that all he did was hit a couple of keys to copy a posting from *alt.activism* into *alt.religion.scientology*, since it was relevant to the discussion there—behavior which on the Net is generally accepted as normal rather than a copyright violation. By the time the meeting with his system administrator took place, email from Netizens had gotten him out of trouble.[25]

By that time, too, regular critics had begun reporting strange incidents in which their long-distance phone companies were asked for information about their bills by unauthorized strangers; one said his neighbors had received visits from a private investigator; and another said the local police had come around bearing printouts of *alt.religion.scientology* postings. One user's real name and hometown (she used her husband's account and a consistent pseudonym for posting online) were divulged by Milne in what she considered to be an invasion of privacy, "for no other reason than asking questions of the wrong group."

And then there was Scamizdat, still jeering and posting anonymously, taking the law into his own hands. A day or so after I let it be known that I'd welcome a quote from this person about his or her activities, an anonymous message landed in my email box. It read: "I am just a netizen fighting a litigious cult in the age of information. While the net has its own perpetual struggles among its orthodoxy and revisionists, it strobes into immobility lawyers and money that darken the battles in the ordinary world. Once a representative portion of the Scientologist cartoon mythology is posted into undeniable digital immortality I will snow crash back into oblivion. SCAMIZDAT."

It took until March 21, 1996, for the CoS to file that expected lawsuit and obtain a temporary restraining order against Grady Ward. The accusation: that he was Scamizdat.

"The only thing I really care about is freedom of speech (and criticism) on the net," says Ward, who categorically denied the charges in a 1996 email interview. He was, however, asked by Judge Whyte not to call the CoS lawyer "Madame Kobrin" in court. Regular *alt.religion.scientology* readers had no trouble recognizing this as a reference to the newsgroup habit of referring to Kobrin as "the 'Ho of Babble-on." On the newsgroup, she is routinely mocked and ridiculed, and people boast about getting letters from her directing them to cease posting portions of the secret documents as a kind of status symbol.

Ward was quickly followed into the courts by Keith Henson. Henson, whose interests in space colonization and cryonics were chronicled in Ed Regis's 1992 book *Great Mambo Chicken and the Transhuman Condition*,[26] welcomed the case, saying by email in 1996, "It will increase my status on the net." Henson has filed a counterclaim for $500 million in damages.

Ward and Henson pose a new challenge for the CoS. Unlike the shocked former Scientologists raided earlier, these two seem to be enjoying their situation enormously. Acting as their own attorneys, they also seem determined to push the CoS as far as possible into producing witnesses and documentary evidence, even successfully demanding that David Miscavige make himself available to testify (Miscavige was deposed in May 1997). The transcripts of the court hearings, available in full on the Net, reveal a true clash of cultures in which the CoS attorneys have to come to grips with the kind of Net humor that posts directions to copies of the secret documents which, when decoded, lead only to the searcher's own computer's directory. It doesn't seem to be easy for them.

These suits must be the first ever to have been reported in such intimate detail on the Net. Every affidavit, every court judgment, and full transcripts of every hearing are all available in one or another archive. If the suits were intended to deter other posters, surely the detail in which they are reported should suffice. But they have not chilled the newsgroup.

Nor has the worst vertical spam in the history of the Net. From the end of May to the end of July 1996 an estimated 20,000 messages consisting of brief quotations from Scientology promotional materials were posted to *alt.religion.scientology*. Posters, who had to pick their way through acres of the stuff in order to continue considering the ramifications of the

Netcom settlement, arguing about Scientology practices, and, of course, flaming each other, were initially as stunned as you might be if you got up one morning to find out that your street had been buried under trainloads of eggplant. Many were convinced that the barrage, eventually dubbed ARSBOMB, would kill the newsgroup entirely.[27]

After a few weeks of panic reactions, a couple of schemes were proposed for by-passing the problem. One is very clever if you don't mind making fun of other people's alien gods. Knowing that Scientologists are not supposed to say the name of Xenu, the alien being Hubbard is said to have named supreme, one poster proposed using it in message subjects to identify non-spam articles so they could be filtered into a sub-newsgroup accepting only those postings. This rather arcane-sounding proposal was adopted and did pretty much work, although it was never more than a stop-gap, as newcomers wishing to participate wouldn't catch on right away.

Over time, the same beings who cancel other types of spam were able to remove most of the worst of it, and it became routine to see messages on *news.admin.net-abuse.misc* detailing huge lists of what material had been removed and by whom.

At the same time, new waves of defiance have seen the secret documents posted in the Netherlands, Sweden, Norway, and on IRC. In a message to *alt.religion.scientology* in early December 1996, a Norwegian poster listed the first month of a program he called "Operation Clambake."[28] One of the more interesting items on the list was a "Random NOTS locator," which would find you a copy of the documents wherever they happen to be posted that day.[29] (In another context, this could be highly useful technology.) In the Netherlands, well-known Dutch writer Karin Spaink and her ISP, xs4all, won in court.[30]

From the CoS point of view, the Swedish case may be the most alarming. When Zenon Panoussis posted the papers to his home pages on the Web, he got the standard response: a request to take them down. Instead, he turned a copy of the papers over to the Swedish Parliament, thereby making them a public document under laws written into the Swedish constitution. The Parliament is accordingly required to show a copy of the documents, for a modest copying fee, to anyone who wants to see them. Although some of the papers were eventually stolen from the Parliament buildings, and Panoussis himself in early January 1997 was awaiting a visit from the bailiffs to seize the documents from his house, Panoussis had given copies to several other institutions to which the same law applies. What once would have been spirited abroad in someone's luggage could now be sent to sanctuary in a matter of seconds.

By then, the Net had lost a stalwart institution (or so it seemed; it was two years old). On August 30, 1996, Julf Helsingius announced he was closing *anon.penet.fi*, after a lower- court ruling gave him thirty days to turn over to the CoS the name and real email address of yet another poster it claimed had infringed its copyrights. With another case from Singapore hanging on the CoS decision (which Helsingius appealed), he concluded that there was no point in running the server if the privacy laws were not strong enough to protect his users' anonymity. Changes in Finnish law to deregulate telecommunications had left what he hoped would be a temporary gap in legislation to cover Internet users' privacy. He hoped the laws would be updated quickly.

What lies ahead for the CoS? Does it make sense for an organization supported by user donations, auditing fees, and book sales to keep using up its resources on legally pursuing Net posters who seem unlikely to give up? If raids and vertical spam don't stop the newsgroup, does it make sense to keep trying the same tactics over and over again? Can the Net take the law into its own hands and render copyrights meaningless? If so, what does this portend for the future of intellectual property?

One scenario sounded so paranoid when it was first proposed on the newsgroup in 1995 by a poster calling himself only "Capricorn" that I dismissed it out of hand. This was that the CoS would eventually try to build a conspiracy case against the Internet and take action under the RICO statutes. At the end of 1996, however, a day before the final hearing on the CoS's demand for attorney fees in the Lerma case, Scientology representatives filed an affidavit from an Internet user identified as Peter Mante, alleging a conspiracy among Internet users to violate Scientology's copyrights. Mante, apparently using the nickname "newkid," declared that he had participated in discussions over IRC in which some of the newsgroup's best-known regulars (a few of whom have denied the allegations) had stressed the importance of continuing to post the secret documents all over the world.[31]

The Irish film censors who banned Monty Python's *Life of Brian* only to see it turn into an underground video hit could have warned the CoS that controversy brings popularity. Throughout 1995 the traffic on *alt. religion.scientology* increased, from an average 2,500 postings a week in March to 2,700 articles a day by August, according to the "Arbitron" ratings posted to *news.admin.misc* by DEC research scientist and Usenet expert Brian Reid throughout 1995. The raids only boosted interest, summed up by one newcomer as the sort of instinct that makes you go take a look at a 200-car pile-up. By April 2, two months after the first raids, *alt.religion.scientology* had moved into the top 40 in the categories of megabytes (no. 40), traffic (no. 8), and per number of readers (no. 18). Some of the fallout landed in *alt.journalism, news.admin.misc, comp.org.eff.talk, alt.current-events.net-abuse*, and even, with the Scamizdat postings, the hacker newsgroup *alt.2600*—which wasn't too thrilled at the incomers, even though the group had to admit there's something like hacking involved in anonymously posting secret scriptures.

However, Stu Sjouwerman, a Scientologist since 1982 and part owner of a computer company, dismissed the affair in an email message in mid-1995 as "less than 0.002 percent of the whole Net. Couple of dogs barking, that's all." Sjouwerman, who is passionate about Scientology's potential to save the planet, runs a closed mailing list for Scientologists, which in early 1995 he said had about two hundred members and a traffic level of fifteen to twenty messages a day. In another message, he commented,

> The issue here is that copyrights are knowingly being violated and we are ready to defend our constitutional rights in court. Listen, have a look at what happened to the Jews in 1933–45. The main reason why this happened is that nobody said a word when it started and let it seep into the German society like a cancer growth. The camps were the terminal stage. We are not going to let this happen again so we are _very_ vocal and will not lie down and die because some people want us to. Remember the Price of Freedom: Constant alertness, constant willingness to fight back. There is no other price.

Homer Smith sees some of this differently, although his starting place, the value and importance of Scientology itself, is the same.

> Scientology is not a scam nor a con, it is a true religion, a very fine one that encompasses the best of man's wisdom to present time on the technical nature of the soul and how to achieve enlightenment for the masses. However, it is also a militaristic religion, like Islam, with a Holy Jihad to take over the planet at all costs. . . . It is a legal jihad to "Keep the Tech Pure."
>
> As for *alt.religion.scientology*, I think what has happened is WONDERFUL on many fronts, not all of which are obviously good. Compared to what *alt.religion.scientology* used to be like two years ago, this is marvelous. The whole world knows about Scientology now, and those that are

able to see the good will find out about it (and probably become Free Zon-ers!) and those that are mad at the bad have something big enough for them to chew the bone with. The Church is a formidable opponent and there are lots of people look just for such a game. (Email interview, 1995)

Former Scientologist (though not a Free Zoner) Robert Vaughn Young takes a darker view, based on his background as a national PR spokesman for the CoS in his membership days. "I am thankful I'm not having to face the Net," he told me frankly by phone in mid-1995. "It's going to be to Scientology what Viet Nam was to the U.S." In the end, "Their only choice is to withdraw. They cannot win." The result, he thinks, will be to "create, for the first time the first place in the world where Scientology can be openly and freely discussed."

The best guess in early 1997 is that Vaughn Young may have been right. The CoS can win court judgments, certainly, but the probability is that as long as the Net's perceptions of the CoS do not change, the more the CoS tries to squelch the distribution of those documents, the more someone somewhere will feel called upon to make sure they are available somewhere on the Net, always assuming that the copies that are circulat-ing are actually faithful copies.

One question that remains is at what point an individual Net poster has the right to assume prerogatives that have traditionally been only the province of journalists and news-gathering organizations. When the Pen-tagon Papers landed on the doorstep of the *New York Times,* the news-paper was able to publish under the First Amendment's guarantees of freedom of speech, and to make a strong argument in court that publica-tion was in the public interest. In the case of Scientology versus the Net, however, a relatively small group of people made that public interest judgment for themselves and were able to muster enough support to use the Net to publish in such a manner that the material probably cannot be recalled, whatever now happens to those individuals. Although the same effect could have been achieved on a smaller scale through widely dis-tributed paper copies, the amplification inherent in the combination of the Net's high-speed communications and the size of the available popu-lation has greatly changed the balance of power.

7

Exporting the First Amendment

There is a place for censors and we only wish that we could tell you where it is.   —Comedian Pat Paulsen, on the *Smothers Brothers Comedy Hour*, 1968[1]

On June 26, 1997, the U.S. Supreme Court struck down, on constitutional grounds, specifically the First Amendment, the Communications Decency Act (CDA), passed on February 1, 1996, as a rider to the Telecommunications Bill and signed into law by President Clinton on February 8, 1996. The CDA would have criminalized the knowing transmission of indecent material to a minor. The notion that we might export American Puritanism is ironic, because in the early 1990s the great fear outside the United States was that the we would, via the Net, impose our tradition of freedom of speech on other countries who didn't want it. Even Britain, theoretically the closest to us, has an Official Secrets Act rather than a Freedom of Information Act, and observing the country that launched a thousand democracies up close makes you understand why the Founding Fathers wrote the Constitution and the Bill of Rights the way they did. Material banned in Britain in traditional media extends beyond the obscenity generally outlawed here; because of Britain's long fight against terrorism, bomb-making information is generally unwelcome (*The Anarchist's Cookbook* is banned in Britain), and its libel laws are much tougher than those in the United States.

Debates about censorship on the Net go a long way back, at least to the mid-1980s (the Pleistocene era, in Net terms) and the creation of the *alt* hierarchy. Besides Usenet, there are many other networks, often forgotten now that the focus is on the Internet, including Fidonet, a collection of an estimated 24,000 or more bulletin board systems (BBSs), which link to the Internet but also have their own newsgroups and email messaging systems, plus the entire collection of electronic mailing lists, some private, some public, and the many tens of thousands of public and private BBSs worldwide. It is presumably with this in mind that Burma has made it illegal to own a modem and China requires all Internet users to register with the police.

It would be a mistake to assume that the development of all these networks depended solely on the existence of a few specific people. Local hierarchies of newsgroups are built all the time, within organizations, by Internet service providers (ISPs) to serve their customers, and by people in specific regions, states, or countries to serve local interests. The owners of those newsgroups may decide whether or not to distribute them outside their organizations; other Usenet sites may decide whether or not to take them. The invention of Usenet, founded in 1979 as a grassroots answer to the Department of Defense–funded experimental network ARPAnet, is generally credited to three students, Steve Bellovin at the University of North Carolina, who wrote the first series of scripts, and Duke University students Steve Daniel and Tom Truscott, who rewrote and extended these in the computer programming language C. Because of its origins, Usenet does not require the Internet to propagate; it is based instead on a UNIX-based program called UUCP (for UNIX to UNIX Copy Program), and many sites still get their Usenet feeds by phoning other sites to exchange news. If Congress today passed a law banning ISPs from distributing Usenet, an underground network of private telephone exchange mechanisms would quickly develop alongside the many mechanisms that already exist for giving people without Usenet feeds access to newsgroups, such as public news servers that can be accessed by anyone with a newsreader (built into most Web browsers these days, and also readily available on the Net).

The situation has always been different on the commercial services. America Online (AOL) and CompuServe, for example, have built their systems by offering royalties based on traffic to those willing to run areas on those services and control what content is available and to whom. Exactly what areas get set up are business decisions that depend as much on the services' assessment of the proposed moderators as on the content itself. Even the WELL, with its much smaller membership, tightly controlled its conference list until early 1996, requiring would-be hosts (as WELL conference moderators are called) to prove there was sufficient interest before sanctioning the conference. Now, the WELL functions the way CIX always has: anyone may start a conference at any time and make it private or public. People seem unnerved by the notion that private areas may exist over which the services have no control, but as long as people who use those areas are consenting adults or children with their parents' consent, it's not clear why they should be subject to any restrictions greater than those imposed on members-only clubs in real life.

It is arrogant and provincial to think that the United States is the only country with the technological know-how and motivation to create information networks. It is virtually certain that all over the world there are people using the same technology in unexpected and hidden ways that we don't know about, even if some have been slower to get started for economic and regulatory reasons (see chapter 13). An estimated 60 percent of 9.4 million Internet hosts—machines or networks that provide Web sites, Usenet news servers, and email services—are based in the United States. That leaves a pretty substantial number that are outside direct U.S. control but from which information flows as seamlessly to U.S. citizens as to the rest of the world.[2]

It was against this background that John Perry Barlow called the First Amendment a "local ordinance" and British newspaper reporter Andrew Brown likened censoring the Net to "making a rule that you can only piss in the shallow end of the pool."[3] One of the more amusing sights on the Net is the American habit of invoking the First Amendment and its provisions like a mantra, even in areas dedicated to international politics or frequented mostly by users from other nations, and even though at least some of those users are not sure that unfettered freedom of speech is an unqualified benefit, and even if they were, certainly wouldn't want to be berated about it by snot-nosed American kids. Similarly, not everyone outside the United States appreciates the arrogance with which American Net commentators dismiss their efforts to control certain types of information—such as the testimony in court cases during trial—as censorship.

Clinton had barely gotten the official fountain pen back into the presidential inkwell after signing the Telecommunications Bill into law before two suits were filed against the Department of Justice seeking to overturn the CDA. The two cases were joined together for hearing in Philadelphia, and the twenty-seven plaintiffs included the American Library Association, the American Booksellers Association, CompuServe, America Online, Microsoft, Netcom, Prodigy, Wired Ventures (the publisher of *Wired* magazine), Apple, the American Civil Liberties Union, the Society of Professional Journalists, and the Commercial Internet Exchange, plus the Citizen Internet Empowerment Coalition, representing approximately

56,000 Netizens.[4] Simultaneously, many Web sites turned their backgrounds to black in protest and posted the now widespread blue ribbons supporting free speech online. Shortly afterward, two more suits were filed in New York.

Testimony was heard over six days in March and April, and, like anything to do with the Net, seems to have had its quirky moments. The author Howard Rheingold (*The Virtual Community*), for example, testifying as an expert witness on the subject of life online, dressed in what plaintiff and reporter Declan McCullagh described on his Fight-Censorship emailing list as "a glowing blue suit, an iridescent pink shirt, and the first tie he's worn in a decade." Others testifying on behalf of the Net were Bill Burrington, director of public policy for AOL, and MIT's Albert Vezza, as an expert witness on the PICS Web content ratings system.

On June 11, U.S. District Judges Dolores Sloviter, Stewart Dalzell, and Ronald Buckwalter in Philadelphia struck down the CDA in the best kind of judicial language. "The Internet may fairly be regarded as a never-ending worldwide conversation. The Government may not, through the CDA, interrupt that conversation. As the most participatory form of mass speech yet developed, the Internet deserves the highest protection from governmental intrusion," the justices wrote. They concluded, "Just as the strength of the Internet is chaos, so the strength of our liberty depends upon the chaos and cacophony of the unfettered speech the First Amendment protects."

The Electronic Frontier Foundation (EFF) summed up the case against the CDA as follows: "[that] the law is unconstitutionally overbroad (criminalizing protected speech), that it is unconstitutionally vague (making it difficult for individuals and organizations to comply), that it fails what the judiciary calls the 'least restrictive means' test for speech regulation, and that there is no basic constitutional authority under the First Amendment to engage in this type of content regulation in any nonbroadcast medium." The EFF and others argued that it would be more appropriate for the standards to be the looser ones generally applied to print media because Net users can choose what material from the Net they view or download. Broadcast media simply spill into people's houses.

Nonetheless, Senator James Exon (D-NE) commented in his press release after the decision, "The Decency Act stands for the premise that it is wrong to provide pornography to children on computers just as it is wrong to do it on a street corner or anywhere else. Hopefully, reason and common sense will prevail in the Supreme Court."[5]

The fear that the CDA would chill discussion on the Net as people began censoring themselves out of fear of prosecution is a real one, in my experience. I have, for example, one friend who will not discuss the subject of child pornography on the Net or ever admit he's seen any because he's convinced that such a statement would get him arrested. On top of that, because of the sheer volume of material on the Net, computers would have to do the scanning. But computers are supremely stupid and literal about following directions, and the CDA would be like an open-meshed trawler net killing dolphins while trying to catch Charlie the Tuna. All kinds of material would be prohibited, including certain literary classics and reports on academic and medical research, as well as more controversial adult humor, abortion information, and gay support groups. If that sounds alarmist, consider that AOL has already had exactly this kind of problem. First its breast cancer support group fell afoul of the system's built-in filters; then British users from the northern English town of Scunthorpe found they couldn't live there for AOL's purposes because of a sequence of four letters in the town's name.

Of course, filters can be defeated by deliberate misspellings, one origin of the kind of writing you see online from would-be hackers or software pirates, something like, "I am a kewl dood looking for warez." A similar situation applies to newsgroup naming schemes; the obscurely titled *alt.binaries.pictures.leek* was for a time known as a group for the illegal exchange of commercial software. Because of this, attempts to block the posting of certain types of material to Usenet by removing specific groups from the newsfeed are generally considered doomed to fail. Conversation about sex didn't happen on Usenet because *alt.sex* was created; the creation of a sex-related discussion group was proposed as a home for the sexually related conversation that was taking place in *soc.singles*.[6]

As Gene Spafford, one of the earliest and longest-lived (eleven years) Usenet administrators, wrote in a long email message explaining his decision to give up his Usenet work, "Attempts to change the real world by altering the structure of the Usenet is an attempt to work sympathetic magic—electronic voodoo."[7]

Doubtless we would have seen more civil disobedience had the CDA not been challenged so quickly. Even so, there were indications that the Net wasn't about to go quietly into regulation as a broadcast medium. Unexpected groups began planning campaigns such as linking to as many objectionable sites (especially if foreign) as possible. The members of *alt.showbiz.gossip*, a newsgroup with a weird sense of irony that allows them simultaneously to indulge in celebrity gossip and laugh at themselves (and the virtual trailer park they live in) for doing it, began using as many swear words as possible.[8]

Other reactions were more timid. System operators began worrying about what material might get them arrested (the day after the CDA's passage an outfit called Oklahomans for Children and Families announced a campaign to eliminate pornography from the Internet, and at least one Oklahoma ISP cut ten of the most controversial newsgroups while awaiting legal advice. In June 1997 CNN reported that the same outfit had obtained a ruling that the movie "The Tin Drum" was illegal under Oklahoma law.).[9] One beneficiary was the Adult Check system, which for $9.95 (payable by credit card) issues you a number certifying you're an adult; these numbers are accepted by approximately two hundred pornographic Web sites. (It's notable that prohibiting pornography has the same effect as prohibiting drugs: the product becomes more expensive and more profitable; it would be interesting to hear the anti-pornography squad's explanation in a public debate on why this is a good thing.)

We found out in 1996 just how many countries want to keep the United States company in regulating the type of information available to their citizens via the Net. The country with one million lawyers started with legislation. Other countries are trying other tactics in what someday may be an interesting guide to national character.

On May 6, the administrators of the two largest French ISPs, FranceNet and World-Net, spent forty-eight hours in detention while police argued that as ISPs they should be held responsible for distributing child pornography despite government statements to the contrary. In protest, most French ISPs temporarily closed their Usenet service; Net users protested by turning their Web page backgrounds black, displaying French flags at half mast, and posting complaints via public news servers and electronic mail. The French Parliament, meanwhile, passed a law in June setting up a central regulatory agency to rate content.

German officials have also threatened ISPs. At the end of 1996, CompuServe subscribers worldwide were temporarily denied access to two hundred Usenet newsgroups after a Munich prosecutor warned the service that the newsgroups contained material that was illegal under German law. (In early 1997 CompuServe's German managing director, Felix Somm, was indicted on similar charges. He left the company shortly afterwards.) CompuServe blocked access to the newsgroups for all its members worldwide while it tried to figure out a mechanism to block them just for German users. CompuServe had actually found an interesting balance; while making the newsgroups available it had tried to eliminate the chance that a young user would stumble accidentally on obscene material by not giving users a full list to choose from. If you wanted *alt. binaries.pictures.erotica* you had to know it existed and type in its name correctly. What was surprising about the German action was that the newsgroups were mostly sexually oriented (including *alt.sex.safe*, which is just what it sounds like).[10] Other types of speech on the Net, such as Holocaust revisionism, are also illegal under German law. (The list of blocked newsgroups became a useful guide for those seeking pornography online, as did, to Chief Inspector Stephen French's clucking disapproval, the list of 133 newsgroups Scotland Yard's Clubs and Vice unit circulated to ISPs in August 1996.)[11]

Since then, Germany has set up a regulatory agency, the Internet Content Task Force (ICTF), and also passed new telecommunications laws requiring ISPs to build in back doors so that state officials can access users' private email if necessary for law enforcement. In early September, the ICTF ordered German ISPs to block access to the Web site at Dutch xs4all, which holds 3,100 personal and commercial home pages including those of *Radikal*, a left-wing political magazine that is banned in Germany. The CEO of xs4all, Felipe Rodriguez, announced that he would investigate the possibility of legal action against the German government, along with plans to rotate his site's IP number (the information behind named addresses that computers use to route network traffic) to make it more difficult to keep the site blocked. In the meantime, many sites began mirroring the *Radikal* pages to ensure their availability.

"This is the effect censorship has on [the] Internet: information is recreated," observed Rodriguez in a widely circulated email message to the ICTF's Michael Schneider, going on to describe technological blocks as providing only "the illusion of censorship." Presciently, earlier in the summer of 1996 both German and Australian ministers suggested that harmonized international standards are needed to prevent Net users from circumventing community standards.

Things only get worse as you move out of Europe, according to a May 10, 1996, report, "Silencing the Net,"[12] produced by the non-governmental organization Human Rights Watch. China requires all ISPs and Internet users to register with the authorities. Viet Nam and Saudi Arabia control access via a single Internet gateway. In July 1996 an Indonesian university lecturer was arrested after distributing email messages about riots in Jakarta to an international mailing list covering Indonesian politics. American journalist Declan McCullagh, who maintains the Fight-Censorship mailing list and the Plague of Freedom pages (http://www.eff.org/pub/Global/Dispatches) lists many more countries interested in censoring the Net, including Cuba, Canada, Kuwait, and Taiwan.

On September 15, 1996, Singapore began requiring all ISPs to funnel their traffic through government-controlled proxy servers that block access to government-disapproved sites; in return, users were promised faster access, as the servers also cache frequently accessed pages. However, after a week Singapore users were already reporting slower access (and therefore higher phone bills) because each clicked request had to be checked against the server's database. Worse, they complained that the proxies deliver out-of-date pages because the pages stored locally aren't updated often enough. Both complaints are common with proxy servers, which are commonly used by networks and commercial services such as America Online to minimize traffic. But think of stock quotes and you'll understand why it's a problem when pages aren't updated frequently enough. On September 25, a Singapore court fined a man approximately $45,000 for possession of pornographic images downloaded from the Internet.[13]

In Britain, handshakes were exchanged in September on a gentlemen's agreement for a combination system involving ratings for Web sites and newsgroups; a hotline for user complaints; and a private, non-profit foundation set up by Peter Dawe, the just-retired CEO of the leading commercial Internet supplier, Pipex, now part of UUNet. The closest similar initiatives are in the Netherlands, where a hotline set up by xs4all for complaints about child pornography online is said to be working well at clearing such material off the Net, and in Belgium, which also opened a similar reporting point on the Web. Britain's initiative, like the CDA, was preceded by a horrendous media report. In the CDA's case, this was the notorious *Time* magazine "Cyberporn" cover story (see chapter 9); in Britain, media pressure came from the century-old *Observer* Sunday newspaper, which on August 25, 1996, ran an outrageous and wildly inaccurate story about child pornography on the Net targeting an associate director at Britain's largest consumer ISP, Demon Internet, and anonymous remailer operator Julf Helsingius. The proposals that resulted in the Internet Watch Foundation (IWF) were announced only a couple of weeks later as a back-of-the-envelope scheme dreamed up by Dawe five days earlier. With a general election looming, it took only two weeks for those proposals to become government policy.

In fact, the British scheme may be the best hope for a regulatory regime because it allows for user choice while seeking public support in enforcing the existing laws. The hotline is starting with child pornography because this is clearly illegal in most countries and there is a substantial consensus that this material should not be circulated on the Net. (In fact, many of the newsgroups with names like *alt.binaries.pictures.erotica.children* were probably started as tasteless jokes and are largely taken up with messages flaming the groups.) How it will work out as the IWF carries out its planned expansion into pirated software, text-based sexual fantasies, and material where the consensus is not as strong remains to be seen.[14]

While Australia and the European Union investigate the potential for classifying the Internet as a broadcast medium and extending similar regulations to it, the trend in many places seems to be toward promoting blocking software and voluntary ratings systems as the favored method for balancing user choice and freedom of speech. Web sites and newsgroups can be rated according to the type of material they generally contain, and parents can use those ratings to limit what their children may access. This will not be a perfect solution; children are not only often better at programming VCRs than their parents are, they are also likely to be better at figuring out how to disable the blocking software than their parents are at figuring out how to enable it. No one seems willing to talk about this, perhaps for fear that this emerging consensus will be damaged, but the fact is that most of these products are trivially easy to defeat by anyone with enough knowledge to edit an AUTOEXEC.BAT file or boot from a floppy—minimal technical skills that are frequently needed for troubleshooting.[15]

Other concerns about today's blocking software are what's getting blocked and why (see chapter 15). However, the hope is that organizations with known agendas will build their own databases of blocked sites. At least one product also enables parents to block their kids from giving out certain types of personal information—a very important function in some, relatively rare circumstances, since prevention is always better than prosecution. Overall, though, while it's safe to say that the software will get better and more sophisticated, it seems unlikely that anyone is going to produce a program that can stand in for parents' involvement in their kids' use of networks.

Just as individual countries are adopting different methods for regulating the Net, so they are picking out different types of information to control. Germany criminalizes Holocaust revisionism, and dry U.S. counties might object to sites covering the details of wine production. Ireland, where abortion is constitutionally banned, spent part of the 1990s battling to restrict information about British abortion clinics. Countries where gambling is illegal might not welcome the news that New York State is setting up an off-track betting Web server. Many, many countries want to make sure that the Net doesn't bring with it new dollops of American cultural imperialism to dilute their own cultures, languages, and traditions.

Another concern is the future of anonymity in a world where posting certain types of information is criminalized. The proposals that led to the formation of the IWF include a note to "Ensure that anonymous servers (e.g.: re-mailers) that they [*sic*] operate in the UK record details of identity and make this available to the Police, when needed."[16] Anonymity on the Net is one area where the standards that apply in everyday physical-world life are not extended rationally—people panic about the potential for abuse of anonymous remailers while simultaneously not questioning the existence on every street corner of devices to support anonymous interactions: mail boxes and telephone booths. It is undeniably true that the use of anonymous remailers can by-pass national censorship attempts; during the Canadian criminal trials of Karla Homulka and Paul Bernado, Helsingius's remailer was used to post trial reports to an electronic mailing list accessible by Canadians denied coverage under the government-ordered media blackout.[17] It's important to remember that under our present legal system, where innocence is to be presumed, it is morally backward to argue that no one would use an anonymous remailer unless they had something to hide (an argument similar to the one made about cryptography).

We should consider learning from Ireland's history. During the decades after independence, Ireland strove to keep itself pure by banning up to two books a day; a classic Irish Senate debate on censorship in 1943 was likened by Irish writer Frank O'Connor to a "long, slow swim through a sewage bed."[18] The worst economic effects of the many bans were felt by Irish writers and the domestic publishing industry, a point that should be considered by American legislators seeking to control what material may be posted on the networks—especially since it is estimated that more than 50 percent of U.S. exports are intellectual property, the kind suited for transmission via the Net.[19] Structures designed to impede the flow of one type of information are likely to impede others by slowing down transmission while the material's legality is being checked, by raising fears of litigation or search and seizure that make people reluctant to use the Net, or by burdening users with added costs. Would you use a telephone that only transmitted certain words and kept user logs?

Or, as University of Miami associate law professor A. Michael Froomkin puts it,

> Almost every attempt to block access to material on the Internet, indeed anything short of an extraordinarily restrictive access policy, can be circumvented easily. Hydras can be killed by heroic measures: according to Greek mythology, Hercules ultimately destroyed Hydra by cauterizing its stumps and severing the immortal head from its body. The Internet, too, could be killed, or a nation can choose to allow access on a restricted basis. Yet, the more a nation pursues a restrictive Internet policy, the less value it will derive from the network and the more it risks being left out of the information revolution.[20]

When, in July 1996, the Net rejoiced over the CDA's defeat in court, it may have cheered too soon: federal legislation typically inspires a wave of similar legislation at the state level. According to the EFF, a number of states, including New York, Oregon, Maryland, New Jersey, Pennsylvania, Washington, Virginia, Montana, and Oklahoma, have now passed or are considering copycat laws.[21] These, too, may eventually be ruled unconstitutional, but it could take some time to get this message across to all fifty states even in the wake of the June 1997 Supreme Court decision. In the meantime, we can look forward to lots of stupid and expensive litigation.[22] Somewhere, one million lawyers may be drooling.

More ideologically, censorship is a quick way to kill the dream of the Net as a clean and shiny new world that can do away with traditional class structures. Censorship automatically creates a class system delineated by access (or lack thereof) to forbidden information. Those with technical skills, the money to buy them, or contacts with those appointed as guardians, can get access; those without can't. The next four chapters examine several such situations, and chapter 13 looks at alternative methods of controlling the free flow of information and the tension between equal access and intellectual property rights.

8

Never Wrestle a Pig

"What is the first thing you notice about a person?"
"Whether the person is male or female" —Spencer Tracy and
Katharine Hepburn in *Desk Set*

If America Online (AOL) users found that they inspired the invention of new prejudices, women were expected to find that they could function in cyberspace as unquestioned equals. In a world where there are no bodies and all that matters is the quality of your written thoughts, the ideal went, all those physical delineators like skin color, gender, or disability would vanish. The thing is, although physical objects don't accompany you into cyberspace, your personality and your experience of the real world do. By the mid-1990s, endless stories began appearing in the media about the predominantly male (and white) nature of Net users and their harassment of women.

There are several different questions tangled up here, of which the easiest is how many women use the Net and for what purpose. The more difficult issues are whether women really are discriminated against in a significant way in cyberspace and how that discrimination is going to be defined. If we're going to object to the U.S. (or any other) government's attempts to set standards for acceptable speech on the Net, should we then award moral guardianship to women (or any other group) instead?

There is no doubt that for a long time cyberspace was predominantly male, although to what degree depended on where you looked. A staff member at CIX estimated in late 1992 that perhaps only 2 percent of the system's users were women. CompuServe has estimated its female membership at 25 percent for the last several years,[1] AOL claims 38 to 40 percent, and best estimates are that women make up about one-third of

Internet users (see chapter 13). The WELL's percentage is thought to be near parity.

But bearing in mind that all these systems are divided up by topic, it's logical that even across a single system women aren't going to be evenly distributed. CompuServe's now defunct Tennis forum had an almost all-female team of sysops and a very high percentage (at a guess, 70 percent) of participating female members. The much bigger *Sports Illustrated* forum, where the tennis topics moved after the Tennis forum's closure, is predominantly male, presumably reflecting the magazine's subscriber base. The media-related forum I co-manage is probably at least a third female.

A quote from Dee Brown's *Wondrous Times on the Frontier* about the lives of women as the American West was opened up offer a good analogy to the earliest days of the Net, when there were almost no women. "Shortages of women in the early days of gold-rush California," he writes, "naturally made them more desirable than in more normally apportioned areas. If a rumor spread that a woman had arrived in any mining camp, men would travel for miles just to take a look at a female form and hear a female voice."[2]

Compare this to Nancy Tamosaitis, in *The Joy of Cybersex:* "Women in the straight or bisexual adult bulletin board world wield an immensely high level of power. According to *Boardwatch Magazine*, only 10 percent of bulletin board callers are female. The other 90 percent who are males are eager, often desperate, to talk with female callers."[3]

Brown doesn't say whether, out of desperation or desire for attention, frontiersmen dressed up in drag. Online, of course, this is trivially easy, to the point where in the early days any lively, provocative female ID was suspected of being a gender-bending male.

Carol Atack, who was one of the first women on CIX because of her job writing computer news, recollected in 1992, "Four to five years ago, there was only a handful of women (or they may have been lurking). Women tended to be fantasy figures created by males to act out." Because of that, "I would get messages from the 'policemen' on CIX to check me out." Because she was lively and noticeable, she found that every time anyone started a new conference she tended to get added to it. In addition, finding that "nearly all the conferences were very male-oriented" (that is, oriented toward cars and computers), she started a conference of her own, *at_home*, a slightly ironic women's magazine–style discussion area; there was a fashion topic (where people discussed what brand of anorak they should be wearing) and an agony topic for people in need of emotional support.

Atack was functioning in exactly the time-honored way the Net has always worked: she wanted something, it wasn't there, she went out and built it. If women feel the Net is hostile, the answer is to build more such places, rather than waiting for someone else, probably a male-dominated technology company, to create "women-friendly" spaces and sell access to them. In fact, some women have: besides women-only resources such as the Systers mailing list for female computer professionals and the many restricted-access conferences on online services, resources such as the Women's Wire and AmazonCity are popping up on the Web to offer women the kind of assistance in making contacts and finding resources that the Net is good at.[4]

More important than the raw numbers is whether women participate proportionately once they're on the Net. My experience says they do, but the research I've seen claims that they don't and blames the difference on intrinsic, gender-specific conversational and interactive styles of the kind popularized by Deborah Tannen's book *You Just Don't Understand*.[5]

Susan Herring, an associate professor at the University of Texas at Arlington who has done several of the most often quoted studies of women online, writes: "My basic claim has two parts: first, that women and men have recognizably different styles in posting to the Internet, contrary to the claim that CMC [computer-mediated communication] neutralizes distinctions of gender; and second, that women and men have different communicative ethics—that is, they value different kinds of online interactions as appropriate and desirable."[6]

Herring goes on to say that after saving and studying a year's worth of messages posted to two mailing lists, Linguist and Megabyte Union, a list dedicated to writing and computers:

> The most striking sex-based disparity in academic CMC is the extent to which men participate more than women. Women constitute 36% of LINGUIST and 42% of MBU subscribers. However, they participate at a rate that is significantly lower than that corresponding to their numerical representation. Two extended discussions were analyzed from each list, one in which sexism was an issue, and the other on a broadly theoretical topic. Although the "sexism" discussions were more popular with women than discussions on other topics, women constituted only 30% of the participants in these discussions on both lists, and in the "theoretical" discussions, only 16% of the participants were women. Furthermore, the messages con-

tributed by women are shorter, averaging a single screen or less, while those of men average one and a half times longer in the "sexism" discussions, and twice as long in the "theoretical" discussions, with some messages ten screens or more in length. Thus while a short message does not necessarily indicate the sex of the sender, a very long message invariably indicates that the sender is male.[7]

Maybe so, but who has the time to *read* any but the most exceptional message that's more than a screen or two in length? The value and impact of a message posted to the Net are not determined by its volume. Brevity is greatly valued on the Net, and the longer you've been online the more you appreciate it. Netizens have also observed frequently that the longest and most opinionated messages are the most likely to be LCW—Loud, Confident, and Wrong.

Herring's results contradict studies carried out by Lee Sproull and Sara Kiesler. In their book *Connections*, a study of the use of electronic communications in networked organizations, they conclude:

> Because it is harder to read status cues in electronic messages than it is in other forms of communication, high-status people do not dominate the discussion in electronic groups as much as they do in face-to-face groups. For instance, when groups of executives met face-to-face, the men in the groups were five times as likely as the women to make the first decision proposal. When those same groups met via computer, the women made the first proposal as often as the men did.[8]

Other women report personal experiences that back up Sproull and Kiesler's research. "Usenet, while it can be nasty, acerbic, uncaring and unsympathetic, is truly a nondiscriminatory society," writes Judy Anderson, who styles herself yduJ ("rhymes with fudge") on Usenet.[9] "It judges you only through your postings, not by what you look like, your marital status, whether you have a disability, or any of the other things that are traditionally used for discrimination."

"On the Internet you are only what you choose to reveal," consultant Frances Bell wrote in an email message to the editor of London's *Independent* newspaper protesting an article about Internet hostility. "People contact me because of what I do and how I do it. Now I may be politically naive, but I thought this was the goal of the ideal workplace: an environment where people of whatever gender are sought-after because of what they do regardless of disability, physical attractiveness or age."[10]

But the image of women confidently striding the Net is not the one projected in the mainstream media. Instead, we get articles like *Newsweek*'s 1994 cover story "Men, Women, and Computers,"[11] which characterized the Net as essentially hostile to women and filled with aggressive, obnoxious, sexually predatory men who like playing with computers and exploring, as opposed to practical, beleaguered women who "just want their computers to work." I have news: that's what everybody wants, man or woman. It's because they *don't* "just work" that it's necessary for us to waste brain cells on the knowledge that our home PC is a clock-doubled 486SX/25 with 16Mb of RAM and almost no free hard disk space so we can explain this to the technical support guy when we can't get our mysteriously silent sound cards to squawk unpleasantly. Not having to know this kind of thing would certainly free up some useful mental space for more valuable information, as Macintosh users around the world are only too happy to remind us with religious fervor.

Much of the scientific evidence purporting to show that women and men are intrinsically different has been challenged, notably in psychologist Carol Tavris's *The Mismeasure of Woman*. "Are women really kinder, gentler, and more interconnected with people and the environment than men are?" she writes skeptically. "Are the qualities of peacefulness and connection to others endemic to female nature, or are they a result of the nurturing, caretaking work that women do because of their social and family roles? For that matter, are these qualities truly more characteristic of women than men, or are they merely human archetypes—stereotypes of female and male—that blur when we look more closely at actual human beings?"[12]

Tavris's conclusion is especially interesting for those studying gender interactions on the Net: "Just as when in Rome most people do as Romans do, the behavior of women and men depends as much on the gender they are *interacting with* than on anything intrinsic about the gender they are."[13] In other words, the difference between men and women online may not be determined by their own gender but by the gender they believe their correspondents are. By this theory, if both women and men believe that the online world is largely male, their behavior may warp accordingly. This makes sense to me, especially since I have trouble with most research that purports to find intrinsic differences between men and women: I always find my behavior a closer match to the supposedly male portion of the spectrum.

Anecdotally, my own experience seems to support the research Tavris quotes. I have twice been startled to find out that a correspondent was female instead of (as I had thought) male. The second time was online; the person in question was someone I had encountered frequently for over a year in a WELL conference. This user had an unusual ID that I couldn't assign to either gender and an even more unusual real name that I couldn't parse. Rather than ask, I just figured eventually cues would appear; they did, when one night, startled, I recognized her on TV commenting on the 1996 election.

Online it didn't matter. What was a shock was the first incident, which concerned a deep-voiced PR person named Chris with whom I'd had several phone conversations but whom I had never met. The day I called and was told "She's in the ladies' room," I got off the phone, stunned, and found myself worrying over all the conversations we'd had and wondering what, if anything, I might have said differently had I known she was female. Although I eventually concluded there wasn't anything, my reaction taught me something I didn't know about how much attention we pay to these things unconsciously, even in situations where the important question isn't gender but whether the review software is going to arrive on time. Online, on the other hand, I am so notoriously poor at noticing the IDs of people I haven't met and connecting those strangers' names to messages that I feel I can safely say that gender really *doesn't* matter.

Tavris's answer to a source for male–female differences is equally interesting: "whenever social scientists have looked beneath (or around) many of the apparent linguistic differences between women and men, they often find that qualities thought to be typical of women are, instead, artifacts of a power imbalance."[14] If it can be extended to online communication, this observation suggests two things. First, both women and men may benefit from having the Net as a safe place to explore new styles of communicating with others and to experiment with interacting in ways that make them feel too vulnerable offline. Second, it would be useful to examine the differences in interactions between men and women in recreational areas where the posters are largely unknown to each other versus professionally oriented areas where those present know each other from working together in the real world and where there are real, professional stakes.

Those stakes are quite different from the kind of problem media reports often focus on—sexual harassment by strangers. This seems to me a huge red herring. Women are likely to be immeasurably safer working online at home late at night than they are traveling across a campus or city. However invasive it feels to have some bozo spewing sexually charged abuse into your email box and out of your computer screen, there's a lot to be said for danger that isn't physical. You have so many more choices online: you can stop and think for a day or two to concoct a choice reply; you can use technical means to remove the harasser from your world; you can complain to the boor's system administrators; you can even, as Ellen Spertus, a researcher in artificial intelligence at the Massachusetts Institute of Technology, points out, use the messages to embarrass the perpetrator.[15] (Always bearing in mind the well-known Net saying, "Never wrestle with a pig. You both get dirty, and the pig likes it.")

Two stories illustrate how this can work—both from the WELL, one accidental, one deliberate. The first was a poster who showed up in the *sexuality* conference and, figuring that women who were willing to *talk* about sex openly might be willing to *do* it, with *him*, emailed a number of female conference participants with a come-on. Unfortunately, the WELL's interface tripped him up, as it has so many, and dumped what he thought were private email messages into the public, open conference for everyone to hoot at. As my father used to say when I missed a smash in ping-pong, "Evil to him who evil thinks."

The second, written up at the time (the summer of 1993) in *Time* magazine,[16] concerned a "cybercad" who ardently pursued several women on the WELL, apparently at the same time, into face-to-face (or, as the WELL likes to call them, F2F) encounters of the most intimate kind, then dumped them unceremoniously. Retiring to the private women-only conference to miserate and discovering they had company, the women decided to out him publicly as a warning to others. The man in question eventually said he had thought the rules were "different in cyberspace"[17] —a clear case of someone's being unable to find the boundary between cyberspace and real life. He may have *met* these women in cyberspace, but the rest of the relationships took place in the physical world. It seems to me it ought to be pretty clear that the moment you pick up that telephone to direct-dial, you've changed jurisdictions. Such a case doesn't mean you shouldn't meet people online or give them your home phone number; but it does mean you should exercise the same caution you would with someone you met casually in a bar. The women on the WELL acknowledged this with great disappointment and a sense of betrayal: they had believed online was safe—the other side of expecting the rules to be different in cyberspace.

Spertus discusses technical means for blocking harassment, such as using cryptographic digital signatures to block out unknown correspondents much the way caller ID blocks out unidentified callers. With such things likely to be available soon, she suggests that women could use shared blacklists and killfiles to exclude known offenders and build networks of trust in which each member is known to at least one other member of the network. While this could be extremely valuable, it is an option with many flaws and is suitable only for a few contexts. We tend to assume that online harassment is trivial and that it won't escalate into physical violence, but this won't be true in all cases. Blocking the harasser's email may block out messages that would alert the recipient to genuine, as opposed to virtual, danger. More, it discards the evidence. In a serious case, like the one reported by consultant Stephanie Brail,[18] whose harasser kept changing originating email addresses, much as spammers do, it may make no difference. Further, blocking messages from unknown correspondents is simply not an option if you are, as many people are expected to become, a freelance professional working via modem for the highest bidder. Such tools are also likely to come easiest and be most readily available to the technically literate, the very people who are already best able to defend themselves if they have to.

It seems to me regressive for women to believe their only safe option online is to move through an edited world like the hothouse flowers Victorian women were supposed to be. It may also be dangerous: the worst threats may be the ones you don't know about and so can't counteract. In any case, the whole point of computer networks is that they connect you to people you didn't know existed; using them to huddle means giving up an important chance to participate in the construction of the electronic corridors of power. This is one area of life where the lack of physical presence should allow women to adventure equally. Most of the women I know online realize this and use the many single-sex areas, which have grown up anywhere in cyberspace that has access control, as only one element of their online lives.

I would argue that the more important hindrances to women's full participation online are lack of access to technical expertise and lack of time. As Ellen Balka put it in a paper examining the issue of access, "Perhaps the greatest issue faced by the women's movement with respect to the adoption of computer networking technology is access." She concludes,

> A widely accessible computer network could increase the number of voices represented in an organization's decision-making process. To realize these goals, however, feminists will need to apply the insights gained from years of productive organizing, and at the same time investigate the social biases of technological systems that, left unconsidered, threaten to create com-

puter networking systems which reproduce rather than challenge the power relations characteristic of western capitalist societies.[19]

Time may be just as big an issue. Women who are already juggling a job, marriage, and children are less likely to be able to find time to hang out online or randomly browse the Web unless they can imagine some immediate practical advantage. It's amusing to report that a small bit of evidence supporting this idea comes from a poster to *alt.transgendered*, who commented in 1994 that the only significant difference in her new life as a woman was the lack of free time. More support comes from a CompuServe November 1995 survey, which found that "according to the survey participants, the primary barrier for women spending time online is not enough free time. The answer was by far the leading factor cited and was selected by 55 percent of respondents."[20]

People who want to sell us things point to online grocery shopping as that practical advantage. (I've done it, and it's not so much a time saver as a much less unpleasant way of acquiring food.) And it is, but the more valuable advantage, if more difficult to convey to the unwired, is the potential for undoing some of the damage done by social constructs. Why shouldn't we have, for example, such an exceptionally valuable thing as a (voluntary) maiden names registry database site? One of the reasons women lose track of their old friends over time is that those friends don't always know what their names are any more. More immediately, as several female CIXen at home with children have said, online gives women in that position a chance to talk via electronic conferencing every day with 10,000 other adults for less per month than the cost of a single night out. Or, if you're the only woman at your level in the corporate structure, online may be the only way you can meet and interact regularly with women at your level in other companies. The online world has far greater potential to change most women's lives than it does most men's.

For this reason, the characterization of the Net as a boy's toy makes smoke come out of my ears, whether the assertion is coming from media sources who tell women to hide behind male or gender-neutral IDs (thereby making cyberspace look even more male) or from addled critics of interface design who think there's something inherently masculine about typed computer commands. If the point-and-click functionality of a graphical interface is somehow inherently feminine, then so is the TV remote control.

I've seen otherwise intelligent women get up at artistic conferences and complain that an interface that uses "kill" as the command to delete a file is too masculine. (Clearly these women are not from New York.) Fine— design your own interface. Women who show up online demanding that those already there alter their behavior are going to get a reception similar to those the government did when it passed the CDA and proposed Clipper. No one really gets to make rules for the Net; backbone Cabalist Gene Spafford, who tried for eleven years by writing the rules of Netiquette, eventually gave up, complaining no one was listening to him. And *he* had seniority and, for a time, real power. That few women have such seniority and technical power is largely a reflection of the make-up of the computer science community.

In a study of gender relations on the Net, Mcgill University researcher Leslie Regan Shade notes: "One of the biggest challenges is widening access to the net for women that aren't institutionally affiliated, whether in industry or academia, where they purportedly have 'ready' access to both the hardware and software, and technical expertise, to successfully learn how to navigate the net."[21]

Speaking of censorship as "an essential condition for democracy," Shade adds,

> While it is true that no external censorship was exercised by the moderators or owners of LINGUIST or MBU, women participating in CMC are nevertheless constrained by censorship both external and internal. Externally, they are censored by male participants who dominate and control the discourse through intimidation tactics, and who ignore or undermine women's contributions when they attempt to participate on a more equal basis. To a lesser extent, non-adversarial men suffer the same treatment, and in and of itself, it need not prevent anyone who is determined to participate from doing so. Where adversariality becomes a devastating form of censorship, however, is in conjunction with the internalized cultural expectations that we bring to the formula: that women will talk less, on less controversial topics, and in a less assertive manner. Finally, although it was not a focus of the present investigation, women are further discouraged from participating in CMC by the expectation—effectively internalized as well— that computer technology is primarily a male domain.

Much though I respect these researchers' attempts to study the cultural phenomenon that is the Net, their conclusions are at such a complete variance with my online experience that I can't help wondering if they're seeing patterns where none exist, or if we use the same Net. On every system I've ever been on I have always known talented, interesting, outspoken women of varying technical aptitude who seem to have no problem expressing what they think and making themselves heard. Asked one woman on the WELL during the dissection of the *Newsweek* piece, how can men dominate a discussion online when there is infinite room for everyone to post as much material as they like?

But indeed we may not be—even should not be—all using the same Net. MIT Media Lab researcher Amy Bruckman, who has founded two virtual communities as part of her research, writes, "When people complain about being harassed on the Net, they've usually stumbled into the wrong online community. The question is not whether 'women' are comfortable on 'the Net,' but rather, what types of communities are possible? How can we create a range of communities so that everyone—men and women—can find a place that is comfortable for them?" She adds, "I'm glad there are places on the Net where I'm not comfortable. The world would be a boring place if it invariably suited any one person's taste. The great promise of the Net is diversity."[22]

I agree with Bruckman wholeheartedly, which is why Shade's comment that ensuring equitable gender access, among other things, "means creating a friendly online environment, one that allows women to speak their thoughts without having to hide their gender"[23] worries me so much. I went online with an obviously female ID before I heard that women are often advised to use male or gender-neutral IDs. Once I had heard that advice, I persisted out of the conviction that if women don't use female IDs the online world will look even more male-dominated than it actually is, discouraging women even further.

It will be a huge waste if we create a set of rules for "appropriate behavior" that make the Net as stuffy and rule-bound a place to be as many in the real world. Surely we want to be equals, not school-marms. Given that the Net is, Bandwidth willing, infinite, it seems to me that there is room for all types of public forums, from the hellfire of *alt.flame* to controlled sites such as AOL's patrolled public areas—or the somewhere-in-the-middle, as *PC World* contributing editor and needlecrafter Judy Heim noted in her discussion of online needlecrafters' forums: "No one will ever, ever pick on you or laugh at you. If they did, they would find 500 women with razor-sharp rotary cutters all over them immediately."[24]

Virtual rotary cutters, of course. In this networked world, the ultimate bid for equality is not to be found in online participation, satisfying though that can be. If we are not to have a new kind of glass ceiling, we need more women who earn their positions in the power structure that defines the Net by inventing and deploying its technological bedrock. There is more control implicit in designing a good piece of newsreader software or an intelligent agent than there is in framing rules of Netiquette and demanding that people obey them. Ellen Spertus writes that her lack of distress at being flamed by a jerk came first from knowing that in real life she and her friends would eventually be in a position to hire and fire him, and only secondarily from knowing that her forwarding his message to his boss got him a disciplinary lecture. To guarantee equality in the future networked world, we need many more like her.

9

Unsafe Sex in the Red
Page District

> We all know what we're talking about. Dirty books are fun. It's
> simply a matter of freedom of pleasure, a right which is not guaran-
> teed by the Constitution, unfortunately.
> —Tom Lehrer, *That Was the Year That Was*

It seems as though every time a new medium is invented people make the horrifying discovery that it's used for sex. Centuries-old
orally transmitted bawdy ballads and poetry, printed books, magazines,
photographs, movies, videotape recordings, floppy disks, bulletin board
systems (BBSs), CD-ROM, cable TV, and now the Internet: the news that
humans are interested, even pruriently interested, in sex should be nothing new.

(Did you turn to this chapter first? You pervert.)

Yet we keep replaying this same Puritanical panic that the new medium
will deprave and corrupt in new and dangerous ways, even though it's ar-
guable that real-life developments—such as the ready availability of reli-
able contraception, or an unpopular war inspiring a period of social
rebellion and insecurity—have a bigger effect on people's behavior. If, as
John Gilmore has so famously remarked, the Net perceives censorship as
damage and routes around it, something similar can be said about sex:
sex perceives regulation as a dam and diverts into new media.

Most, if not all, of the concern about pornography on the Net is coming from people who are not online but have seen press or police reports,
which typically focus on the worst the Net has to offer. It often seems as
though the dark side of online is all anyone writes about. One estimate,
provided by the electronic newsletter *Media Poll* and based on database
searches of the top fifty U.S. newspapers, showed that from 1993 (that is,

before the Web) to 1996, a little over 10 percent of all press reports about the Internet mentioned at least one of the words *sex, terrorism, censorship,* or *pornography.* On the assumption that some of these stories might not focus on the Net, *Media Poll* then eliminated all the articles except those that had the words *Internet* or *World-Wide Web* in the headlines; doing that raised the percentages to slightly over 15 percent.[1]

This particular round of panic has unusual resonance with debates in society at large because the definition of acceptable treatment of women (as well as many other groups) has changed dramatically in the closing decades of the twentieth century. New concepts such as date rape and sexual harassment have altered the landscape since the 1970s, when the keynotes of the feminist movement were equal rights, equal work, and equal pay. The basic unit of communication on the Net in early 1997, barring some graphics and audio, is the word. We are used to thinking of words by themselves as harmless, as in the familiar childhood rhyme: "Sticks and stones may break my bones, but words can never hurt me." But a significant line of feminist campaigning equates words with actions and condemns all pornography as a power play designed to keep women in their place as second-class citizens.

Catharine MacKinnon is a good example to cite: "On the assumption that words have only a referential relation to reality, pornography is defended as only words—even when it is pictures women had to be directly used to make, even when the means of writing are women's bodies, even when a woman is destroyed in order to say it or show it or because it was said or shown."[2] But MacKinnon makes little distinction between textual fantasies that don't involve a woman at all and pictures that do.

MacKinnon is not alone. At an international conference held in London on February 13–14, 1997, to discuss means for policing the Internet, human rights campaigner and University of Rhode Island psychology professor Donna Hughes made it plain that she favors tighter regulations, not just of the Net but of all media, to end international exploitation of and trafficking in women. Her exhibit A: a Web site offering Russian brides for sale and another offering sex tours to the Far East. Yet these are not problems that can be solved by regulating the Internet. These are businesses that must be tackled by the relevant law enforcement organizations, such as the Immigration and Naturalization Service and the destination countries' police forces.

Pornography on the Net is difficult to write about if you love the Net at all, because there has been more bad media reporting on this topic than any other. The temptation is to deny it all and move on. But it's important to be accurate about this, because bad laws are being passed almost daily in the attempt to control the online circulation of pornography, and those media reports are often used as the prime evidence for why regulation is needed.

There are four basic things to say about pornography on the Net. First, it's out there. Second, it's easy to avoid. Third, it's a relatively small percentage of the many gigabytes of data flowing around the world. (At a recent count there were 168 Usenet newsgroups with sex-related names —but there are 20,000 newsgroups overall.) Fourth, pornography on the Net is not an isolated phenomenon, but must be placed in the wider social context of real life, with all the other sexually explicit media and lifestyle choices that make up our complex world.

To go with those basic truths, there are a number of myths about pornography on the Net that impede intelligent debate on the subject and therefore need to be debunked. Many are rooted in technical ignorance or misunderstandings.

First, there is a serious disparity between the amount of pornography available on the Net and the amount of attention it gets in the press. It's sensational stuff, and the transparency of the Net means we find out about cases that otherwise would have been private. There was the woman whose husband sued for divorce when he found logs of her cybersex sessions on the family hard drive; there was Sharon Lopatka, the Maryland housewife and part-time decorator who looked for and found someone to torture her to death in one of the sex newsgroups on Usenet; there was Jake Baker, the University of Michigan student who was prosecuted for posting a sick and violent fantasy using the name of a classmate (the charges were later dismissed);[3] there was the $7 million that writer Jeff Goodell figured sex was putting in America Online's coffers every month.[4] Those sex-and-death stories dominate media coverage of the Net for the same reason that they dominate the coverage of celebrities' and politicians' lives, as well as the plots of movies: they shock, they get attention, and they sell.

Second, the Net is not like television. A surprising (to Net people) number of non-Net users believe that you hit a button to connect to the Internet and pornography just flows, unwanted and unbidden, across your computer screen. This is not what happens, as anyone who's ever had to research pornography on the Net for a living knows. In general, pornography on the Net is like anything else on the Net: if you want to find it, you have to go out looking for it, and most of what you find will be useless crap or stuff that's better quality offline.

Things may change when there's a digital camera and a high-speed Internet link in every bedroom, but for now most of the available material is fairly poor quality, mostly scanned-in photographs from magazines (where are those copyright police when you need them?) and remarkably repetitive amateur (text) sexual fantasies that go to show how bad the teaching of sex education and anatomy in our schools really is. Material that is in any way unusual tends to keep recycling, in the way of the Net, so that even what's there is less than it seems. A newcomer might be stunned by the amount of material; return visitors will notice how much of it is repostings of stuff that's already made the rounds a number of times. A single example: in December 1996, I went looking for a specific fantasy I'd seen in 1994 about a young male who took a pill to turn himself into a female. (As a she, he became gorgeous, stacked, and in such a constant state of arousal that he couldn't do anything but hit the sack with bar pick-ups, but that's another unlikely story.) I found it recently reposted to the fantasy newsgroup *alt.sex.stories* with little trouble. It's fair to say that a lot of the shock about pornography online is coming from people who are unaware of what pornography is available offline.

However, it's also true that many Net users overestimate how difficult it is to find pornography online, partly because they never see any (since they're not looking for it), and partly because a few years ago it genuinely was much harder than it is now.

The first time I went trawling the Net for pornography was in late 1994 (for an article for the British magazine *Personal Computer World*);[5] following that, in early 1995, a BBC researcher came over to my house in quest of pornography on the Net. We spent three hours wandering uselessly around the Web not finding shocking pictures. The BBC researcher nodded solemnly, admitted he hadn't realized how hard it would be to find salacious material—and then used only the twenty seconds in which we were successful, made possible only because of a tip-off from a friend.

At the time, one of the limiting factors for pornography on the Net was, ironically, the popularity of any site that carried it: there wasn't much motive for a non-commercial site to supply the necessary overhead in hardware and network connections. For example, around that time one of the relatively few pornography Web sites in existence, part of a larger fine arts archive at the Netherlands' University of Delft, had shut down because the archive was so popular it was swamping the university's network. "The archive is transmitting unrestricted amounts of pictures (30,000 pictures per day)," wrote the archive's administrator on the (otherwise empty) Web page shortly after the closure, explaining the decision. "The network traffic generated by this archive was accounting for well over half of the total network traffic of Delft University. With over 10,000 visitors per day, this is (was?) one of the busiest Internet sites in the world. I don't like censorship at all, but closing the access to the pornographic pictures seems the only way to do something about the complaints above. During the past 1.5 years, the top 50 chart never contained a single non-pornographic picture."

Back then, if you really wanted sexual material you got out your credit card and coughed up for a subscription to an "adult" BBS—something most children wouldn't be able to do. At that time, the easy service on the Net was Gopher, a (text) menu-based indexing system that's still in use today, although most people now access those servers via a Web browser. (Back then the Web didn't have search engines—Yahoo! went up in 1994, and Altavista started up in December, 1995—so finding things required getting Web addresses by word of mouth.)

When you searched on the word "sex" across all of "gopherspace" using an engine known as Veronica, you got back an impressive-looking list of several thousand documents. These must have looked very tasty to tabloid hacks, but only a small amount of investigation showed they were such exceptionally titillating things as academic papers on the feminization of tadpoles, statistical surveys of postings to Usenet newsgroups (how often, how many kilobytes), and the FAQ files from the *alt.sex* groups. I mean, just fabulous stuff. The most salacious sounding entry on the list—"INTERNATIONAL PHONE SEX LINES"—was a series of Usenet articles from the tail-end of a thread with practically no content whatsoever. Even the FAQs, which of course are still around today, updated, aren't exactly fun: pages and pages of computer programmer–style revision history, such as (from the *alt.sex.fetish* FAQ), "May 21, 1994: added lots of shoe types in the vocabulary section," followed by the group's rules about what kind of material to post, plus information of interest to its readers—like how to take care of latex. The average twelve-year-old would find this stuff weird but disappointing. He might ask awkward questions, of course, but then so did my friend's six-year-old daughter the day she cut a story out of the newspaper to take to school for an assignment and demanded to know what an abortion was and what they meant about reducing the time limit.

Usenet was another story, or seemed to be: subscribing to a newsgroup like *alt.binaries.pictures.erotica* was simple enough, but you can't just post a picture or program file to Usenet any more than you can send it across the Internet by email without finagling. Both email and Usenet were originally designed to handle straight ASCII text; to post or email binary files[6] you have to use a converter program to encode them into text for transmission. There's also a size limit, so really large files have to be split into pieces. If you're reading a newsgroup with a traditional newsreader such as those UNIX programs without the vowels (someone actually named newsreader programs nn and trn), what you see looks like PGP-encrypted gibberish. To turn the garbage text back into a picture for display, you have to collect all the pieces and run them through a decoding program that also splices them back together. In addition, few people back then had enough hardware overhead to store, manipulate, and display those images.

A lot has changed. The same systems (Altavista, Yahoo!, Hotbot) that make it easy to find the ninety-two pages that mention your own name also make it easy to search on words associated with pornography (try "sexxxy"). We still don't have systems that can take descriptions like "naked women with big tits" and return matching photographs (although it's probably only a matter of time), but since humans tend to behave in stereotypical patterns, it's relatively easy to guess what words might figure in any text lurking near the photographs and pull up enough hits to scare Hugh Hefner.[7] But here again, the text may not match the pictures, and most links only lead to the front doors of commercial Web sites, which typically give you just a few samples before demanding your credit card.

At the same time, today's new generation of Net users generally aren't using those arcane UNIX tools; they're doing everything through a Web browser, including reading news, and the browsers have decoding and splicing facilities built right into them. For a substantial percentage of today's users, to click on a binary posting is to see it displayed. The next generation of services, real-time live video, is already beginning to appear, and it's even easier: hand in a credit card number and sit back and watch a small, grainy, live strip show.

Those changes aside, it is nonetheless true that many journalists have made the mistake of estimating how much pornography there is online based on the results of text searches, and then have written influential diatribes about the dangers of the Net. Two examples, among many, are

Time magazine's July 3, 1995, cover story, "Cyberporn," and the London-based tabloid *News of the World*'s "exposé" of sex online in 1990, which focused on the CIX conferencing system. The CIX story was laughable to anyone who knows the system, as it singled out two conferences from among thousands, shredding in the process one of London's senior computer journalists, a married man with two daughters. Named as a moderator of one of these two sex-related conferences (he moderates tens of others besides), he had bricks thrown through the windows of his house.

The *Time* story, which arguably helped influence the passage of the Communications Decency Act (CDA), relied heavily on a badly flawed and quickly discredited study called "Marketing Pornography on the Information Superhighway" by Martin Rimm,[8] then a thirty-year-old undergraduate student in electrical engineering at Carnegie-Mellon University. Rimm's analysis of 917,410 items, found primarily on commercial adult BBSs and, he said, representing 8.5 million downloads,[9] led him to claim, among other things, that 83.5 percent of images posted to Usenet were pornographic, and that pornographers were using transaction logs to compile sophisticated databases of user preferences to determine which type of images to market more aggressively.

Rimm's study was immediately widely criticized both on Usenet and, especially, on the WELL, where a jury of writers and experts, led by Vanderbilt University marketing professor Donna Hoffman and Electronic Frontier Foundation (*eff*) general counsel Mike Godwin, confronted *Time*'s reporter, Philip Elmer-DeWitt, with a startlingly well-researched critique of the article, the Rimm study, and Rimm's background in less than a week. The story made it into Congress even faster, however: The same day it hit the stands, it was quoted in the Senate as evidence that the Net needed regulation. The WELL discussion eventually pushed Elmer-DeWitt into writing a full-page partial recantation acknowledging that the study had "damaging flaws."[10] These are worth going into, because the *Time* story is still being quoted by politicians and would-be regulators, and because there are so many misperceptions about pornography on the Net.

Hoffman, whose academic background is in behavioral statistics, and her partner, Thomas P. Novak, both associate professors at the Owen Graduate School of Management at Vanderbilt University, wrote a paper listing the major flaws in Rimm's work, based on the extensive WELL analysis.[11] First and foremost, they wrote, the study was not peer-reviewed, normally considered vital authentication for any scientific study. Instead, they note, it was embargoed for six months before its publication in a (non–peer reviewed) law journal and its use by *Time* as the basis for the "Cyberporn" story. Many of Rimm's statements, they went on, were unsubstantiated. Methodological flaws made it difficult to determine exactly what Rimm did in carrying out his study, rendering his results difficult or impossible to replicate; replication of results is the basis of the scientific method by which we build, painfully, our store of common knowledge. Further, data were misinterpreted; Rimm's definition of "pornography" was not consistent; there was confusion between the readership of Usenet at one university and readership worldwide; there was confusion between Usenet, the World-Wide Web, the sixty-eight adult BBSs he claimed to have actually surveyed, and the Information Superhighway. Finally, they questioned where Rimm derived his assertion about those databases of user preferences the porn merchants were said to be compiling from transaction analysis.

Hoffman and Novak also pointed out that *Time*'s reporting failed to note its own inconsistencies: the article reported that "only about 3 percent of all the messages on the Usenet newsgroups [represent pornographic images], while the Usenet itself represents 11.5 percent of the traffic on the Internet," but then did not draw the logical conclusion that less than 0.5 percent (3 percent of 11 percent) of the messages on the Internet are associated with newsgroups that contain pornographic imagery. To put the claim that 83.5 percent of Usenet images are pornographic into further context, Rimm derived those figures by examining the postings to seventeen out of the thirty-two Usenet groups that typically carried image files over a seven-day time period.

DEC research scientist Brian Reid noted in his trenchant criticism of the study, "I have been measuring USENET readership and analyzing USENET content, and publishing studies of what I find since April 1986. I have spent years refining the measurement techniques and the data processing algorithms. Despite those 9 years of working on the problem, I still do not believe that it is possible to get measurements whose accuracy is within a factor of 10 of the truth."[12]

A few weeks later, investigative journalist Brock Meeks, then Washington bureau chief of *Inter@ctive Week*,[13] revealed in the award-winning electronic newsletter he publishes and writes, *Cyberwire Dispatch*, that Rimm had made a second contribution to the world's literature out of that data he'd collected from adult BBSs: *The Pornographer's Handbook: How to Exploit Women, Dupe Men and Make Lots of Money.*

An excerpt from the book posted to several BBS-related newsgroups and later verified by Meeks read,

> In this book, you will also discover the trade secrets of the most successful adult BBS in the business. You will learn the secrets not only of facial cumshots, but of 62 other types of images that you need to be aware of in marketing your adult BBS, from portraits to oral to anal to transsexual to fisting. You will learn about supply and demand curves, histograms, contingency table analysis, mean popularity indices, cluster analysis, and a host of other sophisticated marketing techniques never before applied by any adult BBS. And above all, never before published.

Other posted sections of the privately published book were far more offensive than this.

Ironically, as Meeks pointed out, Carnegie-Mellon University was simultaneously funding a different study called HomeNet, a field trial studying Internet use by a group of families in the Pittsburgh area who were supplied with the hardware, software, telephone, Internet connections, and training necessary to get them started online. HomeNet's September 1995 report found that "the sexually oriented newsgroups do not hold their readers."[14] Although thirteen of the top thirty newsgroups the 157 participants in forty-eight families accessed during the first five months of the trial were sexually oriented, the report notes that only four of the list of thirty newsgroups that were followed (that is, accessed three or more times) over the five months covered in the report were sexually oriented. In fact, it says, "less than 50 percent of the sample ever accessed a sexually oriented newsgroup, and only 20 percent accessed a sexually oriented newsgroup three or more times." Similar stories used to be told of the early days of satellite TV.

None of that changes the perception that the Net is really a sewer at heart or that children are put at risk when they're allowed out to play with geeks bearing .GIFs,[15] even though many of them face much worse from real life in the form of abuse, neglect, and poverty than they do from the worst images the Net has to offer.

But what is pornography, anyway? You may know it when you see it, but can you find twelve people to agree with you? In the wake of the tabloid attack on CIX, people got cautious. One friend worriedly reported to the management, for example, a cartoon-style picture he'd found on the system of a small, pastel-colored stallion doing to My Little Pony what a generation of unsentimental parents would probably have liked to do themselves. Is that pornography? I'd call it hostile-parent humor. Similarly, I'm not really sure what people talk about in *alt.sex. bestiality.barney*, but surely that purple thug must deserve it. Or how would you classify Heartless's Holey Haven's explicit and alienated tips on when it's not worth the trouble to give a blow job? We also need to consider the difference between consumption of pornography—browsing pictures on Web sites, downloading video clips—and the mutually consensual interactive fantasy sessions that take place in real time.

Is society as a whole well served by the prohibition on sexually explicit material? Just as personal computers put the means to produce respectably elegant publications on all sorts of desks, and the Internet has given a worldwide platform to those who could never have afforded to buy their own radio or TV station, today's technology means that pornography does not have to be the sole production of a small band of men who make millions out of its forbidden aura. Does it make sense to pursue those who post sexual material to online public areas for no financial return while leaving alone the commercial producers and distributors of films, videotapes, and magazines? This is an area where the existence of the Net can change the debate.

But the perception is that these other media are controlled, that a child attempting to take a copy of *Fanny Hill* out of the library or buy a copy of *Bestiality Monthly* would have to get past a gatekeeping adult, while on the Net anything can happen. One of the sillier tabloid newspaper articles of 1994 attacked the BBC Networking Club for selling access to pornography.[16] Its manager, Julian Ellison, after pointing out that the Club had cut sex-related newsgroups out of its newsfeed, said, "It seems to me that this obsession with pornography is found among those who have never used the Internet," adding that even though it's easier to access pornography through a public library or newsstand, "the combined sensationalism of porn and technology strikes fear into people."

The fact is that because the Internet is vast and the systems for measuring it poor (see chapter 12), we may never be able to gauge accurately how much pornography is out there, any more than we know offhand how many of our neighbors have vibrators in their nightstands. But granted that parents have a right to be concerned about what their kids see, and that people in general have a right not to be barraged with material they find offensive, the question more usefully might be what kinds of systems to put in place to enable those things.

The first answer is that in general the Net organizes itself rather well.

People who are paying in time, even if not phone and access charges, really don't appreciate logging into a newsgroup called *rec.sport.tennis* or *soc.feminism* and finding photographs from *Hustler*, any more than the *alt.binaries.pictures.erotica* people want pictures of Mickey Mouse shoved in front of their noses. Such postings generally attract flames and, if the user is persistent, complaints to the *news.admin.net-abuse.** hierarchy, followed by the attention of one of those Net-approved cancelers. The invasion of newsgroups like *rec.pets.cats* aside, there isn't (so far, anyway) a gang of Net users who think that areas likely to attract children should be invaded with explicit material. Many Netizens are parents, too.

The big exception to this logical sorting is the commercial services moving onto the Web who seem to feel that spamming newsgroups and sending out junk email indiscriminately are appropriate ways to advertise their services. The existence of those Web sites or newsgroups like *alt. binaries.pictures.erotica.male* doesn't impinge on most users' Net lives at all; but parents have every right to object if their twelve-year-old logs on to read messages from his friends and finds a host of stupid messages from "Lisa" or "Tiffany" with smiley faces in the subject lines and which, when opened, advertise "hot babes." These are pernicious because they are intentionally designed to fool people into thinking they are messages from friends, and the senders, like other junk emailers, don't seem to care whether they damage the Net as a whole or bring down regulation on our heads. Most of these messages come from a known set of domains, all served by the same upstream provider, and for a long time that provider seemed uninterested in replying to complaints about this abuse (it was gratifying to note in mid-1997 that this ISP had finally suspended its spamming users until they could show they had installed better targeting and opt-out procedures). The sites themselves, however, aren't free: they generally give casual visitors access to a small set of photographs of the type you see in *Penthouse* or *Playboy*. For anything more, you need to supply a credit card number. In the one genuine case I know of where a young child stumbled across a pornographic site, it was one of these types of sites; she was doing a school project and searched Altavista on the word "Smarties," only to find the rather sleazy *smarties.com* site. A change of domain name would easily solve that particular problem.

Granting parents the right to control what their children see is not a controversial idea on the Net, although there is a great deal of controversy over what precise material children shouldn't see—you might want to block the Banned Books Online exhibit where someone else would rather block the National Rifle Association. What is controversial is the notion that one group of adults should have the right to determine what another group of adults may see. What you think is the best solution—technical, legislative, or social—depends on how you define the problem, as well as how you think about the Net. For kids, the ideal, of course, is parental guidance; but many parents haven't got the time to understand what their children are looking at, or else do not have the kind of relationship with their children that allows the children to feel comfortable asking for help if they run into situations they can't handle. That is a broader problem for which controlling what material is available on the Net is largely irrelevant.

The logical answer is to find a technological solution that builds on the Net's existing structure but can be configured by individual users to their own tastes. The most common proposal is a mix of ratings systems for newsgroups and Web sites and blocking software that could go beyond those ratings and also keep out some of those offensive ads wherever they appeared. While the idea is sound and logical and fits with net.culture—that bedrock of user choice—anyone who's reviewed the blocking software knows that there are several problems with this approach. First and foremost, of course, is the fact that the parents who want to do the blocking are less likely to understand how the software works (and how to disable it) than the children the software is supposed to protect. Second is the fact that any child who is remotely curious will, upon seeing that certain sites are blocked, try to figure out how to gain access to them. (Ratings will almost certainly generate software that looks for the "bad" sites.) This software may be the right approach, but it needs to get a lot better.

A new problem with this type of software surfaced in the summer of 1996, when Brock Meeks in tandem with journalist Declan McCullagh, then working for *HotWired*,[17] got hold of a copy of the CyberSitter database and deconstructed it to find that the company's blocking facilities extended to such non-pornographic material as the sites of the National Organization for Women and even the Gopher server belonging to the WELL, lending fuel to those who believe that censoring sexual material leads inexorably to censoring other types of controversial content. In Meeks's widely read and influential electronic newsletter, *Cyberwire Dispatch*, Meeks and McCullagh argued that parents should have the right to know what kind of material is being blocked.[18] McCullagh reported some months later that Solid Oak, CyberSitter's publisher, threatened them with criminal prosecution for reverse- engineering the database.

Held out as hope for the future along those lines is the notion that ratings systems such as the W3 Consortium–backed PICS might be sensitive and configurable enough to allow third parties whose views are known, such as, say, the Christian Coalition or the Boy Scouts, to supply filtering services. Blocking software and other types of filtering mechanisms will have to get much better, with more standardized interfaces, before this is a reality, but it would be a good approach. The current situation, where some of these companies treat their databases of blocked sites the way the National Security Agency wants to treat cryptography, will continue to create trouble.[19] In late 1996, Solid Oak began blocking the site of a high school student who put up a list of sites blocked by CyberSitter (and other, similar products). The incident was reported by McCullagh in a story for the *Netly News*.[20] A few months later, when the city of Boston installed the competing "censorware" product Cyber Patrol (which blocks the AOL-sucks and Planned Parenthood sites) on all the city libraries' computers, McCullagh announced *Netly News*'s new Censorware Search Engine, which allowed people to find out if their Web sites were banned in Boston.[21]

However imperfect a solution this kind of software is, individual choice is the only strategy that's likely to work in the long run. Blunt-instrument approaches are likely to fail for the same reason and in the same way that the attempts at removing the Church of Scientology's secret documents have failed: there are too many sites and too many people who believe that access should be allowed, whether or not they themselves want to make use of that specific material. Besides, countries disagree widely on what pornography is and what should be banned.

Ultimately, the Net doesn't create real life, it only reflects it. We may not like what it shows us, or the fact that online technology—Internet Relay Chat, Webcams (little digital cameras whose output is posted on the Web), those text-based shared worlds known as MUDs, conferencing, even email—gives people freedom to explore their sexuality in new ways. It may be an unpleasant revelation that Nebraska housewives want to fantasize about bondage with like-minded people in AOL chat rooms, or that so many strangers want to retire to private channels to indulge in frenzied one-handed typing, or that men want to post pictures of other men posing in full glory in front of woodpiles. These days, such activities seem safer than sex in the real world. But the question to ask is what the Net is teaching us about the society we built before we got wired.

10

The Wrong Side of the Passwords

Don't you think that for your first crime you shouldn't attach your
name and address and mail it to several thousand strangers?
—Dogbert, in Scott Adams's *Dilbert*

If pornography on the Net scares people, hackers scare them
even more. The word "hacker" has slipped its meanings from the culture
of engineering and technology building recounted by Steven Levy in his
1984 book *Hackers*. Robert Bickford, a California software developer
who runs an annual conference for that sort of hacker, defines it as "any
person who derives joy from discovering ways to circumvent limitations."[1] That definition, as Bickford writes, includes software engineers
and systems analysts as readily as the archetypal anti-social teenage
hacker of media stereotype. In the context of the Net, such a definition
takes in PGP creator Phil Zimmermann, the students who made the first
UUCP connection to start Usenet, anonymous server operator Julf Helsingius, John Gilmore, the Computer Emergency Response Team that
cleans up after computer break-ins, and even Bill Gates, who managed to
subvert IBM's licensing procedures and make Microsoft rich. But that's
not the popular image; press reports focus on the so-called "dark-side"
hacker who gets arrested for cracking into others' systems—like Kevin
Mitnick, whose arrest in February 1995 in Raleigh, North Carolina,
made worldwide headlines and spawned three books.[2] Bickford would
exclude the criminal hackers and keep the technologically gifted inven-
tors in his definition.

Although the Net makes it easier for certain types of information—
passwords, system-cracking software tools, and information about security weaknesses—to change hands, the hacker community isn't really kept
together by the Net. Instead, its center of gravity is a small-format printed

magazine called *2600: The Hacker Quarterly*, published out of New York by its editor-in-chief, Emmanuel Goldstein.

Emmanuel Goldstein is, of course, not his real name, which might (or might not) be Eric Corley. Corley, a New Yorker who looks a little like Arlo Guthrie and some days talks to journalists with all the enthusiasm of Arlo facing the draft board, borrowed his professional name from George Orwell's *1984*. (In Orwell's book, Goldstein was the author of the *Book of Forbidden Knowledge*; an apparent subversive, he eventually turned out to be in cahoots with the all-controlling Party.) Besides running the magazine, this Goldstein does a radio show on WBAI in New York called "Off the Hook," in which he, guests, and callers talk about technology and complain about telephones.

In this subculture, no one is fond of companies like IBM and Microsoft, but the arch-enemy is the telephone companies. Hacking's roots are in what used to be known as "phone phreaking," the practice of coercing the telephone system into giving you free phone calls. Anyone who was in college in the early 1970s probably remembers one of the earliest manifestations, phony credit card calls, but the more dedicated and technically gifted were able to construct boxes that mimicked the sounds of coins dropping into the slot to fool operators. The magazine *2600* derives its name from 2600Hz, the tone which, when blown into a telephone receiver, used to trigger the phone system into accepting your commands as though you were an operator. Curiously (and famously), for a time whistles tuned to exactly that tone were distributed as prizes in boxes of the cereal Cap'n Crunch; the early phreaker who discovered this, John Draper, was for a long time known by that name.

These days, much of hacking is about computers and the Internet, but the basic character of the scene hasn't changed. Robert Schifreen, whose 1984 arrest for hacking into Prince Philip's Prestel mailbox inspired the writing of Britain's Computer Misuse Act, says, "It's still that desperate mentality of sitting there and doing it for hours on end."[3] Goldstein, too, talks of hacking as "searching out information and wasting a lot of time."

Hackers challenge: they stress-test security systems, they evade detection when they can, and they try to find out things they're not supposed to know. In that, they're probably not so different from any adolescent boy who ever took apart the new school radio or stripped down a car and rebuilt it. They also challenge our faith in the systems we try to trust every day, our notions of the freedom of information, and our certainty about where the line should be drawn between exploration and crime. Can we assume that someone who has a copy of a file of 20,000 credit card numbers is automatically bent on theft of goods and services? Can we assume that someone who has the designs and $200 worth of electronic components, available at any Radio Shack store, necessary to counterfeit a cellular phone is automatically going to steal thousands of dollars worth of phone calls? Mitnick is alleged to have stashed a copy of just such a credit card file in a little-used directory on the WELL, although he is not thought to have ever used the information. Another hacker, Bernie S., was arrested for having such a set of components, and served jail time. Bernie S.'s career in jail, like those of Mitnick and other hackers, is tracked on the 2600 Web site,[4] with much the same flavor as Amnesty International's tracking of political prisoners. Uncannily so: the Web site noted in late 1996 that Bernie S. was beaten up in jail and denied the medical care he needed, and that Mitnick had been put in solitary confinement and his books taken away. However, over time a few companies such as IBM have come to accept the notion that hackers may offer a useful service in finding holes in their security systems and even employ them to do so.

As computer networks become the underpinnings of all our most vital services, what scares people is the thought that someone with no moral conscience could hack into a cancer hospital and tamper with patients' records, or tap into one of the nation's big repositories of credit information and change you at a stroke from a financially trustworthy citizen into a deadbeat. In a *Harper's* magazine forum held electronically on the WELL in 1990, John Perry Barlow wrote about the superstitious awe he felt when Phiber Optik, one of the young, visiting hackers, uploaded Barlow's credit history, retrieved from the major credit information database TRW, into the discussion: "I've been in redneck bars wearing shoulder-length curls, police custody while on acid, and Harlem after midnight, but no one has ever put the spook in me quite as Phiber Optik did at that moment." Later, when he'd gotten to know Phiber Optik a bit better by phone and in person, he mused, "His cracking impulses seemed purely exploratory, and I've begun to wonder if we wouldn't also regard spelunkers as desperate criminals if AT&T owned all the caves."[5]

In fact, it took me two hacker conferences a year apart and three hacker meetings before I saw anyone do anything illegal. When I did, they were "cloning a Mars bar," as they call it in hacker-speak, which means reprogramming a cellular phone so it works on a different phone number than the one it was originally assigned. That may not sound like much, but this kind of reprogramming is said to cost the world's mobile phone companies millions in stolen phone calls and lost air time every year.

It wasn't a very impressive procedure, and I only spotted it by accident when I turned around from my table at the McDonald's they'd chosen for their meeting. A guy had loaded his laptop with a piece of software downloaded from the Net that can send pulses down a cable to the cellphone, reprogramming the EEPROM[6] inside to a new phone number and ESN (the serial number that distinguishes phones). These numbers have to be paired correctly or the phones don't work. The phone had been acquired, legally I guess, second-hand; the cable was handmade. There was only one brief glitch, to check that he had the right area code, before he hit the button to send the numbers and the phone was tried and pronounced to be working at some poor schnook's expense.

The phone reprogrammer was young, with the roundness and not-quite-finished features of a movie-image schoolboy. He told us he got the numbers from "contacts." Retrieved from the garbage outside a company? Purchased on the street? Procured from the phone company by pretending to be a technical engineer? One of the others in the group told me if you're good at pretending to be one of their engineers on a job you can get them to read you matched pairs over the phone.

A brief discussion about morals and ethics followed: at a previous meeting, one of them kept insisting cloning phones wasn't illegal or wrong. Everyone had a shot at explaining to him why it was not only morally but legally wrong, but he was adamant: the time was paid for and the owner wasn't using it, he argued. I have heard the same argument applied to computer systems: they have security holes their owners don't correct, so they deserve to be hacked; hackers are performing a public service by highlighting the risks. In some ways I do believe that. If my bank is, out of arrogance or stupidity, failing to protect my money (which, after all, spends most of its time as digits floating around cyberspace), I want to know this. Emmanuel Goldstein spends a lot of time defending 2600's publication of security information and instructions for building gadgets to crack into systems on just those grounds of high-tech consumer advocacy.

One of the others at the table, a thin, sharp-featured redhead, burst out suddenly, "Oh, great. Do this right in McDonald's in front of a stranger." A chorus of voices: I'm not a stranger. They know me.

"Even worse," I said, when the babble died down, "in front of a *journalist*."

"You're not a real journalist," he said. The thing is, I agreed with him. But the evidence suggested I might be wrong. The others insisted that yes, they did know me, I was a journalist. One of them even had a couple of my articles on his Web page. I seem to have hacked the media.

"You're probably the Feds," he said, unconvinced. I don't know if he meant it or not. Would the Feds send a forty-two-year old *female* on a mission to penetrate a hacker group? For the rest of the evening, though, he referred to me repeatedly as "the Feds." Maybe half joking. Maybe.

These guys are a mixed bag. The youngest looks maybe eighteen, the oldest forty-plus, not that I'm any judge of ages, and they range from hovering jobless on the edge of the Net to being employed by the U.S. Navy. They're drawn together by the same love of computers and obsession with tinkering with their innards that sets them apart from the rest of humanity.

"Do you worry about getting caught?" I asked the cellphone programmer. He was wearing a smug smile.

"No," he said. "I'm too well protected." Perhaps he is. I still didn't even know his email address, let alone his name, where he lived, or his phone number. On the other hand, I thought he genuinely risked getting caught that night, and I wondered about overconfidence. It had only been a matter of a few weeks since one of the well-known names on this particular hacking scene had what they call an "accident with a cellular phone."

"What was the accident?" I asked the hacker who told me about it.

"He got caught."

The archetypal hacker is supposed to be introverted, solitary, unable to make human connections. And yet the hacking scene seems to me very social, especially compared to writing: they have meetings, travel to conferences, get together to go scouting for old equipment being thrown out, and chat on Usenet and mailing lists and, even more so, on Internet Relay Chat (IRC).

What they don't have a lot of is contact with women. You can have a lot of arguments about this: girls are less often encouraged to use computers; girls are more interested in social lives; girls have different expectations placed on them; girls mature faster; girls are taught to obey the rules, whereas people think breaking rules is part of growing up for boys. But the fact remains: so far, relatively few women develop the kind of exploratory, obsessive persistence that leads these guys to spend endless hours repetitively dialing phone numbers looking for modems.

One of the guys at the next table leaned over and said, "The question is, who is the hacker? The one who wrote the software, or the one who just downloads it and uses it?"

"The one who wrote it," I said, without a second's hesitation. The subject dropped, but it reminded me that I'd heard from a telephone company security specialist that the hacker channels on IRC are frequently used to exchange just this sort of software. Being able to retrieve such software lowers the technical barrier to this kind of petty theft to anyone who can work IRC, handle a soldering iron, and run a DOS program on a laptop (still a distinct sub-group from the majority of the population). That's always provided you can convince other hackers you're worth exchanging software with.

Go through any public area on the Net with anything related to hacking in the title, and you'll find nothing but contempt displayed for people logging on looking for quick and easy answers. However hostile the Net is to newcomers, multiply that by a factor of ten for the hacker groups, who add a hefty dose of not unreasonable paranoia to the normal intolerance for repetitive questions and a resounding contempt for people who are not willing to do their own homework. Guys who march into one of these groups asking for the addresses of "warez" sites (sites where pirated software is available) or collections of passwords to get free time on America Online (AOL) are quickly dismissed as "lamers" and ignored or slapped down. On *alt.2600* the FAQ warns that if you want information, you must include details of an Obligatory Hack, usually shortened to Ob-Hack, to establish yourself as someone worthy to receive information. These aren't always computer-related, illegal, or even impressive. A guy who just wants someone else to give him a stolen password for AOL isn't a hacker, he's a thief (or a "phisher" in hacker lingo)—and a lazy one, at that. He could at least take the trouble to use a bisk to get him onto AOL and try to socially engineer the natives.

Real respect is reserved for someone like Dan Farmer, who wrote a little program he called SATAN (for Security Administrator's Tool for Analyzing Networks, a stretch-to-fit acronym if there ever was one) that goes through a network configuration and lists the holes and makes suggestions for closing them.[7] In the hands of the network administrator at whom Farmer primarily aimed his program, this is a useful warning about what needs to be fixed or patched; Farmer's Web site contains information and advice about how to do this. Common software like the UNIX program SENDMAIL has known bugs that can be exploited by would-be crackers, and although patches are available and warnings have been sent out, some administrators still either haven't known or haven't bothered to install the fixes.

Just as a screwdriver can take the lock off a door, in a knowledgeable cracker's hands, SATAN shows exactly where to start poking. Its release onto the Net in early 1995 was so controversial that Farmer, who demonstrated his routine at the 1995 Computers, Freedom, and Privacy Conference to a stunned audience, got fired by his employer, computer manufacturer Silicon Graphics, for it. (He was almost immediately re-hired by one of Silicon Graphics's competitors, Sun Microsystems, and makes a brief appearance providing accommodation to Tsutomu Shimomura in the book Shimomura and *New York Times* journalist John Markoff wrote about the 1995 capture of Kevin Mitnick. Shimomura, who has no trouble condemning Mitnick as a criminal, describes Farmer's firing as "a fit of corporate cowardice.")[8]

I have yet to see a hacking tool on the Net that was easy enough for someone with no technical knowledge to use, other than anonymizing services such as encrypted remailers or services that allow you to browse the Web without revealing any personal information. But you don't necessarily have to have specialist tools to do a lot of damage; the two-way nature of the Net means that some functions are there to be used or abused.

For example, I know a twelve-year-old who's set up his Web page with a Java script[9] that is programmed to open and close Netscape until it crashes. He found it on the Web somewhere, and copied and pasted it into one of his own pages using functions built into most Web browsers and that are important in helping people study Web pages to understand how they're constructed and share clever, new things they've thought up. This kid's friends know which of the many buttons to push to get the script to stop, but strangers choosing to load that page have to guess. The same kid got in trouble with a friend's parents for forging their email address on offensive email to a female classmate.[10] Will he now become a dangerous hacker, or a software technician writing useful code? The question seems to me on a par with trying to predict whether a teenage joyrider will become a car thief or an auto mechanic, or change direction altogether and become an accountant. It's impossible to tell.

Goldstein often talks about hacking as a kind of consumer service: who but hackers will tell you that the phone company is overcharging you and why, or publish the information that a file of 20,000 credit card numbers, stolen from an Internet service provider, is floating around the Net? Some of the information they circulate is very persuasive: you don't have to see someone wave a radio scanner and pick up neighboring cellular phone conversations more than once to realize analog mobile phones aren't the place to talk about your personal secrets, even if Newt Gingrich and Britain's Royal Family seem reluctant to get the message.[11]

A lot of people get tired of the argument that hackers are performing a useful service by exposing security holes. John Austen, the detective who arrested Schifreen all those years ago and set up the world's first dedicated computer crime investigation unit, says, "If I were driving past your front door and saw it open, I don't go in and remove something and then say, ha, ha, I've removed it. What I should do is try to find you and say, you've left your front door open, please don't leave it open any more. . . . They go around telling everybody else about it, and they think it's fun. And there seems to be some idea, some sort of moral bug in people's brains, that this is a clever thing to do."

But sometimes it *is* funny. A lot of people laughed when, in 1996, the Web pages belonging to the CIA and the Department of Justice were hacked, and did again when the US Airforce and British Labour Party sites got hit.[12] Things like this are embarrassing, but they're Net jokes. (With 56,000 Netizens against the DoJ over the CDA, of course they're going to think it's funny when the DoJ gets publicly renamed the "Department of InJustice"?) What worries me a lot more is the prospect that some group of hackers might doctor a site nearly undetectably, so that small bits of disinformation would seep out to journalists and others who used the site, slowly poisoning the world's body of knowledge. This is one reason why reporting on the Net is as much about traditional journalistic skills and training as it is about knowing the Net; when, in late 1996, some hoaxer sent out a message advertising customized child pornography for sale from a forged AOL address, it took both types of skills to deconstruct the hoax.[13]

Forums do exist for alerting administrators and others interested to security risks. The Computer Emergency Response Team releases periodic alerts that every system administrator should read to find out about known bugs and fixes. More generally oriented, the Risks Forum[14] recounts tales of unexpected loopholes ready to catch the unwary, such as poorly constructed sites that return their password lists in Web searches and warnings about the Year 2000 bug, a problem concerning the pattern of programming computers to use only the last two digits to represent the year's number. Sharing that kind of information is what the Net was built for; it's valuable to all kinds of people for all kinds of reasons. You could decide, perhaps, that technical information should be restricted to licensed professionals; but doing that wouldn't slow down hackers, who are going to look obsessively for the information until they find it, nearly as much as it would make it difficult for ordinary computer users to control their own machines. Yes, a kid can find out how to defeat any of the censorware products on the Net; take the information off the Net and it's still right there in every DOS manual ever printed.

Cracking things open, no matter how much persistence and technical knowledge it requires, doesn't win universal respect. Austen said in 1993, "The difficult things in technology are actually creating something yourself, not poking around in somebody else's system or trying to break a control system that somebody else has made. That's like saying that if I'm a carpenter I can make a beautiful door for your front door and I put some locks on it ... do you say that the guy who comes along with a sledgehammer and knocks it down is more creative?"[15] Goldstein echoes this: "A lot of people are into hacking right now, but it's only the people who are into searching out information and wasting a lot of time who are hackers."[16]

The pettiness of some of these efforts was underlined for me when one member of the hacker gathering, the Navy security guy—now married and, he assured me, respectably monogamous—launched into a long, inchoate defense of inflating his status in the Navy to bag women: it's dazzling, and it's a faster way to achieve the desired result than might have been possible with the truth. Then he tangled this all up with conquest and challenge, "the way men like to approach women," the fun of the chase. "It's a one-night stand. You just want to get in quick." But if it's the challenge and the chase that appeal, why cheat to make it easier? If anything, you should be cheating to make it harder. By analogy, if it's the challenge these guys want, why go the easy, pre-programmed route? Some of the answer is that the cloned cellphone is only a means to an end: the ability to wander untraceably around the Internet trying doorknobs via a hacked university account. It turned out there was another reason: our cloner had already had his cellphone cut off for non-payment three times.

These are, of course, small-time hackers, and although they do present a risk, they're far from the biggest threat to computer systems. Disgruntled employees, current and former, do far more damage (just like rape, you are more at risk from someone you know and who knows you); the

Year 2000 problem surfacing because computers were not designed to handle dates past 1999 will be far more expensive to fix; system crashes due to faulty or badly designed software lose more data. In a General Accounting Office (GAO) report on computer security released in May 1996, the Computer Emergency Response Team estimates that at least 80 percent of the security problems it addresses involve passwords poorly chosen or poorly protected by computer users.[17] That's a sobering thought, especially since the private cryptographic keys on which our future digital identities will depend are also protected from fraudulent use by passwords and passphrases.

That same report estimated that military systems may have experienced as many as 250,000 hacker attacks. Based on the Defense Information Systems Agency (DISA) data taken from attacks it carried out itself, DISA estimated that the attacks were successful 65 percent of the time, and that the number of attacks is doubling each year as Internet use and the sophistication of hackers and their tools increases. The figure of 250,000 attacks was widely reported, but when you look closely there were actually only 559 officially reported attacks in 1995.

The FBI view is grim: at a tutorial on law enforcement at the 1996 Computers, Freedom, and Privacy Conference, computer crime specialist Richard Ress told us, "A villain armed with a computer and a small squad of hackers can be as dangerous and disruptive as any adversary we've faced since World War II." And further, "We must dispel the notion that hackers are kids having fun and recognize that they are resourceful, talented, and dangerous." But some of them *are* just kids, and the Electronic Frontier Foundation was founded on the concerns about the rights of innocent users during search and seizure operations, especially the disposition of electronic mail stored on, for example, a system being taken down.

I'd argue that there are worse things to be scared about. The GAO report also mentions that the Department of Defense was warned as long ago as 1994 that its security was inadequate and that its policies were not suitable for the networked environment in which it now finds itself. The report adds, however: "Absolute protection of Defense information is neither practical nor affordable. Instead, Defense must turn to risk management to ensure computer security. In doing so, however, it must make tradeoffs that consider the magnitude of the threat, the value and sensitivity of the information to be protected, and the cost of protecting it." In other words: no one is safe, and there is no perfect security.

The latest twist on hacker scares is infowar. Paul Strassman and

William Marlow, in a paper presented at a January 1996 conference at Harvard University, laid out just how vulnerable we may be becoming: "Information terrorist attacks can be expected to become a decisive element of any combined threat to the economic and social integrity of the international community. Nations whose life-line becomes increasingly dependent on information networks should realize that there is no sanctuary from information-based assaults. Commercial organizations, especially in telecommunications, finance, transportation, and power generation offer choice targets to massive disruption."[18] In the light of the GAO report's comments on security, this is a disturbing scenario. Strassman and Marlow go on to argue that anonymous remailers are a dangerous "pathology" requiring public-health style measures of inoculation and quarantine.

Europe, too, contemplates requiring traceability as the price of allowing the use of anonymity, and it became plain in late 1996 when the Church of Scientology won its court order against Helsingius how much pressure any anonymous remailer operator who functions within the borders of a single country may face from his or her national authorities. The CoS was alleging yet another set of copyright violations, a civil matter. Helsingius had believed that Finnish law would place privacy above civil—though not criminal—violations. But changes to Finnish telecommunications law earlier that summer had removed this privacy protection, and although Helsingius expected it to be restored in new laws, there was a gap during which his users weren't covered.

"We need to work out the rules for who's responsible for what and when you can actually get access to that information," Helsingius said shortly after the server's closure. "I feel that working with the authorities and within the law is the only way you can do something like this in the long run."[19]

One big issue that faces us is distinguishing the areas where passing laws makes sense from those where it's better to use a technological fix—the same kind of balance that privacy advocates are trying to find between data protection legislation and spreading the use of encryption. It's stupid, for example, to outlaw the use of a readily available item like a radio scanner to eavesdrop on a mobile phone conversation if you can deploy encryption to garble the conversation so that even if anyone hears it they can't understand what's being said. On the other hand, it's wasteful to deploy an expensive technological fix if it's not needed. One thing is for sure, especially in view of the GAO report's conclusions: we should not be designing systems on the presumption that we can make them so perfect that they will never fail; we should be designing systems that incorporate elements that minimize the damage when they do fail. Because fail they will, somehow, sometime, whether rats chew through a vital cable or someone forgets to disable the default accounts supplied on a new system (a common point of entry for hackers). Or, in the words of the WELL's press release after Mitnick's arrest: "Public computer systems, by their very nature, are impossible to entirely secure." The argument that we should design systems to minimize the damage of failure was persuasively made about software design in the 1995 book *Fatal Defect*,[20] and it applies even more to computer networks; it was, in fact, precisely the principle on which the Internet was built.

This is particularly true because the insane pace of technological development means that new technology is deployed before anyone can consider the consequences. That twelve-year-old's Java script was relatively harmless, but why should we assume all such things will be? In December 1996, Edward Felton, head of Princeton University's Safe Programming Team, announced he had discovered major flaws in the design of the World-Wide Web that could allow a spoof server to insert itself between a Web site and a visiting user and intercept (and potentially alter) traffic passing between them.[21] A different risk was found in early 1997, when in a twist on 800-number scams a sex-oriented site required users to download a viewer to access its pornographic pictures; when they did and ran the software, it silently disconnected their modem and redialed long distance to Moldova, racking up huge phone bills whose profits went to the site itself (and the relevant phone companies). Around the same time, a team of German hackers announced that they had been able to write a script to use Microsoft's Active-X controls (a system for producing small programs to run animations and manage interactive features) to access information stored on a user's hard disk in the personal finance software Quicken and transfer funds from the user's bank account. Microsoft's answer was to recommend allowing your Web browser to run only code that had been signed by a reputable source—but how users are to determine this (other than mindlessly Just Buying Microsoft) isn't clear. (My own current solution is to disable Active-X and to keep all really private information on a computer that does not go online.)

These schemes put a new spin on old crimes, and as technology advances faster than we can think about its effects, there will be more such uncomfortable stories. They are particularly scary if you're accustomed to thinking of the Net as a portion of the outside world you can control through your computer; it's a different matter if the Net can reach inside your bank account and help itself. Otherwise, most of the crimes you hear about in connection with the Net are not new. Fashion designs aren't stolen and copied because of the Internet; the process is simply speeded up.

As soon as you move away from the theft of information or its misuse, things become much more straightforward. Modems, computer files, and phone lines do not abuse or rape children, just as they do not blow up buildings. People do those things, and while the Internet may eventually be the primary source of all information to all people, at the moment it is far easier, more anonymous, cheaper, and faster for most people to find bomb-making information in the public or school library and pornography of any type in magazine or videocassette format. In fact, it would be more logical to look at the transparency and built-in tracing capabilities of most of the Net and conclude that it would be safer if we required everyone to get all their information that way instead of in those old, uncontrollable media like books, where anyone can make a copy and you can't find out where they sent it.

And there are such double standards about this, which have more to do with a general fear of change and new technology than with any kind of reasoning. When the *Sunday Times* reported that child pornography was being exchanged on IRC, it found several system administrators to say they were considering dumping the chat lines. Yet a few weeks later, when newspapers covered the trial of a British diplomat caught coming into Britain with a suitcase full of child pornography on videocassette, no one suggested banning VCRs or home video cameras.

11

Beyond the Borderline

> Sanity is like a clearing in the jungle where the humans agree to
> meet from time to time and behave in certain fixed ways that even a
> baboon could master.
> —Wilfrid Sheed, *In Love with Daylight*, 1995

Hackers may scare people, but they have at least vaguely understandable motives. Even if most people don't share their obsession for taking computers apart and making them jump through hoops, most people have had at least some irrational, overriding interest at some point in their lives that can help them understand. Less easy to understand, because their motives are opaque, is the small percentage of people who cannot function in cyberspace. I don't mean that they can't learn how to configure an Internet connection, or that they can't grasp the notion of newsgroup names or use a computer; I mean that they seem unable, for no discernible reason, to conform to such rules and conventions as the Internet has. These nuts—I'm sure someone will be along in a minute to come up with a more politically correct word—have the kind of personality problem that leads some drunks to get into vicious fights in otherwise peaceful pubs. You'd think that in the sprawling infinity of cyberspace you wouldn't notice, but they make sure you do.

I'm leaving out here people who are delusional, paranoid, or just plain weird but who function in cyberspace. For example, a lot of people on *alt.religion.scientology* think one regular Dutch poster, a former Scientologist named Koos Nolste de Trenite, is nuts: he believes he is channeling the spirit of L. Ron Hubbard. He posts frequently, in blank verse, what he claims to be Hubbard's thoughts on various Scientology members and *alt.religion.scientology* critics. At one point or another, he has declared almost everyone on the newsgroup to be a Suppressive Person. People get tired of this procedure. But in Net terms, he's essentially harmless. He doesn't (unless he has another identity no one's recognized) go berserk and suddenly start spattering the newsgroup with reams of hatred; he doesn't wake up on a Saturday morning and decide to post his messages to 10,000 groups across Usenet; and he doesn't spark off fights among other people, who are generally used to him. Newcomers are alerted to his presence in the FAQ. I would say that this person functions perfectly well in cyberspace, even if he's not making friends for himself and his grasp on reality is a little unusual.

But take this case: when I first got involved with running CompuServe's Fleet Street forum for UK media, we had a guy who had already been banned twice by the previous management.[1] He was unpredictable. He would write long, trenchant messages that set everyone laughing— and then the next minute he would turn on people, attacking them with viciously foul language and making them understandably uncomfortable and insecure. After a month, easily 60 percent of the forum's messages were to, by, or about him. A lonely wannabe, perhaps? Nope. He was the real thing: a genuine Fleet Street photographer, and personally known to a few of the old hacks in the forum.

I have a theory of online moderating, which goes that it takes every new moderator (or sysop) one nut to find out that you don't have enough time in your life to work with people who can't or won't function in a moderated online setting without creating huge amounts of trouble: if they're not demanding your time and attention policing their postings, they're setting other people off in similar behavior. This was my first time out sysopping, so I thought, I can work with this person; he just needs some respect. We exchanged email. I explained that service policy was not to allow swearing or personal attacks in the public areas. He agreed to tone it down. I discovered the distracting obsession of logging on twenty-three times a day to check up on what was happening in the forum. But he seemed to be settling in, and I left a couple of encouraging comments to some of his more interesting messages. Well, we all get a kick out of believing we've fixed things.

Then our friend was told by someone at headquarters that I had banned him from the forum (I hadn't). Volcanic email followed, threatening the downfall of the forum and my personal ruin. Shown it was a mistake, he repented. This precipitated warm, cuddly messages about his being an old softy, far more disturbing than the vicious ones. In the meantime, he'd forged a message stirring up trouble between two other forum members, requiring phone calls, explanations and hours of my time. And on and on. He was asked to leave, prompting an emotional farewell followed by periodic returns, promises of no more clones, then new IDs. By this time, we were used to his style: he had a chip on his shoulder about journalists' attitudes toward photographers and liked to boast about the tough qualities of paparazzi. So his next clone appearance was spotted within two messages; challenged, he went back to checking quietly now and then.

Then one evening in early 1997, nine months after his official farewell, he suddenly posted a batch of abusive messages. "Be warned I eat fucks like you and shit them on my real problems," he posted to a sysop who tried suggesting he stop. When I asked him to leave, he replied, "You would NEVER dare to tell me where I could go face to face. Or let's say we will put that to the test soon" and "I am a top pro with massive power darling, don't ever test it. I will eat you alive." I asked him if he was drunk. "No darling. I don't drink, I promise," he typed back. Then we kicked him offline, we hoped for good. There just isn't enough time.

I don't think anyone in the forum was in any doubt that this person had a problem; some who knew him in his professional life seemed to suggest this was not a surprise. He wanted to be liked, but was deeply suspicious and contemptuous of anyone who tried, the way some people are who have been hurt a lot. When I offered to direct him to some areas of the Net that were less structured and where he might find his personality fit in better (I was thinking of *alt.flame, alt.tasteless,* or *alt.fan. howard-stern*), he wasn't interested in that. I surmised that to some extent he enjoyed having rules to break and the attention that came with it.

There is no defense against someone like that until they do something provably illegal and someone is willing to make the complaint. They are incredibly disruptive, and on a service like CompuServe people are paying extra just so that professional sysops will give them a useful, pleasant environment.

It's become apparent to me since that the appearance of CompuServe (and I'm sure America Online and other online services with moderated areas) as a trouble-free zone is hard won by the sysops. Our local psycho, who became a sort of online tourist attraction when I consulted some experienced online professionals for advice, was not even close to being the worst offender, galling though I'm sure he'd find that news. I've heard reports of people running as many as twenty-five accounts at once, aided no doubt by free trial disks, and of people coming back time after time using ID after ID and name after name. The really extraordinary thing is how instantly recognizable these people become online once you're used to their psychological profile and posting habits; perhaps those repeating patterns are part of what ails them. Our forum members recognized clone number four within two messages; others report similar experiences. One day soon there may be a science of analyzing posting patterns the way there is a science of graphic analysis, or the way professional investigators track people down by following their known hobbies and professional interests. Such patterns are one way police could develop for piercing the Net's veil of anonymity in a criminal investigation, an effort that will be helped by the existence of services such as Reference.com and Deja News, which could be used to develop leads by searching archived material on known patterns of language or interests.

Then we got our second nut. This was a guy who persistently and provably lied about himself and his qualifications, billing himself loudly, in capital letters, as an "INTERNATIONAL PHOTOJOURNALIST," with a list of famous magazines he was supposed to have worked for. In a forum full of national-level journalists who didn't feel the need to trumpet their qualifications, this behavior aroused immediate suspicion, so someone checked up on him and found the claims were bogus. What do you do in a controlled forum if someone is annoying but not abusive enough to ban, but is consistently lying about himself? While it seems obvious that you should warn your members about the risks you know of, it's dangerous to give them too strong a sense that you can protect them from every nut that may pass. Someone who does not draw your attention by posting in the open forum may go on for months, quietly reading members' messages and compiling mental profiles of their personalities before opening a correspondence with them that may or may not mention your forum. Small, older, text-based systems and many emailing lists have a useful feature here, in that users can generally retrieve a complete list of discussion group members, even those who don't post. You can't do this on Usenet, where there's simply no way to tell who may be reading what you write, and newer, graphical systems haven't bothered to implement such capabilities.

Every system has its share of similar stories, many of them worse than these. They undermine the social groupings of the networks by damaging the trust and openness that are the first enchantments the online world holds for many new users, and by setting everyone else off.

In 1996, CIXen lived through months of prolific postings from a guy who specializes in the kind of petty malice that turns every normal person into raving, gibbering Furies. He just knew exactly how to *get* people. Eventually, some of them decided to get him back by making him look stupid.

On CIX, as has already been said, anyone can start a conference and make it open, closed, or secret. A small, annoyed group started such a conference and using standard CIX commands faked a lot of messages to make it look as though CIX's management were censoring messages in secret conferences (a serious violation of the system's basic norms, if it had been true). They then added him to the conference and waited. He promptly went into an open conference for technical support and laid his accusation against the management, something CIX's owners, unaware of the joke, regarded as so libelous that they threw him off the system on literally twenty-eight minutes' notice. (Their outsized reaction was undoubtedly colored by having had to deal for months with this user and the fallout of complaints from other users on the system about his behavior.)

There ensued a weird and contentious few weeks, when half of the system argued passionately that disliked though he was, he shouldn't have been thrown offline just for being a jerk. The other half was too delighted he was gone to care about fairness. One user summed it up this way: "WHAT DO WE WANT? <USER> BACK! WHEN DO WE WANT IT? Difficult question . . . "

After a few weeks his account was reinstated, prompting more decisions. In one large, closed conference where a vote was held, 5 (out of 160) of the conference's participants voted to white-ball him, so the moderators gave up and cloned the conference, leaving it up to individual members to choose whether to frequent the original conference, where he was reinstated, or the new copy, where he didn't exist.

Curiously enough, the experience did improve this particular user, though not instantly, especially because the twin conferences' moderator took the trouble to explain to this user what had been done and why. A few months later, he was able to venture the small joke that he was staying on the system, "just to stop a large chorus of cheers from starting." A reply came from one of CIX's oldest users: "every community has its village idiot." By early 1997, this user had improved to the point where fully half his messages had useful information in them rather than random sniping. The situation can only improve as this user's old reputation fades over time, as has happened to others who began online as nuisances and grew to become pillars of their communities.

For this kind of community pressure to work, you need some very specific circumstances. You need a relatively small online service, where
everyone knows each other so it's not easy to escape to a completely new
area where no one knows your previous behavior: CIX has 16,000 members, which sounds like a lot but actually feels quite small. You need a
subgroup of professionals within that system whose opinion matters to
the problem user so that he is willing to change: this was the case on CIX.
Finally, you need someone who is willing to spend the time to teach some
manners: in this instance, the job fell to the conference's host.

Because Usenet is so much bigger, it's had a lot more village idiots, most
of whose stories are recorded in the "Net.Legends FAQ," subtitled "Noticeable Phenomena of Usenet."[2] The "Net.Legends FAQ" catalogues notorious Usenet posters, including the good guys (like Gene Spafford), the
harmless (like Homer Wilson Smith), and the obsessed; the list was compiled from answers to a call for nominations in *alt.folklore.urban*. There
was, for example, the case of Serdar Argic, who apparently managed to
run a daily search on all of Usenet[3] for mentions of Turkey, and followed
up all such messages with lengthy and historically inaccurate diatribes
about genocide against the Turks. Computers being what they are, his
messages were as likely to follow up articles detailing Thanksgiving menus
as they were postings to *soc.culture.turkey*. Since the system administrator at the site Argic used, *anatolia.org*, was, as the "Net.Legends FAQ"
puts it, "*not* cooperative in the least with the wishes of the rest of
UseNet that Serdar get a real life," a petition began circulating around
Usenet in the spring of 1994 addressed to the administrators at UUNet, the
upstream provider for *anatolia.org*. The request that they put the pressure
on Argic to stop flooding Usenet with these rants missed its target: *anato-
lia.org* apparently disappeared in April 1994.

Usenet has gotten a lot of entertainment making fun of its loons. A less
polite example is the *alt.usenet.kooks* newsgroup, which exists specifically to make fun of people whose behavior seems to merit it. The
alt.usenet.kooks FAQ defines a net.kook as "Anyone who posts uniquely
strange, perfectly incomprehensible articles, or who manifests a persistent, extreme, and somewhat bizarre obsession."[4] The FAQ goes on to
say, "It is important to note the subtle distinction between a net.kook, a
net.cretin, and a clueless newbie. The newbie, one hopes, can acquire a
clue on the installment plan even if he can't afford to buy one for cash;
the cretin is merely stupid and/or irritating; but a true net.kook has a spe-

cial fascination derived from his or her utter ineffability. Their behavior is irrational, if not downright weird, but they are seldom merely boring." And finally, "A net.kook may or may not be clinically insane."

Since April 1994 the newsgroup has voted monthly on the Kook of the Month award, which has gone to folks such as Earle Gordon Curley (October 1995), a self-styled psychic posting regularly to *sci.skeptic* (getting himself sued by paranormal investigator James Randi in late 1996), and Dr. Dmitri Vulis (May 1996), who campaigned so vigorously for a candidate he had chosen for the award that he wound up being nominated himself. According to the awards page, after some unsavory incidents involving forged votes and postings to *soc.culture.pakistani,* more than 800 votes came in for "this rather unimportant award," and Vulis won by a margin of 30. In late 1996, Vulis achieved what many would have thought impossible: he got himself thrown off the anarchy-loving, 1,200-member cypherpunks emailing list by its owner, ultimate anti-censor John Gilmore, for persistently and egregiously attacking everyone in sight.

Three Kook of the Month awards have been won by notable figures on *alt.religion.scientology:* Koos Nolste Trenite (February 1995), the Dutch channeler of L. Ron Hubbard; Peter Nathan Haas (December 1995), who made a name for himself by attempting to insist that everyone on the newsgroup be polite; and Scientology attorney Helena Kobrin (August 1995). Kobrin is also immortalized on the "Helena Kobrin Love Page," maintained by British poster Martin Poulter. Satirical and offensive, it also includes a note on how to complain to the California bar about Kobrin.[5]

What can you do with people who are unfit for cyberspace and take everyone else along with them? Making fun of them blows off steam but is not in any way a satisfying solution if what you hope to achieve is a Net on which everyone can find a spiritual home. Holding them up to ridicule, if anything, alienates them further from the social norms. In a moderated forum, it's up to the sysop to retain enough impartiality to settle the inevitable fights and put brakes on what sadly seems to be a normal, human tendency to nominate the person who stands out as a whipping boy. Anyone who was ever stuck on the receiving end of malicious treatment in school or camp should be sympathetic enough not to inflict similar behavior on other people; unfortunately, in my experience it doesn't work that way online.

Keeping that balance is desperately difficult. It's hard to convey how disruptive these people can be, or how little they seem to register the provocative effect they have on other people. They are always sure you're picking on them unfairly; after all, didn't that other guy just tell them to FOAD? And the answer is, Well, yes, he did—but only after you'd called him names for two weeks and needled him maliciously every time he said anything. You can say that, but they just won't see it that way.

One standard suggestion is to give these attention-seekers their own area to dominate; then those who want to can talk to them and those who don't can easily avoid them. Some people do enjoy roiling tar pits of violent electronic discussion, just as some people like to watch car crashes or burning buildings. Areas for just that type of mentality exist in cyberspace already—on Usenet, you have newsgroups like *alt.flame* and *alt.tasteless*; on London's CIX you have the *abuse* conference. The thing is, the welding torches who frequent *alt.tasteless* and *alt.flame* are not loose screws or unable to function in cyberspace: like all subcultures, they have their own rules, even if the workings of these aren't clear to outsiders. It wouldn't have worked with our psycho, who seemed to like having rules to chafe against. How can you make nuts stay where they're put? If what they want is attention, sooner or later they're going to come out and bother someone: even *alt.tasteless* did that when it invaded *rec.pets.cats*.

The mature thing is to ignore them, either by humanly controlling your reactions or by using a killfile. Deprived of the attention, cyberwackos are as likely as anyone else to get bored and go away or adopt more acceptable behavior. This approach requires a lot of discipline, mutual support, and trust on the part of the other local residents, and is therefore most likely to work only in older forums full of experienced onliners. In an area full of newcomers that hasn't cohered yet in any significant way, people are likely to feel that they deserve to have *their* temper tantrums, too.

But a killfile won't help you if the misfit is destructive enough. In September 1996, some nut unleashed a cancelbot (an automated software robot message-canceller) one weekend that probably wiped out about 25,000 postings on newsgroups relating to Asian and Jewish topics. The newsgroups were completely disrupted for a couple of days, until Chris Lewis, the best-known active canceler of spam and other mass postings, was able to resurrect the canceled postings. This kind of thing—and there have been other cases—is not something that can be handled by individual restraint or peer pressure; it's the online equivalent of trashing a public space, and the answer is likely to lie in technical improvements and traditional policing.

The problems posed by electronic misfits will only become more acute as the Net increasingly becomes the dominant medium for social interaction and general communications. We can help those without access to computers by creating public terminals. We can help those unable to operate computers by giving them better systems and human aid. We can even teach caution and the use of X-no-archive headers on Usenet postings to keep truly personal material from being permanently searchable on services like Deja News.[6] But how will we handle those whose self-destructive instincts make them a danger to any online community in which they operate?

My own feeling is that at least some of the answer lies in fostering the survival of diverse, smaller communities. The more diversity there is, the more likely it is that everyone will find some area where they fit in. It's a waste of the infinite flexibility of the medium if everything is global; we have something like that, and it's called CNN. One suggestion posted in late 1996 to the main newsgroup for discussing spam and related issues, *news.admin.net-abuse.misc*, was that Usenet spam could be defeated if we abandoned Usenet's hierarchical structure entirely and just threw articles into a massive pool, which users would search by keyword using an engine like Deja News to bring up articles of interest. This is a massively wrong-headed idea, because the current structure helps foster a sense of community across the world among those who share specific interests. Besides, it would be hugely inefficient, since computer searching just isn't that good yet, and it would cut out of Usenet smaller sites that can afford only a partial feed.

Smaller communities also tend to allow people to get to know each other better, just as it's much easier to be anonymous in a large city than in a small town. This can make a big difference. I've seen several cases where people's bizarre behavior turned out to be completely understandable and even tolerable when their offline circumstances were explained by someone who knew them. That kind of personal knowledge only comes over time with regular contact in a familiar environment.

One principle that could usefully be built into our networks, which would help foster that sort of community, is reimplementing the functions we're now losing. Just as we lost a lot of functions for a while on PCs when mature DOS programs were translated into immature Windows programs, the conversion of the predominantly text-based Net of the early 1990s into a predominantly graphical environment is costing us features that actually mattered. The WELL's new graphical interface, Engaged, may be easier for newcomers to pick up, but it has yet to install real-time communication (known in WELL lingo as "sends") and the facility for seeing who reads a conference and when they were last there. More real-time features have been lost with an early 1997 decision to change the WELL's mail system in a way that makes it less immediately responsive.

On the Net at large, the now widespread use of graphical software and a desire to minimize the information about systems' users available to hackers have made it less likely that you can look up a user (via the Finger utility) and see if he or she is currently online. (One good feature about America Online is that it not only makes this easy, it gives you an automated routine to do it with.) There is a loss of privacy implicit in this; a reasonable tradeoff might be reciprocity, so that if someone looks up information about you, you can find out they've done it. (This is possible on older UNIX systems and is a basic principle implemented in a futuristic system of badges developed at Britain's Olivetti Research Labs, which register the staff's whereabouts and make the information available over the Internet.) Such a set-up would have the advantage of warning you if someone were obsessively watching you.

The difficulty is that the smaller the community, the more disruptive a misfit can be. One example of this was the well-known 1993 story of a virtual rape on LambdaMOO, the biggest and oldest shared fantasy world. The incident and its consequences (lots of discussion and the eventual elimination of the erring player) led to the formation of a system of government that consists of petitions and ballots whose results are binding on the system administrators, who are bound to carry out whatever the population decides.[7] If a system of social, as opposed to technical, government ever evolves on the wider Net, we will have to find a better way of handling the misfits who inspire its formation.

12

Garbage In, Garbage Out

> James Hacker (prime minister): The statistics are unarguable.
> Humphrey Appleby (cabinet secretary): Statistics! You can prove
> anything with statistics.
> Hacker: Even the truth. —From *Yes, Prime Minister*,
> by Jonathan Lynn and Anthony Jay

In August 1995, when the first paid-for advertising banner appeared on the original Web indexing service, Yahoo!, someone posted a memorial notice to Usenet: Yahoo! had gone commercial, and the Net was Dead. At the time, one of the most significant concerns on Netizens' minds was that sweeping commercialization of the Net was going to wipe away the existing culture by taking what was a free, public resource, sticking a meter on it, and selling it back to the people who had created it.

The Web's potential as a commercial medium was evident already, even though no systems were yet in place for handling secure transactions or heavy-duty product databases. It all happened very fast. In late 1995, you could browse a couple of pictures of flowers on a Web site and place an order by telephone; at the end of 1996, you could buy from Land's End's entire catalogue with intelligent ordering that told you if an item was out of stock and transmitted your order using encryption built into both your browser and the company's server. People want to do these things: half of everyone I know is desperately envious because in late 1996 a major supermarket chain started trying out selling groceries over the Net for next-day delivery in my particular residential area (the other half can't imagine why anyone would want to buy food this way).

Simultaneously, the Web's dominant nature has morphed: in 1994, most information sites were built by academic institutions or amateurs and hobbyists. By the middle of 1996, almost every media company was scrapping to set up a professional-quality news service, and journalists, who in 1994 were told they were about to become extinct, were being paid to supply these sites' content. There are no records of who was first to get paid to write for the Web; I can only say that when I started writing for *d.Comm*, the *Economist*'s Web-based newsletter, at the end of 1995, I figured I was probably in the first fifty.

This complete reinvention of the Web brought with it a new set of clashes. Consumers in general don't want to pay for content on the Net; they want to be able to browse freely. Things may be different when Web-based services have been around longer and people know what they'd be buying, but in general there are too many unknown quantities for people to be willing to fork out for a subscription. There are exceptions; the *Electronic Telegraph* reports that people will pay small amounts for access to specialized pockets of content such as fantasy football leagues. The dominant answer so far is advertising sponsorship on a business model similar to that of radio and TV (as opposed to print, where being able to charge for the publication offsets some of the costs).

But advertising sponsors want the one thing most Net users don't want to give up: detailed demographic information. Net users hate this, partly because we're all so conscious of the amount of junk mail and junk telephone calls we get; the last thing we want is to be pestered over the Internet, too. Over time, actual sales sites have an advantage here, since you can't really order a new anorak from L. L. Bean without giving them at least some information about yourself, such as color preference, size, and shipping address. But if you're a business considering making the investment—anywhere from tens of thousands to millions of dollars—to set up a Web site, you want to know the make-up of the population that's going to use it. Cue another major cultural shift.

Most humans like to count things. Since the people using the Net in the early days were computer people, what they counted was primarily machines. In the excitement of watching the Internet spread like mold on damp bread, they counted the number of Internet hosts (machines or networks attached to the Net) and the countries in which they were located. The famous 1988 Internet Worm, which temporarily paralyzed part of the Internet and inspired a wave of computer crime legislation and hacker crackdowns, was a botched attempt to map this spread.

But companies don't market to machines (however much we wish they would); they want to count people. At least, that was the thrust of an argument constructed by Donna Hoffman and Tom Novak, associate professors at Vanderbilt University's Owen Graduate School of Management, in an article published in *Wired* in November 1994, in which they called for a net.census.[1] "It is time to act," they wrote. "The Internet has changed dramatically in size, character, and economic importance, but may not evolve further without careful measurement of its users. Until then, the lack of accurate and credible information about Internet users is likely to hinder the continued health and positive development of electronic commerce."

Hoffman and Novak are unusual fixtures on the Net's landscape, Hoffman in particular: she not only analyzes the Net but shows up every day on the WELL, where she sometimes styles herself "data geek." While others did the investigative footwork that was partly responsible for discrediting Martin Rimm's study of pornography (see chapter 9), it was Hoffman's knowledge of marketing research and statistical analysis that exposed the study's many technical flaws. While we browse, Hoffman and Novak are busy researching the marketing implications of commercializing the Internet, a specialty that didn't even exist a couple of years ago, as part of Project 2000, a five-year research effort sponsored by, among others, Daimler-Beng, HotWired Ventures, Sun, and the National Science Foundation.[2]

The immediate impetus behind Hoffman's and Novak's call to numbers was an article in the *New York Times* in which cyberspace correspondent Peter Lewis contrasted estimates of Net usership based on two competing surveys of Internet hosts.[3] Both surveys counted machines, rather than users, a process Hoffman and Novak compared to conducting a real-world census by counting buildings ("without regard to their function or contents") rather than people. One of the two surveys, Mark Lottor's July 1994 Internet Domain Survey,[4] put the number of hosts between 707,000 and 3.2 million; the other, John Quarterman's TIC/MIDS Internet Demographic Survey, administered by email in January 1994, put the number at 1 million to 1.4 million.[5] Depending whether you guessed 3.5, 5, 7.5, or 10 users per host (all common estimates at the time), you would get anywhere from 2.5 million to 32 million Internet users—a difference roughly equivalent to the population of Colombia or California.

In 1994, when the National Science Foundation pulled out of supplying the Net's backbone—the major arteries through which data is transmitted—in favor of commercial suppliers, some of these technical measurements became less easily obtainable because there was no longer a single main road through which all traffic flowed. At the same time, it became more difficult to count hosts using standard Internet utilities such as Ping (a network-testing routine that lets you determine if a system attached to the Internet is alive) because increased security on many sites blocked such inquiries. But this was also the moment when the Internet was being turned into a business, creating a new interest in such numerical data.

Noting that few Internet users at the time were interested in counting people rather than machines, except in the limited context of counting visits to individual Web sites, Hoffman and Novak complained, "It is foolhardy to be content with an 'adequate' number of visits to a site. In the explosively evolving Internet environment, we expect that the novelty of many commercial sites will soon fade, and then the real competition to attract visits to commercial sites will begin. In this competitive environment, accurate information on market potential and user needs will be critical." However, they added, "surveying the size of the Net will be difficult, complex, and costly."

Nonetheless, Hoffman and Novak proposed that such a survey should be attempted, taking into account why and how people actually use the Internet and how they react to its commercialization. They proposed the formation of an advisory panel and the development of a set of protocols and standards for measuring the Internet, with the key proviso that the information so developed should be made public. "Privatizing this information," they say, "flies in the face of the anarchic, yet democratic roots of the Net and may be the surest path to a monolithic, mass-market vision of a commercialized, yet sadly 'de-evolved' Internet." The point here is this: if the good demographic data are private, then the only people who can afford access to it are the major corporations. For the small, Mom-and-Pop operation to be able to compete equally—one of the dreams of the Net—the data have to be free.

Hoffman and Novak thought they'd gotten their wish when, in early 1995, they got the CommerceNet consortium, of which they are members, to agree to supply up to $100,000 to fund the study. Out of twenty-odd proposals, the committee of five (including Hoffman and Novak) selected A. C. Nielsen, the well-known TV ratings company, which they felt had the best proposal and also had significantly underbid the rest of the field.

Nielsen's methodology was a familiar one: select a nationally projectable sample and conduct telephone interviews using a carefully designed survey questionnaire. In order for the sample to be projected accurately, however, its makeup has to be compared to known census data for the target population (in the Nielsen study's case, the adult population of the United States and Canada). If, hypothetically, 20 percent of your sample were under twenty-five, but official census data shows that in the general population 30 percent are under twenty-five, you need to take this difference into account when you project the results of the survey onto the larger population. While you would probably refine your selection procedures to choose a more representative sample in the case of such an egregious discrepancy, it's typical for samples to vary slightly from the make-up of the larger population. This difficult but well-established process of analyzing the statistics, making these comparisons, and adjusting the results to take these differences into account is called weighting. If this all sounds too complicated and mathematical, think of it like balancing a tire and applying weights to eliminate small imperfections that are unnoticeable at ten miles per hour but make the car vibrate noisily at fifty-five.

When Nielsen weighted the data and released the results in November 1995, they were unexpectedly high: the number of Americans and Canadians sixteen or older with access to the Internet was projected at 37 million, of which 24 million used the Internet, 18 million used the Web, and 2.5 million had actually used the Web to make purchases.[6] Hoffman and Novak, who had proposed the study and were expected to endorse it, immediately challenged these figures. In April 1996, they released a reanalysis of the same data claiming the figures were inflated due to errors in the weights. "The average inflation due to deficient weighting alone is 20.6%, the average inflation due to inconsistency alone is 13%, and the average total inflation in the original CNIDS [CommerceNet/Nielsen Internet Demographic Survey] estimates, when adjusted for the combined effect of these critical flaws, is 38%," they wrote. "As such these estimates lack validity and are of little value to decision makers."[7] Imagine you're running a business, and you're thinking of advertising on *Roseanne*, and you're basing your marketing plans and advertising expenditures on the assumption that the audience is more than a third larger than it actually is. Hoffman's and Novak's corrected estimates were 28.8 million with access, 16.4 million actually using the Internet, 11.5 million using the Web, and 1.5 million who had used the Web to purchase something. Nielsen, which had priced copies of its full report at $5,000, disagreed with this reanalysis,[8] but Hoffman and Novak's paper was accepted for publication in the peer-reviewed journal *Communications of the ACM* and Nielsen eventually revised its estimates.

One reason Nielsen's figures seemed so high was that several other surveys, released around the same time, came out with much lower numbers. Specialist Internet publisher O'Reilly and Associates 1995 study came out with 5.8 million adults using the Internet; consulting and research service FIND/SVP estimated 8.4 million adults and 1.1 million children use the Internet; and Times Mirror came up with 25 million adult Americans online.[9]

The wide variation among those numbers illustrates a different problem: there is little agreement on how to define such basic concepts as "Internet access" and "Internet user." All of America Online's 8 million users have Internet access, but that doesn't mean they use it. Leaving net.prejudice aside, AOL members who send email and have chat sessions only with each other aren't using the Internet, they're using AOL. Similarly, a business may connect its network to the Internet but give genuine access only to a small subset of employees. There are also subtle but real distinctions to be made between types of Internet access: indirect access via a gateway from an online service or bulletin board system (BBS) gives you a more restricted set of functions than direct access via an Internet service provider (ISP) that puts your machine directly on the Net; direct access may or may not give you your own domain name and permanent numbered Internet address, allowing you to host a Web or FTP site on your own machine instead of on a service provider's setup.

The O'Reilly survey, with the lowest numbers, defined an Internet user as someone eighteen or over with direct Internet access, excluding users whose access was solely via an online service such as AOL or CompuServe. FIND/SVP included all those eighteen or over who used at least one Internet application in addition to email, with no restrictions on whether that Internet access was supplied by an online service or a direct ISP. Times Mirror's substantially larger estimate was based on the broadest definition: anyone eighteen or over who ever used a computer from home, work, or school to connect to online services, BBSs, or the Internet.

Raw Internet usage was not the only element these surveys studied; they also looked at the overall demographic makeup of those who use the Internet, including gender, education, income, and age. Stanford Research International (SRI) analyzed the Nielsen and O'Reilly surveys along with two sets of figures from the Graphic, Visualization, and Usability (GVU) Center at Georgia Tech looking for overall trends. Among other things,

SRI found that the percentage of women on the Net was rising; that the average age of Internet users was likely to decline, slowly dropping to slightly below a median age of thirty; and that average income of Internet users might also decline. SRI concluded, however, that "educational attainment continues to be the fundamental demographic driver of Web access and activity."[10] Its prediction that women would make up half of all Web users by the end of 1996, however, has not come true; best estimates at the end of 1996 were that a little over a third of Internet users were women. Of the areas SRI studied, it found the most difficulty in drawing conclusions about income, which, they note, "remains an ambiguous and unreliable measure of the value of the Internet audience."

Darrell Huff, whose short, entertaining book *How to Lie with Statistics* ought to be required reading for anyone who is bemused by the many numbers we see in newspapers every day, wrote, "Many a statistic . . . gets by only because the magic of numbers brings about a suspension of common sense."[11] Using a common-sense yardstick, most Internet users probably thought Nielsen's estimates were high, just as most experienced Usenet posters know instinctively that Rimm's claim that 87 percent of Usenet traffic is pornography can't be right. Personally, the most valuable of these surveys is the SRI meta-analysis, which looks for trends rather than focusing on specific numbers.

In his analysis of the Rimm pornography study (see chapter 9) DEC research scientist Brian Reid goes on to point out that useful information can be derived by studying trends—for instance, comparing the results over time for a single newsgroup, or comparing the results from a single time period across newsgroups. While Reid's comments were limited to Usenet, a very different ball of wax, until we have independent analyses of Internet usership that are non-commercial and equivalent to the decennial federal population census, bearing these principles in mind seems to me a good idea. Although, pretty much all the surveys agreed, with the exception of Nielsen. Time will also help; a few years from now, companies that have been selling via the Web, such as L. L. Bean, Land's End, and the bookselling service Amazon, will begin to report the results of their experiences.

It is, of course, in the interest of anyone selling the Internet as a commercial medium to show that there are lots of women (the primary shoppers in many households), high income levels, and all those other things that advertisers like. SRI's caution, in the midst of so much Internet hype, is therefore particularly welcome.

In the end, what constitutes success for advertisers is people buying their products. Measuring this kind of success on the Web turns out to be no easier than measuring Internet use. When Hoffman and Novak set out in mid-1996 to survey Web-based advertising, they discovered there were more than ninety sizes of Web ad banners, little consistency among sites in pricing advertising, and little demographic information about customers. Sites don't even necessarily charge the same way. While most charge by the thousand "impressions"—the number of times an advertising banner is displayed on a page downloaded by a visitor to the site—some charge by "clickthrough," that is, the number of times a visitor clicks on an advertising banner to go to the advertiser's own site, the disadvantage being that the sponsored site loses out if the advertiser's design is too poor to attract those clickthroughs.

Differences and inconsistencies like these led Hoffman and Novak to call, in September 1996, for the development of standardized techniques for measuring Web use. "First, there are no established principles for measuring traffic on commercial Web sites that seek to generate revenues from advertising sponsorship," they wrote. "Second, there is no standard way of measuring consumer response to advertisements. Third, there are no standards for optimal media pricing models. Finally, the complexity of the medium in general hinders the standardization process."[12] Nonetheless, they note, estimates are that Web-based advertising will grow substantially over the next few years, and predictions put advertising revenue for the year 2000 at $1.7 billion to $5 billion.[13] To put those numbers in perspective, in 1995 U.S. companies spent $31.2 billion on direct mail and $11.1 billion on radio advertising. In 1996, Web advertising was a tiny fraction of those, and two-thirds of that went to the top ten sites.[14]

This is one of the reasons that predictions that large corporations will fare badly on the Web will probably be proved incorrect. The Web's lack of familiarity and raw immaturity as a medium reward familiar names disproportionately. Buying groceries through one of the few trial systems available at the end of 1996 meant choosing products from a list offering little auxiliary information; the inevitable result is to gravitate toward national brand names and known quantities.

In order for Web sites to have a shot at turning commercial—sites like the Internet Movie Database and the search engine Yahoo! started as personal projects—they have to collect demographic information to show potential advertisers that they attract the kind of visitors those advertisers are interested in. The simplest way of collecting this information is the registration forms required by many sites, especially those publishing new, professionally written material—what they call "content."

Unfortunately for site owners who are trying to find a way to pay themselves a living, this kind of information isn't exactly what a lot of Net users want to supply. Attempts to log user characteristics are seen by many Netheads as an unwelcome invasion of privacy; in fact, this was named as the most important issue facing the Net by 26.2 percent of respondents to the October 1996 GVU survey of user attitudes. Besides, people hate looking at ads; that's why we now have VCRs that mark the ads and automatically spin past them. The Net equivalent is services like the Anonymizer and Internet Fast Forward,[15] which allow anonymous browsing, and intermediary services that allow you to register once and then browse using a single, numbered ID. The third-party service makes only the aggregated demographic data available to its subscribing sites, while users only reveal their personal details to one centralized site.

Many Web wanderers don't realize just how much information Web sites can acquire about them while they're visiting, even without registration forms. Most of this is pretty harmless—do you really care if the Alien Abduction Web site marks down that you're using Windows 95 and Netscape 3.0 while it's asking you to sign up for a date and time to be abducted?[16] But it spooks people to think that a Web server can read information like that off what they think of as their private, personal computer systems. Web sites can also typically tell what domain you're coming from (though generally not your precise email address) and what pages you look at and when.

A certain amount of this information gets stored in a file called a "cookie." A lot has been written about this, but in fact, cookies aren't as big an invasion of privacy as they sound at first, especially because they're actually stored on your system, not on the Web site. If you've used the Web since about the middle of 1996, you probably have a cookie file in the directory on your hard drive where your Web browser is stored; it's called COOKIES.TXT and is just a text file full of arcane information that won't mean much to you but helps the Web site give you a somewhat personalized service. The idea is that, for example, a site's "What's New" page might reflect what's new on the site since you last visited, rather than since the last time the programmers updated it.

But precisely how much people dislike giving up personal information can be shown by the fact that, in GVU's Sixth WWW User Survey,[17] roughly a third of respondents reported lying on Web site registration forms. (It also raises questions about direct marketers' glib statements that people really like to receive unsolicited product information.)

These GVU surveys take a different approach: instead of counting the size of the Internet population, they are interested in studying the values and attitudes of those already on the Net. Because their surveys depend on voluntary response from a self-selecting sample, rather than from a scientifically selected and weighted sample, there are inherent biases. People who dislike answering surveys, never use the Web, or use it only in highly rigid ways (such as looking only at a company's preprogrammed sites) won't appear, and those paying timed access charges may be deterred from answering the lengthy sets of questions. GVU did try to counteract this effect by advertising the surveys in a carefully chosen set of newsgroups, announcing them in non-Net media such as newspapers and magazines, and using advertising banners on high-traffic sites such as the main search engines. Nonetheless, it's well known in demographic research that a self-selecting sample of people interested in answering surveys is unlikely to be representative of the general population.

In her book *Tainted Truth*, an examination of the effects of corporate sponsorship on the results reported by scientific research, journalist Cynthia Crossen looked at the complex interplay between question design and sample selection:

> To show how much difference poor questions and a non-random sample can make, consider this question posed by Ross Perot. In a mail-in questionnaire published in *TV Guide*, the question was "Should the President have the Line Item Veto to eliminate waste?"; 97 percent said yes. The same question was later asked of a sample that was scientifically selected rather than self-selected, and 71 percent said yes. The question was rewritten in a more neutral way—"Should the President have the Line Item Veto, or not?"—and asked of a scientifically selected sample. This time only 57 percent said yes.[18]

Unrepresentative or not, the sixth GVU survey still contains surprises indicating that the make-up of the Net might be different than we tend to think. One such example is the political leanings of Net users. A lot of expectations derive from the writing that appears in *Wired* magazine or from net.prophets such as John Perry Barlow, who has said a number of times that the Net's infective culture has spawned 30 million libertarians. GVU's sixth survey tells a different story: the largest group of Web users, 38.4 percent, identified themselves as centrist, with the next largest groups being left-liberal (27.3 percent) and libertarian (25.1 percent).[19] Other findings are less surprising, though they should sound a warning note for commercial interests: only 9.88 percent report reading junk email messages, nearly 4 percent retaliate, and, most significantly for the future, younger users are less tolerant of junk email than older ones.

As another twist on what is commonly believed, the Net may not re-capture younger consumers for news media. The GVU survey reports that the younger generation consumes less news online, just as it does in tra-ditional media. Further, only about 20 percent of those questioned in a survey commissioned by the Radio-Television News Directors Founda-tion said they'd be willing to pay even a nominal fee for a news-on-demand electronic service; most would prefer that such services be supported by advertising. GVU also reported that 67.6 percent of re-spondents said they were not willing to pay fees for accessing Web sites, although it qualified that by pointing out that it was unclear whether this was because of a perceived lack of value of the information supplied (which might change over time) or because people were already paying for access to the Net through online service fees and telephone bills.

Either way, these attitudes suggest that an interesting battle lies ahead between two net.obsessions: freedom of information and privacy. Com-mercial interests don't want to give their information away; if advertising is going to pay all those costs, then Net users must be prepared to give up their demographic secrets. If users want privacy and anonymity, they may have to pay extra for it. On the Net, there is no reason why both ap-proaches shouldn't exist simultaneously.

13

Grass Roots

> An AT&T survey of U.S. broadcasting in 1926 determined that ap-
> proximately one-half of U.S. stations were operated to generate
> publicity for the owner's primary enterprise, while one-third were
> operated by nonprofit groups for eleemosynary purposes. Only 4.3
> percent of U.S. stations were characterized as being "commercial
> broadcasters," while a mere one-quarter of U.S. stations permitted
> the public to purchase airtime for its own use.
> —Robert W. McChesney, *Telecommunications,*
> *Mass Media, and Democracy*

It was clear to most people on the Net even before anyone
started doing fancy demographic surveys that most early online users
were white, well educated, relatively affluent, and male. As soon as Vice
President Al Gore started talking about a National Information Infrastructure, one of the first questions was how to ensure universal access, a
dream all net.visionaries share, even if some of them do hate America Online. (The best-known dissenting view comes from physicist Clifford
Stoll, who argued in his 1995 book *Silicon Snake Oil* that schools and libraries should be spending their money on books, not computers.)[1] Part
of the reasoning behind this dream is the notion that universal access
means increased democracy and freedom with greater public access to
public information than has been available before, and that this greater
accessibility may overturn today's power structures. And yet, many of
these same net.visionaries reject government regulation or intervention as
an aid to this process, and believe instead in the force of free markets and
competition: what may be more important than universal service is universal interoperability, so the Net's standards remain ever open.[2]

"I've been very encouraged by the way in which the demographics of
the Internet have shifted dramatically over the last couple of years," John

Perry Barlow said in a July 1996 debate at Harvard University on the future of presidential campaigning in a networked world. "There are many more languages . . . available than there were two years ago, and it's shifting rapidly. But it's not shifting because of any governmental or political process. It's shifting because the users are making it so." Barlow's copanelists represented the Democratic and Republican national conventions, and the focus of their comments was notably on the Net as a way to broadcast candidates' campaign material, not as a collaborative two-way medium where candidates might enjoy a new level of interaction with their constituents. Or, as Barlow put it, "The Internet is not a mass medium. And everything I've heard today talks about treating it as though it were. It's not a broadcast medium, and it's not part of the United States. It is cyberspace, which is an extra-territorial and anti-sovereign condition that may completely eliminate anything but the most ceremonial role for the presidency of the United States."[3]

Or perhaps not. Great democratic advances were predicted for radio, too, and yet in the United States it became a commercially dominated medium largely controlled by a few corporate interests. This could also happen to the Net. The cooperative, pioneering spirit in which people wrote tools for their own use and shared them freely is already dying in the rush to cash in and find advertising sponsorship. The focus on the Communications Decency Act drew attention away from the other provisions of the 1996 Telecommunications Bill, which greatly deregulated the telephone, cable, and broadcasting industries.

Journalism professor Robert McChesney has compared that bill to the Federal Communications Act of 1934, which paved the way for today's tight commercial control of the broadcast media:

> The debate in Congress over the future of telecommunications policy has disregarded issues of democracy and fairness. Lawmakers have focused instead on gutting regulations that impede the profitability of companies seeking to develop new communications technologies. And so, the current legislative process has been guided by the same assumptions that led to the disastrous Communications Act of 1934: namely, that competition among corporations in the marketplace will provide the most efficient and democratic communications system. The tightening oligarchy of telecommunications companies that arose in the wake of the 1934 law shows how misguided that assumption was. And there is no reason to believe that a new law based on the same logic will be any more viable as a guide to opening up the digital frontier.[4]

But Barlow still has a point. Even though the original backbone of the Net was built with government money, far more of it has been created (or cobbled together) by commercial and personal interests, and there's no certainty that governments will be quick to provide access to what we think of as public data. The earliest appearance online of such important databases as the Securities and Exchange Commission database of companies was not provided by a government outfit but by the dedicated Carl Malamud. Malamud was also one of the first to experiment with Internet broadcasting and was responsible for setting up the Internet Multicasting service in 1994, using a public radio approach of listener and corporate sponsorship to broadcasting senate and congressional sessions as well as music, Internet Talk Radio and "Geek of the Week" interviews.[5]

Across Europe, although there is a greater tradition of public broadcasting (in return for a TV license fee), there is not such a great tradition of regarding data that was collected at the taxpayer's expense as publicly owned. In Britain, for example, laws and government papers are subject to copyright and are published by the Stationery Office at relatively high prices calculated to help recover costs.[6] Distributing the material via the Net for free was therefore a matter for debate (early reports are that the Stationery Office, like other publishers, is finding that putting the material on the Web actually increases sales). Similarly, there is less local and regional programming of all types, and the kind of public access U.S. cable TV companies are required to provide is nonexistent; however, cable TV companies are allowed to provide telephone services and are giving British Telecom the first competition it's ever had in that market.

The big question is what universal access means and what form it might take. We're certainly nowhere near such a situation today. Jock Gill, one of the people who masterminded the White House's connection to the Internet in 1993, estimated then that there were some pockets in the United States where as much as 20 percent of the population didn't even have telephones.[7] More recently, a 1995 Department of Commerce survey noted that the lowest telephone penetration is in inner cities (79.8 percent), while the lowest ownership of computers and modems is among the rural poor (4.5 percent).[8]

This is not a uniquely American pattern. Electronic Frontier Ireland (EFI) points out that although Ireland has made an international name for itself with telemarketing and hotline technical support services (Dell and Gateway are only two example of companies that use Irish telephone sales and support services), ensuring equal access is a high priority. The local dialing areas for Ireland's Internet service providers (ISPs), as EFI noted in 1995, are all in cities, but the Irish population is spread thinly across the countryside. This disparity worried the planners.

> It will be no exaggeration to say those who fall behind will form an underclass: it will be very difficult for people not familiar with the technology to secure anything but the most menial of jobs. Moreover, as the technology becomes part of our social and political structures, these people could find themselves cut off and disenfranchised. Clearly, such an underclass could become the main ingrdient [*sic*] in a cocktail of social, political and economic disaster. It is a scenario we must avoid at all costs.

EFI's planning document concludes that universal access must be extended from the traditional telecommunications services to the new medium.[9] The report also states that costs must be reduced to as little as a quarter of current (1995) costs and blames high prices for slow take-up, noting that *Scientific American* compared telephone use in the United States and the United Kingdom and found that the average American household used its phones for more than an hour a day, compared to less than fifteen minutes for U.K. users. Irish phone rates, as the EFI noted, are higher than the United Kingdom's; however, the report fails to consider that local calling is billed differently (more cheaply) in Ireland, even though long distance calling is as much as 50 percent more expensive. For city residents with local dial-up to an ISP node, therefore, Irish users may be better off than their British counterparts.

EFI is, however, correct when it says that "those living in rural areas, who have most to gain from telecommunications, are penalized for taking advantage of it." This is just as true in the United States, where rural areas often are not served by local dial-up Internet access. Add the fact that rural libraries usually have less funding and are therefore less able to supply Internet connections, and the fact that salaries are often lower, it's obvious why those who already have the most real-world services—urban residents—also have the best Internet access. Ithaca, New York, the home of Cornell University, didn't get a CompuServe node until about 1992; the town where some friends of mine live in southeastern Ohio will probably never have one. Both those communities now have dial-up Internet access from their local colleges, however.

At least one survey has shown that these costs matter. An Organization for Economic Cooperation and Development (OECD) study released in June 1996 showed that although Scandinavia has just 5 percent of Europe's population, it has 25 percent of Europe's Internet hosts. It also showed a strong correlation between competitive telecommunications markets and lower prices, and between Internet penetration and competitive telecommunications markets. In addition, the report found that "a major reason that a sufficient amount of local content is not available in some countries is because domestic producers and users do not have efficient access to networks."[10] In other words, better access means better opportunities not only for getting information but for publishing it. This issue of local content is an important one in most countries outside the United States, who fear that the predominantly American character of the Internet may overpower local languages and cultures the way it already dominates the entertainment industry. However, it's equally possible that the Internet will continue to do the job it's already doing of uniting dispersed subcultures and making them stronger, whether it's by allowing a tiny Scottish radio station to broadcast popular Scottish performers to the rest of the world or by helping scholars to preserve obscure languages.

The European Parliament is already aware of this problem: "If the development of information highways is not sufficiently well structured, it could lead to all types of abuse and undermining of democracy by creating a gulf between those who are able to master this technological instrument and those who are not," runs the resolution it drafted in 1995,[11] stressing the importance of protecting European cultural values, ensuring easy access, low costs, and the provision of some basic services free of charge (while simultaneously proposing to tighten up copyright law and crack down on piracy). However, the European Parliament's criteria for success are economic rather than idealistic: "In conditions of unemployment such as those prevailing in the Union at the moment, the information revolution will prove its worth to society and ultimately consolidate itself only to the extent that its impact on the employment situation turns out to be on balance, positive." In other words, people can't live by electrons alone, something that will only be surprising to people who have been on the Net so long at a stretch that when they get hungry they type "pizza" at the nearest system prompt and expect food.[12]

But granted that public Internet access can be provided via public terminals situated in libraries, schools, or even corner kiosks coupled with local Free-Nets to provide email and a basic set of functions, raw access isn't much good if everything online has a price tag.

The problem is that these concerns about equal access come at a time when intellectual property laws are being reexamined and tightened.[13]

Copyright protection has been extended, and the Software Publishers' Association is pressuring ISPs to police their systems for potential infringements. At the same time, the culture that surrounded the UNIX operating system and the Internet generally, in which researchers created tools because they needed them personally and then gave them away to the community at large, is fading in the rush to cash in. A Supreme Court decision in 1981 opened the way for patenting software (in Europe, software is generally protected by copyright instead), creating problems in deciding what elements of a product may be copied for the purpose of making it intuitive for users who are used to specific conventions.

Opposition to this way of managing the software industry led to the formation of the Free Software Foundation and the League for Programming Freedom, set up specifically to continue the tradition of creating free, high-quality software for widespread use. John Gilmore, whose name pops up in so many other contexts, was involved in setting up Cygnus Support, a company specializing in selling services and support for this free software.

We may be facing a similar privatization of information. Although it's generally been held that facts are in the public domain even though the precise words expressing those facts may be copyrighted, a database treaty proposed to the World Intellectual Property Organization (WIPO) by the U.S. government at the end of 1996 was aimed at changing this. The proposed database treaty did not pass at WIPO's December 1996 meeting. But the possible ramifications alarmed organizations such as the Electronic Frontier Foundation (EFF), which claimed it could potentially reduce access to information as diverse as stock quotes, sports results, and even government information via Freedom of Information Requests.[14]

"This treaty would completely undermine the 1991 U.S. Supreme Court decision in *Feist Publications, Inc., v. Rural Telephone Service,*" the EFF noted. "In *Feist,* the Court rejected a claim of copyright for data from a telephone directory's white pages, finding that facts cannot be copyrighted and that obvious items, such as lists of names, addresses, and telephone numbers in alphabetical order, are not sufficiently creative to qualify for copyright protection." It's worth noting that this situation doesn't prevail in all countries; in Britain, for example, the telephone directories are copyrighted by British Telecom (although an intrepid individual could compile his or her own directory from independent sources) and the database of postal codes is copyrighted by the Post Office. The result so far has been to keep this information off the public Net; it is possible, however, to access British Telecom's database via paid services.

The EFF was also concerned that the treaty as proposed would have included prohibitions against "the importation, manufacture or distribution of protection-defeating devices"—which, the EFF concluded, could mean anything from white-out to a pair of scissors (which could be used to remove copyright notices).[15] It's hard to imagine the law being enforced to such an extent, but that clause, together with provisions for holding system operators liable, has an ominous ring to many.

For all of the advantages of placing public data on the Net, it does have its downside. For example, it also allows much faster and more efficient invasion of privacy. In mid-1996, Oregon resident Aaron Nabil created a small media storm when he paid the $222 necessary to extract a magnetic tape copy of the state's database of license plates from the Division of Motor Vehicles (DMV), wrote a script to search the database, and put the whole thing up on his World-Wide Web pages so any visitor could type in a license plate and get back the owner's full name and address. His motive, he said on the page at the time, was personal: he wanted to speed up tracking down motorists who whizzed dangerously down the street where his little sister liked to play. The data were, as Nabil pointed out, readily available to anyone who walked into a DMV office and paid $4 for an individual record. But many people didn't realize how public this information really was until it was placed on the Net. The risks that this kind of public access—as well as services like Switchboard and Four11, which provide the equivalent of nationwide telephone directories, some of them with easy access to local street maps—poses to individuals from potential stalkers or known abusers should be obvious. None these are data that couldn't be found easily offline, but the effort it would take to assemble the information might deter some.[16]

Americans are particularly vulnerable to this because the country has so few privacy laws. But given the Net's international character, even stiffer laws like the European Community's planned data protection directive may not be able to offer much protection. The directive will cover data collected in or exported from a European country—for example, a German subsidiary office wanting to send marketing data on to its American headquarters may run into problems because of the United States's lack of regulations concerning its use. But no amount of European legislation can cover a Web site based in the Philippines using a .COM address and collecting personal information directly, and that company would be free to sell on that data however it likes. It's not a difficult situation to imagine: the site might be conducting medical or other surveys, where the visitor believes there will be some benefit in filling in the form. And people do supply the most incredible information about themselves online without asking many questions: the *Survey.net* site, for example, has collected a huge range of personal responses covering everything from drug use to masturbation.[17]

The ready availability of search engines also has its downside. They have aggregated what were thought to be ephemeral communications into great repositories of personal profiles. On the Usenet archiving service Deja News,[18] you can hit a button to display a listing of all the postings made from a particular email address back to March 1995—a time when surely everyone expected their words to be expunged after a few days. A similar service, Reference.com,[19] searches mailing lists, whose members typically expect their comments to be seen only by other members. It can't be long before personnel directors start using these services to check out prospective employees—tomorrow's equivalent of today's failed urine test may be the discovery that you once posted a message to *alt.drugs*.

Meanwhile, the Net's technical direction poses a different set of problems. The same graphical interfaces that make computers easier to use for the non-technical also demand more powerful computers and make disabled access more difficult. The common denominator of the Net used to be text; older systems such as CIX, the WELL, and most BBSs demand that you interact with them by typing in commands. One of the earliest Web browsers, Lynx, is still used on such systems to access the Web. It's not as easy or pleasant as pointing and clicking, but it does the job. And, more importantly, text can be fed into a text-to-speech processor or displayed on a Braille output device for the blind, or magnified for the partially sighted. Probably about a quarter of the Web's users browse using only text at least some of the time, either because they're limited to a Lynx system or because they turn off the graphics (and therefore the ads) in order to get pages to download faster; try this and you quickly find how many developers don't bother to insert text to display instead of graphics (via the ALT tag in the formatting language for Web pages, HTML, added after campaigning by the Yuri Rubinsky Insight Foundation) so text-based users can navigate.[20] The W3 Consortium, the MIT-based group that manages the Web's future, is well aware of the problems the Net poses for disabled access as audio and video are deployed and is working to form an worldwide coalition to cover this area, but the effort is in its infancy.[21]

In the meantime, a set of professional standards needs to be defined. Few people, when they open an account on an online service or Internet provider, think about what will happen if they decide to close it in order to change services. There are no standards governing ISPs' responsibility for forwarding email after the account is closed. I don't know of any that even offer such a service, even though forwarding is standard in the postal and telephone industries. There isn't even any agreement on what constitutes Internet access. If a provider says it offers a certain speed of connection from its servers to the Internet, should it be required to submit its claim to third-party certification? A situation like this arose in the United Kingdom in 1995, when a small outfit based in the south of England conned even some experienced online users into believing it had large amounts of bandwidth; the truth was it had one small 64K line to a bigger service provider, which eventually shut it off for not paying its bills. Similarly, should a commercial Web site charging fees for access be required to guarantee a certain level of performance for its subscribers? What information about its service standards, protocols, and security measures should an ISP be required to divulge to its subscribers?

None of these areas have yet been considered as ones where governments or independent commissions might regulate the Net, and yet they are fundamental questions. When it comes to considering universal service, there are more, some of which are being discussed. Should the online industry be required to finance expansion of the Net into areas that otherwise will be deprived of access? What should constitute a basic Internet connection? In areas where there is only one provider, are there basic services it should be required to supply? One British ISP announced at the end of 1996, for example, that it was going to drop its entire Usenet feed because it refused to supply access to pornography. Leaving aside the fact that this is a more or less meaningless gesture (as well as a gross exaggeration) in Net terms, if this ISP were the only one available to a region full of users, should it be allowed to make such a decision? Businesses may prefer the Web because it more closely models the media they're familiar with, but Usenet is the town square of the Internet. The only question that has received significant attention is that of ISP liability in cases of copyright infringement or the distribution of illegal, offensive, or defamatory material. For the rest, the focus has generally been on what material to block, not what should be made available.

The same problems that exist on a domestic scale are replicated worldwide. Varying intellectual property laws around the world mean that pressure is being placed on countries like China to crack down on software piracy; India, Thailand, and Brazil don't recognize pharmaceutical patents; and not all countries have the same laws Western countries do about trademarks, marks of origin, and unfair competition. In a survey of these differences, law student Nicolas S. Gikkas concludes, "No doubt the Western legal tradition of intellectual property rights will be foisted on developing countries as the price of admission into the world market controlled by the countries of North America and Europe."[22]

That may not, as former World Health Organization (WHO) medical officer Christopher Zielinski points out, be a good thing.[23] Just as politicians and major corporations moving onto the Web seem to have difficulty grasping that the most important characteristic of the Net is its two-way nature, Western countries seem to assume that information resources follow the same pattern as economics. Zielinski believes it is a reflection of existing prejudice to presume that all the useful information is going to flow from the First World to the Third. He points to the history of scientific research where, in a vicious circle, non-Western research doesn't get indexed, so it doesn't get cited or widely reviewed, so it's even less likely to get indexed.

An August 1995 article in *Scientific American* traced the results of these subtle barriers and prejudices: "Although developing countries encompass 24.1 percent of the world's scientists and 5.3 percent of its research spending, most leading journals publish far smaller proportions of articles by authors from these regions." Research from Third World science journals made up only 2.5 percent of the Science Citation index in 1980; by 1994 it had fallen by 40 percent.[24]

With new diseases traveling from the Third World to the developed world, local research may be especially important. While at the WHO, Zielinski pioneered a relatively low-cost CD-ROM based indexing service of 223 journals; the revenue from the disk was split among the journals, and researchers were allowed to copy articles free of charge. Similar initiatives were started in the fields of agriculture and general science and technology. In 1996, Zielinski negotiated to make the CD-ROM's full text available on the Internet.[25]

If there is endemic prejudice by peer reviewers, it won't go away just because the journals are more accessible. And while the Net can help by making all types of scientific research more accessible, it won't if major databases of periodicals remain under corporate control. Much of America's court decisions, for example, are indexed by Westlaw, which claims copyright on the system of citations it uses. Proposals for revamping science publishing to speed up the system and provide better and wider peer review have already suggested schemes for authenticating reviewers' comments, which might reinforce, rather than revamp, the current system by specifying reviewer qualifications that reflect our existing prejudices.[26]

Zielinski, meanwhile, is equally concerned that new levels of copyright protection will choke off access to knowledge for anyone who can't pay Western rates for them. "My picture of the information superhighway," he wrote in 1996, "is a one-way flow of traffic coming down both lanes and both sides of the road from the West. The traffic on this road consists of locked security vans stretching to the horizon, steered by armed guards who speak only in cryptograms and credit card numbers. The only ordinary vehicles are being driven by a few obsessives, nerds, saintly aunts and crazed deviants. There is nothing moving in the opposite direction, no equal and opposite flow of Third World information from the South, no contraflow of counter culture."[27] Zielinski recommends a system of local pricing, free access to scientific and medical information, and free dissemination of information across the Internet, because, he notes, "information that is essential to human wellbeing should be freely accessible to all."

14

The Net Is Dead

Reports of my death have been greatly exaggerated.
—Mark Twain, in a cable
from London to the Associated Press

It's axiomatic that at any given time, someone somewhere on the Net is predicting its imminent demise. If it's not the apocryphal modem tax (a rumor that recycles around the Net about as often as Dave Barry's column on the beached whale they blew up in Oregon or the long-since recovered Craig Shergold's dying request for business cards), it's death by regulation, mismanagement, or lack of bandwidth, the measure of how much data can flow across a connection at a time.

High bandwidth means lots of data; video and audio that a user can interact with in real time, that is, instantaneously, are high-bandwidth applications. Barry's text column is small, a page or so of text taking up only a few kilobytes of computer memory or disk storage space; the three-minute video clip of the Oregon TV news coverage of the exploding whale takes up 11.7 megabytes, enough memory or disk space to hold twenty-three copies of this entire book, and demands a lot of bandwidth if you want to be able to watch it as if your PC and the Internet were a giant broadcasting system. When, in 1994, I retrieved the file via FTP, it took more than an hour to transmit to my computer.

Bandwidth (and where more of it is going to come from) is intimately bound up with the political and legal questions of equal access. The key issue is who is going to pay for it. A growing lobby is claiming that the Internet's cooperative structure can't work in a future of high-bandwidth applications such as real-time voice and video, and that the Net will shortly be swamped by its own success if it doesn't "grow up" and adopt a pricing structure that more accurately reflects the costs of expansion.

One of the more vocal members of this group is networking company

3Com founder Bob Metcalfe, inventor of Ethernet, the world's most popular local area networking standard, and now a columnist for *Info World*. In his acceptance speech for the Electric Frontier Foundation's 1996 Pioneer award for his inventions, Metcalfe hit the assembled Net lovers at the 1996 Computers, Freedom, and Privacy Conference with a shocking prediction: the Internet would start to collapse in 1996. Quizzed a little more closely, he modified this statement. It wouldn't exactly collapse, but it would start experiencing the network equivalent of the blackouts and brownouts the power grid sees when it gets overloaded. In the ensuing months, when Netcom and America Online (AOL) both experienced major downtimes (AOL for more than nineteen hours one day in August), a lot of people took that as evidence that he was right.

But these networks are not the Internet; they are just some of the many networks attached to the Internet. AOL later attributed its long outage to configuration errors: the service was installing high-capacity switches within its local area network when its network access provider, ANS, misconfigured routing information destined for AOL. Because the entire system was down, the diagnostic systems that might have caught the error were not in place, and it took many hours for technicians to identify what was wrong and reconfigure the routers.[1] Members were given a free hour on the service in compensation, but as many commentators pointed out, if you had come to depend on email, a free hour on the service doesn't go any distance at all in recompensing you for a day's lost work.

However, it is probably accurate to say that AOL's problem might not have happened in an earlier era, when its system was smaller and updates and tweaks could be done by hand. It certainly would have mattered less with fewer people dependent on the service specifically and email in general. In the automated system now necessary because of the service's size, no one knew what had happened. A couple of months earlier, Netcom was out for five hours with, reportedly, a similar problem. These stories also highlighted how many points of failure there are for Internet connections, which depend on the electricity supply and telephone connections, as well as the reliability of the Internet service providers (ISPs) on both ends of the correspondence.

In a paper presented at MIT in September 1996, research affiliate Sharon Eisner Gillett and Lotus founder and EFF co-founder Mitch Kapor examined the organization and management of the Internet and concluded that 99 percent of the Internet's management could be—was designed to be—handled by automated means.[2] The remaining 1 percent includes tasks such as coordinating routing when there are software errors, creating standards for protocols and service quality, and coordinating the assignment of domain names and addresses. Gillett and Kapor argued that any proposals for change should distribute authority to avoid creating situations where resources are scarce (as in defining protocols that limit the number of available new addresses, for example) and provide a path for technical evolution, which they see as key to keeping the Net alive.[3]

Although Metcalfe was made to eat his words publicly in early 1997, lots of complaints about the Internet did surface in 1996. But they didn't come from users, who continued to flock online even though it meant learning why the World-Wide Web is so often called the World-Wide Wait. Rather, they came from the telephone companies, who complained that the combination of flat-rate pricing for Internet access and free—or at least, flat-rate—local calling encouraged users to stay online for lengths of time far beyond those the network was designed to manage. Just how big a difference was explained to the Federal Communications Commission (FCC) Bandwidth Forum, a January 23, 1997, meeting that assembled the points of view of a variety of telephone and online industry figures as well as consumer advocates.

Lee Bauman, vice president of local competition for Pacific Telesis, summarized the problems his company faced in grappling with California's 1 million active Internet users, who averaged sixty-two minutes a day connected to their ISPs whereas average residential customers typically originated only twenty-two minutes' worth of calls. "We last year had 23 billion minutes of use going to Internet access providers in California," he told the meeting, estimating that the company would have to spend $130 million in 1997 to beef up its network to handle the increased traffic. "We believe that a good portion of that money could be much better spent for the benefit of the country in building the new forms of data networks."[4]

The telephone companies' preferred solution is to charge ISPs, or "enhanced service providers," usage charges for access to the phone network, charges that presumably would be passed on to Internet users in the form of per-minute access fees. This would reverse five years of falling prices for online services of all types, and the concern is that higher costs might mean inhibiting the growth of the Internet.

This is not just a theoretical assumption: Internet use has grown much more slowly both in rural America, where users frequently have to pay long-distance charges for access, and the world beyond North America, where local calls are metered and charged by the minute. Conversely, when AOL switched from metered, per-minute charging to a flat-rate plan at the beginning of December 1996, the service immediately got blocked up by users who went online and stayed there. Discovering that it could be difficult to get through to the busied-out service, some users apparently began camping out online for even longer periods. AOL's CEO, Steve Case, begged AOLers to be responsible and log off as quickly as possible until the service could be upgraded; within weeks, junk email was going out advertising a program to keep your AOL connection open continuously.

Commenting on the Bandwidth Forum discussion, Shabbir Safdar, co-founder of the lobbying organization Voter Telecom Watch, wrote in the organization's newsletter, "At risk is the actual design of the Internet. Will it continue to be open and available to anyone with a computer and modem, or will it be stratified by pricing such that it is available to fewer people than are [*sic*] available today?"[5] Of the telephone companies' specific suggestion for usage charges, he wrote,

> This solution places the majority of the cost on today's Internet users and businesses without adequately defining what the money will go to pay for. Worse, it runs the risk of focusing costs on a single group for a benefit that will be appreciated by everyone today and in the future.
>
> This is analogous to a city bus that gets a flat tire on the way to work. The solution isn't to ask everyone on the bus at that moment to pitch in to pay for the new tire. However it isn't inappropriate to build the price of the new tire into the overall fee structure for the city's bus system.

In an aside, he adds, "Let's not kill the Net just so we can get broadcast-quality video into grandma's house."

Telephone access charges, however, were not what Metcalfe had in mind, because he wasn't talking about congestion on the telephone network. He was talking about the many ways he figured the Internet could die—overloading, sabotage (by hackers or even ISPs fighting for market share), the advent of audio and video, or the bugs he's convinced will surface in the software that runs on routers, the computers that figure out where traffic is supposed to go. The first of those he attributed to the absence of what he called a "messaging system" between supply and demand, and what he had in mind as a solution was to introduce "settlement."[6]

Settlement is the financial structure underpinning the workings of the post office and the telephone companies. When you drop a letter in the mail box that's destined for, say, Britain, you pay the U.S. postal service to carry it to your destination. The British postal service, however, carries the letter for part of its journey and bills the United States service for that portion. Long-distance phone calling works the same way. Huge sums of money change hands in settlement payments each year; according to The Economist, in 1994 U.S. phone companies paid out a net $4.3 billion to foreign carriers.[7]

On the Internet, life is a barter system: service providers carry each other's traffic without payment on a cooperative basis, and everyone is more or less equal. This principle lets you send an email message to Australia as cheaply as to the kid next door, and it makes real-time voice connections—known as the Internet phone—no more expensive than browsing the World-Wide Web.

The Internet phone is a good example of the bandwidth-hogging applications of the future. You hook a microphone and sound board to your PC, install one of several readily available software programs, and either log onto a Web site and see who's available to talk or, with more recent products, dial an ordinary telephone number. Some Netheads who are online all the time use the Internet phone as their normal telephone—essentially, you just page them for a private conversation. The telephone companies will tell you that the quality isn't as good as their direct connections, and while that's true there's something about paying local call rates to talk long distance that attracts people. In June 1996, the American Carriers Telecommunication Association, an organization of 130 long–distance carriers and local phone companies, got riled enough by it to petition the FCC to step in and stop the growth of Internet telephony.

But settlement may be more of a new set of problems than a solution. For one thing, it might well split the Net, because not all service providers will agree to accept such a system. For another, chances are good that the financial burdens of installing the necessary administration and accounting systems would land disproportionately on the smaller service providers; one reason so many direct ISPs charge flat rates is that they are cheap to administer. There are more reasons than just increased access costs for Net users to be concerned about this; the best protection for net.freedoms is as much decentralization as possible. High administration costs would make it more likely that the Net would wind up in the hands of just a few big players. To some extent this is happening already: although there are still an estimated 3,000 ISPs in the United States alone, some are consolidating and others are expanding overseas. The leading U.S. domestic ISP, Netcom, has opened up in the United Kingdom and Brazil; CompuServe is worldwide; AOL has opened international services with partners in the United Kingdom and Germany; Britain's Pipex has been swallowed up twice by progressively larger U.S. telecommunications companies; and Microsoft has alliances with just about everybody.

Ironically, the suggestion that the Internet should adopt settlement comes at a time when, according to the *Economist*,[8] the telephone industry is considering scrapping settlement in favor of a sender-keeps-all system. American companies complain that they are subsidizing inefficient foreign carriers by having to fork out those billions every year. At the same time, the magazine notes, the much higher cost of leased lines outside the United States means that it's more expensive for those countries to add bandwidth than it is for the United States to do the same. Since about 60 percent of all Internet sites are in the United States, connecting to the United States is a higher priority for non-American carriers than connecting to the rest of the world is for Americans. The upshot is that the costs of upgrading international bandwidth fall disproportionately on overseas carriers, who complain that the rest of the planet is subsidizing the United States. Until the United States cares as much about connecting to the rest of the world as the rest of the world cares about connecting to the United States, this situation is likely to remain.

In a massive article for *Wired* on the laying of the world's longest wire—the first privately financed (by a consortium of companies including Nynex, New York–based Gulf Associates, and others from Saudi Arabic and Japan) high-capacity fiber optic cable from the United Kingdom to Japan—science fiction writer Neal Stephenson pointed out that settlement has also backfired on the telephone companies in the form of "callback" services, which take advantage of the price differentials between the United States and elsewhere.[9] Someone subscribing to such a service in London, for example, dials a computer in the United States, which immediately dials back with an open line from which the caller can dial out to any number. Even from London, which probably has some of the cheapest telephone rates outside the United States, such services can cut the cost of a call to a third of the price. Such services are illegal in many places, but just as Netheads find ways to alter spellings to bypass computerized censors, the callback services find ways to counter blocking mechanisms local telephone companies put in place. Given the international nature of the Internet and its connections, it's hard to see how the Internet equivalent of such services could be stopped if settlement became a way of life on the Net.

Another problem with settlement is how to charge. Services like CompuServe ran complex, tiered pricing schemes for years. On CompuServe, you pay for the amount of time you spend in some areas and the amount of material you download in others. Contributing files is free. But that's on a single proprietary system that was designed from the outset to handle such billing. The Internet was not so designed, and is not a single system that can be easily metered. Charging by the amount of traffic is also a complex matter on something like the Web, where a user may send a tiny amount of information one way—a URL—and get an unpredictably large amount back. Charging by the packet wouldn't lead anywhere useful, since each one is acknowledged by the return of another packet.

At least some of the bandwidth problem posed by the Internet phone and other applications such as video conferencing via products like CU-SeeMe, fancy advertising using Java, complex graphics, computer animations, and the potential resource guzzling of automated software agents and robots[10] will be solved technically. Better compression to cut down on the amount of data, local storage of popular audio and video files, and new developments such as satellite broadcasting of some sites will take some of the load off the Net. But part of the solution has to be structural: if millions of people worldwide use the Internet for real-time multimedia applications the network will have to be upgraded to cope—particularly if, as many old-time Netizens hope, there are to be two-way broadband connections to each home so that any consumer can also be a publisher. Ironically, the same advertising that may sponsor free content on the Net may add to access costs by requiring bigger bandwidth. The money to create that will have to come from someplace, and if it's going to come from commercial entities such as telephone companies they want evidence that they will be able to make the money back. Charging ISPs for access to the phone network is one way; being able to sell information services such as video on demand and home shopping (if you count those as information) is another.

Speaking at the FCC Bandwidth Forum, James Love pointed out that at the same time the telephone companies were complaining about congestion caused by ISPs' flat-rate connections, those same phone companies were trying to get into the business of selling flat-rate Internet access. Pacific Bell, for example, the worst-affected phone company, was simultaneously offering cut rates on installing second home telephone lines, with an offer of five months' free Internet access thrown in. Similar schizophrenia seems to be repeated in telephone companies around the world. The head of British Telecom's research labs, Peter Cochrane, has complained bitterly many times that the Internet is a "parasite." And yet, British Telecom itself is in the flat-rate Internet access business and by early 1997 had lowered its prices to match those of the original low-cost British domestic ISP, Demon.

But telephone companies live in what they must think are strange and disturbing times, as country after country sheds its regulated telephone monopoly in favor of new competition. AT&T got MCI, Sprint, and ACC to compete with; British Telecom got Mercury in the long-distance market and, in the market for local calls, Britain's new cable companies, which are offering the first free local calling the country has ever had. True, this service is limited to evenings and weekends and to calls between subscribers to the same cable company (the country is divided up by region), but it's a start. Meanwhile, direct satellite services are talking about using some of their spare capacity to broadcast the most popular Web sites, a few electric companies are experimenting with delivering entertainment and information services, the privately financed Britain–Japan fiber optic cable is challenging the phone companies' traditional hegemony over the telecommunications infrastructure, and wireless networks are the most likely telecommunications future for Third World countries where building the kind of wired telecommunications infrastructure we take for granted in the West is too expensive.[11] According to 2600, getting a telephone line in São Paolo, Brazil, can cost $2,000 to $6,000 (or $1,200 if you're willing to wait a couple of years) compared to $300 for a cellphone.[12]

These changing times have led to a large amount of cross-ownership, which is another potential threat to the Net's current, decentralized infrastructure, just as cross-ownership has put much of the media into the hands of a few large players. Shortly after the Telecommunications Act passed, several of the so-called "Baby Bells," the regional telephone companies formed in the wake of the 1982 court-ordered break-up of AT&T, forged alliances; the same companies have bought local wireless networks, and, in the case of Nynex, even expanded overseas by buying cable companies—Nynex owns a number of the United Kingdom's cable franchises.

It doesn't help that there is a fundamental difference of approach between the telephone networks and the Internet. Telephone networks are circuit-switched. When you place a call, you open a two-way circuit to the person you're calling, and that circuit belongs to you until the call is finished. In a human conversation, as MIT Media Lab director and *Wired* columnist Nicholas Negroponte likes to say, silence is meaningful. The Internet, however, is a packet-switched network. Any data that gets sent, whether voice, text, or full-motion video, gets divided up into little packets that take any available route to their destination, where they are reassembled into the original message. The consequence is that the Internet is inherently more efficient in the way it sends data; but there is a price, however slight, in terms of the time it takes to do all that work. Further, running an Internet connection over a dial-up phone line is inherently wasteful: all that silence spent reading a Web page is not meaningful to the computer at the other end.

At the FCC Bandwidth Forum, Love raised another point having to do with the number of people who can be connected at any one time. Any network is engineered to handle only a percentage of its paid users at a time—even on Mother's Day just after the rates go down, the whole country doesn't get on the phone at once. The telephone network is engineered to handle about one-seventh of its customers at a time, while most ISPs have enough modems, or ports, to accommodate 5 to 10 percent of their subscribers. AOL was an exception: its metered per-minute rates limited its members' usage, and until the switch to flat-rate pricing it got away with much lower levels of access provision, roughly 3 percent. The $350 million infrastructure upgrade AOL announced in January 1997, for completion in July 1997, would take the service only up to the lower end of that industry standard. Love's argument was that even the high end of ISPs' network provision, 10 percent, was lower than the one in seven Bell Atlantic was claiming.

Settlement is not the only pricing option that has been proposed. Hal Varian, an economist at the University of California at Berkeley, has been arguing for some years that the Net needs priority-based pricing, which would give higher-quality service to those willing to pay for it. In a sense, this type of service is arriving already with the private, value-added networks being built by companies like IBM and GEIS, which sell data network services at a higher price, promising better security and faster transmission in return. These services route data over their own networks as far as possible, handing over to the Internet, if necessary, at the last possible moment. But Varian points out that this structure of alternative networks doesn't suit the home-based consumer, who ideally should have a choice of quality of service over a single line.[13]

Bill Washburn, the founder of the Commercial Internet Exchange, an industry body usually known as CIX set up in 1991 to promote the commercialization of the Internet, believes a lot of the talk of doom is misplaced. "I think this is just a recent variation on the Net Is Dead comment —or the Net Is Dying or the Net Is About to Die—that they've been saying for years. It's a tradition—this will kill the Net."[14] He believes that the current pricing structure has been a vital one: "Flat-rate pricing made new kinds of activities and services possible and freed the imagination."

Nonetheless, it may be too easy for Netheads to trust that whatever application they come up with will eventually attract the bandwidth it needs by some kind of divine mandate, and to underestimate the risks of placing all their faith in what is arguably a Heath Robinson contraption.

As Stephenson traced the his way through the Middle East and the wilds of Cornwall, he studied the map of international connections and concluded: "Netheads have heard so much puffery about the robust nature of the Internet and its amazing ability to route around obstacles that they frequently have a grossly inflated conception of how many routes packets can take between continents and how much bandwidth those routes can carry." In mid-1996, the entire state of Minnesota was cut off from the rest of the Net, he notes, when its single primary connection went down. "If Minnesota, of all places, is so vulnerable, one can imagine how tenuous many international links must be."[15]

15

Networks of Trust

> "Did you see me come into your shop?"
> "Yes, I did."
> "Good. Now, have you ever seen me in your life before?"
> "Never in my life."
> "Then how do you know it is *me*?"
>
> —Idries Shah, *The Pleasantries*
> *of the Incredible Mulla Nastrudin*

Sometime in 1996 a London reporter emailed Bill Gates to check a fact. The point is not that he got an answer at 3 A.M. Seattle time, nor that Gates ought to have had better things to do. It's that this is the utopian vision of the Net: it flattens the world so you can talk to anyone and be heard. The middlemen can be put on a spaceship and sent to crash on another planet, like they were in the *Hitchhiker's Guide to the Galaxy*.

The startling thing about this story is that it happened in 1996, by which time that utopian vision was already being drowned. It's really the kind of story that harks back to when the Net was young, when a person could read all of Usenet in a single day, sending an email message required knowing the names of all the machines it had to pass through to reach its destination, and the Net community was so small and homogeneous that you could trust that any email that came in was going to be worth the trouble of reading it. Now, with millions of email addresses, long-time email users get megabytes of the stuff, email software comes with automated filtering and re-routing features, and secretaries are back in business.

Everywhere you look on the Net you see the same story: the simple volume of data makes it impossible to read or assimilate everything, and even the search engines that are supposed to make meaningful selections from that data do the job badly, especially compared to traditional library indexing systems. There's a parallel problem with people and businesses: whereas in a small community, online or real, you assume that everyone you meet is trustworthy unless proven otherwise, in a large one, you assume the reverse. The difficulty is that no matter how infinite and populated cyberspace becomes, it always feels small, partly because we experience it in the privacy of our own computers, and partly because everywhere you look people are dividing themselves up into small groups: newsgroups (which often split if they get too big), conferences, IRC channels and chat rooms, and now small online discussions on Web sites organized around those sites' official content.

In times like these, trust is precious: trust that when my computer links to yours your security will be good enough that my system won't be compromised; trust that the information I receive and pass on is accurate and true; trust that if I give you personal information about myself I won't find my privacy betrayed. As we've already seen, these are not simple things in a world mediated by technology. But the hardest one, as the Internet experiments with what works and what doesn't, is trust that your communication will be worth my time. As trust erodes, it's middlemen who will fill the gap and sell our trust back to us. They will be the brokers in the new power structure that is already forming on and around the Net, however much people might like to think that all Netizens will always have an equal shot in the meritocracy of ideas. The advent of electronic commerce is hastening the change: companies know that in order to trade successfully online, customers will have to believe they are trustworthy, both in terms of handling customer data and in terms of the quality of their merchandise.

This is an area where familiar names have a huge advantage. The mythology of the Net is that it equalizes competition, so that a Mom-and-Pop outfit in Singapore has the same reach as General Motors. In intellectual property, that may be at least partly true: companies like Netscape, Superscape (a publisher of virtual reality software), games publisher id Software, and many other companies got to their multi-million-dollar status by sending out their products over the Net and letting people try them. But would you buy digital cash for more than a trivial amount of real money from a company whose physical address you didn't know? Even though what we now think of as "real" money spends most of its time in cyberspace as the ones and zeros that ultimately make up computer data, to turn over that money you have to believe that the virtual banking outfit is trustworthy and that there will be enough places to spend that digital cash for you to get your money's worth. As the Net continues to grow and evolve, people will have more and more at stake, personally, professionally, and financially; the more there is at stake, the more necessary third parties will be for such familiar functions from the real world as authentication, verification, and credit checking.

A. Michael Froomkin, who has written several papers on the legal problems posed by the Net, says, "I think there are going to be a lot of things that you wouldn't do in your right mind without a middleman."[1] He sees these middlemen as enablers.

As Froomkin points out in his paper "The Essential Role of Trusted Third Parties in Electronic Commerce,"[2] third parties are already setting up shop in the area of authentication and verification: certifying a company or personal digital signature—essentially, notary services for the Net—or verifying for a vendor that your digital wallet is good for the $4.50 you want to spend (that latter function is designed into most digital cash schemes). Credit card companies are also scrambling to figure out how they could handle microbilling, that is, charging tiny amounts—a tenth of a cent, say, to pick up the tennis results every day, or a nickel to listen to a radio program. A lot of sites would love to implement something like this, but no one's quite figured out how yet because transaction costs are too high. Microbilling would open a lot of commercial possibilities for electronic content beyond the current models, which are generally limited to subscription, advertising sponsorship, and no-charge. With microbilling, you could charge someone as little as a fraction of a penny to, say, use a special font just once in a document being formatted.[3] A 1996 Forrester Group report predicts the rise of Internet transaction brokers,[4] whose function would be to consolidate these purchases into a single bill—also a possible future role for the traditional online services, especially CompuServe, which has long had structures in place to aggregate charges, albeit somewhat larger ones.

The W3 Consortium, which guides the development of the Web from its home base at the Laboratory of Computer Science at MIT, has drafted a proposed standard for microbilling called the Micro Payment Transfer Protocol. In the draft, a third-party broker would keep accounts for both the customer and the merchant.[5]

Other payment systems take different approaches, but all involve the intervention of third parties in one way or another.[6] The SET (Secure Electronic Transaction) standard, developed by companies like Master-Card, Visa, and IBM, adds a layer of security for both parties of a transaction using existing credit card accounts and banks. Credit card users don't give participating merchants actual credit card numbers, but rather identifiers that the merchant can present for verification to the bank, which also dispenses a certified receipt to the purchaser. The first trials using SET began in January 1997, when the combination of MasterCard, IBM, and Danish Payment Systems opened their doors to between 500 and 1,000 customers in Denmark.

Also based on existing financial services is CyberCash, which allows a user to select from a list of already registered credit cards and authenticates the transaction for both merchant and customer, also certifying the agreement of both merchant and customer to the exact details of the transaction. A CyberCoin system, available only in the United States in early 1997, gives customers an electronic wallet from which smaller amounts—under ten dollars—can be spent.

Financial third parties are only the beginning. The many proposals for key escrow (or "key recovery," as Clinton dubbed it in his December 1996 policy announcement) will require trusted third parties to store and manage cryptographic keys. Even if key escrow doesn't become an international regulatory requirement, there are so many good reasons to escrow keys that there is going to be demand for those services.

Placing large numbers of cryptographic keys—which in a digital world will be our identities—in the hands of trusted third parties is going to create a new set of institutions with the kind of power and responsibilities currently associated with banks. (In fact, European proposals for trusted third parties have tended to assume that those parties would be the traditional banks.) The original Clipper proposals expected that keys would be escrowed with two government departments; one objection to these centralized stores was how much of a target they would be for criminals and spies. It would be more in keeping with the decentralized nature of the Net to opt for diversity and user choice. Some people ask a friend to hold copies of their house keys or store their money in the freezer; why shouldn't I choose to store a copy of my cryptographic key in my lawyer's safe or in a friend's kitchen drawer? With or without mandatory key escrow, building an infrastructure for escrowing and managing keys is an area demanding a carefully thought-out legal framework. No company—and there will be businesses built on key escrow services even if they don't become mandatory—is going to go into this sort of business without a clear understanding of what its liability will be in a case a key is lost, damaged, or stolen.

John Brimacombe, managing director of Cambridge-based Jobstream PLC, a company specializing in financial services with a particular interest in cryptography, is one of those energetic individuals who sees commercial opportunities for even small companies everywhere he looks. Of trusted third parties, he says, "One of the essences of trust is that it's a personal relationship. The bigger the organization the more impersonal it is. The desire to understand the organization you've trusted with your secrets is a reason for having smaller escrow providers" (telephone interview, 1996). Governments may be thinking in terms of banks, but if you have something as private and sensitive as the key to your most intimate communications, who would you rather kept it for you? Your bank, where probably no one knows you? Microsoft? Brimacombe, who is interested in becoming a trusted third party, believes that along with that go a panoply of ancillary services, such as authenticating transactions along the lines of notaries public, providing data backup and storage, and mediating contract negotiations online.

Companies are already beginning to operate in the related area of certification. Here the idea is that an individual Net surfer could be issued a certificate that guarantees some particular fact or group of facts about that surfer's identity. In the case of Adult Check, the service that sprang up in the wake of the passage of the Communications Decency Act, you pay $9.95 (by credit card) for a one-year ID certifying that you're over twenty-one. Then, when you want to visit any of the roughly 200 (rather sleazy) Web sites that accept Adult Check, you just type in the ID number and the site checks that it's valid without having to know anything more about you. Adult Check promises to keep all data confidential, and the Web sites can show prosecutors they are making the effort to keep out minors.

A more interesting example of third-party digital identification is the RSA Data Security spin-off VeriSign, the first commercial certificate authority.[7] As of early 1997, they offered three classes of certificates, the simplest of which just attests that a user's email ID is unique. The next level verifies your street address and a few other personal details. The third requires personal presence or registered credentials.

When someone applies for an ID, VeriSign uses a public-key cryptographic system to generate the usual pair of public and private keys (see chapter 4). The company then sends the registrant a personal identification number via email, which, when entered at the Web site, unlocks access to the user's new digital ID. This ID contains the user's public key —the one the user can give out—along with whatever public information about the user is appropriate for the class of certificate the user has chosen. The ID is signed with VeriSign's private key, which is kept on a secure server. Any time someone wants to check the ID's authenticity, they can do so, through facilities at the Web site.

VeriSign's IDs are intended to be used for all sorts of authentication, such as verifying the source of email, identifying paid-up customers to Web sites, gaining access to virtual private networks (secure business-to-business networks operated over the insecure public Internet), and guaranteeing the origins of downloaded software. In early 1997 VeriSign claimed to have issued 500,000 such IDs to individuals and another 14,000 to Web sites.

This is an area that will benefit from industry standardization, so that you could choose an organization you already trust and tell your browser to accept only certificates issued by that organization. Or, using IDs issued by an outfit like VeriSign, which issues several classes of certificates, you might want to set the browser to refuse financial transactions in which the other party's certificate isn't, say, level two or better. That kind of setup would build a Web of trust in much the way the Internet itself has grown up; the advantage would be a much tougher cyber-societal fabric than the hierarchical structures most businesses today are used to. Widely accepted digital IDs should also add a layer of convenience: instead of filling out a new form at every Web site and being issued with a new ID and password to forget, you fill out one form once and use the digital ID thereafter. (It's fair to say, however, that any time we try to automate anything we find ourselves frustratedly coming up against the problem that computers just aren't flexible the way humans are. It's easy to imagine a setup where your browser will not let you carry out an urgent transaction because it's one penny over the limit you've set. We will be living in interesting times while that sort of thing gets figured out.)

Another type of central registration scheme with a wholly different purpose in mind is DoubleClick,[8] an advertising network set up early in 1996 when a division of the New York ad agency Poppe Tyson merged with a small software start-up. The result is a network of some thirty sites including those belonging to companies like Intuit and General Electric and advertisers like IBM, Intel, and United Parcel Service. DoubleClick's service offers a demographic twist: the company maintains a database of Internet users that tracks their specific interests. When one of the claimed 6.5 million users in that database lands on a DoubleClick site, the company's software looks up the user's email address and produces customized ads that are supposed to appeal specifically to that user. Advertising companies pay by the number of impressions (hits) delivered, which DoubleClick tracks. Naturally, this is behavior that's seen by a number of Netheads as intrusive, so there are now anonymizing services such as the Anonymizer and Privnet,[9] both of which block the site's ability to retrieve information about visiting users.

Many Net surfers don't realize it, but the average Web site can tell what browser you're using, what domain you're coming from, and what type of computer and operating system you're using, as well as what pages you looked at and for how long. A lot of Web sites put this information into a small bit of text called a "cookie" and store it on your hard drive, to streamline your next visit to their site, which some people feel is an invasion of privacy.[10] No one's suggested it (yet), but in the way of the Net it's easy to imagine a future in which Net surfers could choose among several different types of centralized registration services to gain access to the same networks of commercial Web sites. One service might charge you extra but give you freedom from advertising; another might give you free access to content as long as you accept advertising with it; a third might pay you a tiny percentage in return for your personal details and the right to rent them out to direct marketers as part of a commercial database.

More traditional anonymizing services, used to protect the real-world identity of emailers and Usenet posters, introduce another class of middlemen. Services that assign a permanent pseudonym, as Julf Helsingius's *anon.penet.fi* did, allow users to interact over long periods. As Helsingius noted when explaining the reasons for closing his server,[11] such services must work with the law if they are to survive in the long term. A different situation applies to anonymizing services that strip all identifying information, keep no logs, and allow users to post but not receive replies. Hackers, who are some of the interested users of these systems, keep tabs on the systems' throughput and security level. However the servers work, you have to trust the owner's integrity, security, and determination not to hand over personal information to police or other questioners without the proper court or other orders. There would, after all, be some impressive scope for a blackmailer running an anonymous server and keeping tabs on its users.

Advertising is already bringing a whole new class of middlemen to the Net: specialist ad agencies such as DoubleClick and Burst! Media, which match Web sites with buyers.[12] Burst!'s approach is a bit different from

DoubleClick's, in that it specifically has chosen to work with smaller companies and sites. Burst! matches advertisers to its network of more than 500 sites by looking for network members whose demographics fit the advertiser's desired profile. The company characterizes its sites as independent content producers—homegrown sites covering topics like genealogy, fashion, fishing, or gourmet cooking.

Jarvis Coffin, Burst!'s president and a former director of advertising for the *Los Angeles Times*, says, "We are entirely betting on the fact that the Internet is going to be about a tremendous diversity of content" (telephone interview, 1996). Burst! works on commission; it stores the ads—small banner graphics—on a server at BBN Planet, one of the original contractors for the precursor to the Internet. When you load a page from one of Burst!'s sites, a few lines of code in the Web page call up the ad from Burst!'s server, load it, and count the hit for auditing purposes.

All those advertising services will require another category of middlemen: third-party auditors to verify the number of times a particular company's banners have been seen on a given site and on which pages. And another: organizations who are concerned about the future of truth-in-advertising. Britain's Advertising Standards Authority, which responds to public complaints about ads and false claims, regards Web sites run by British companies as falling within its territory.[13] Similarly, medical authorities, including the Food and Drug Administration (FDA), are concerned about the potential for selling unapproved drugs and quack health cures in an unregulated environment.[14]

One non-regulatory solution to this might be some kind of branding by trusted organizations. In an international medium, you can only control sites run by companies from your own country. Under a branding scheme, sites containing reputable information could be endorsed by third parties with known reputations, such as the FDA and its counterparts elsewhere. This is similar to the ratings and classification systems already being discussed for Web sites, where you might choose a ratings system based on the known agenda of a particular church, government body, or cause organization. Surveying all those Web sites is a time-consuming job, but here again, a standardized interface so that any organization could custom-build a database of sites and plug it in would go a long way toward ensuring maximum user choice. Today's specialized software packages have already been criticized for blocking material that doesn't obviously fit the categories they say they're blocking, such as sex and bomb-making instructions.

An alternative to blocking software is a different class of middlemen that already exists on the commercial online systems: moderators and sysops, who get paid to monitor specific areas to make sure they conform to what's expected of them. Moderating is a hard enough job (trust me, I know) that few people want to do it for any length of time without pay. The business model required to support paying these people, which awards them royalties according to the amount of time people spend in their areas, is what keeps CompuServe and kept America Online so comparatively expensive. AOL's conversion to a flat-rate service at the end of 1996 requires the service to find new ways to pay its content providers; the most likely will be through selling advertising space. What effect sponsorship will have on online debate remains to be seen.

Some traditional middlemen are likely to survive, even though early predictions were that they would no longer be necessary. These are primarily information specialists, such as librarians, researchers, and journalists. The thinking was that no one would need these filters because the information would all be right there on the Net, and good computerized searching would make it easy to sort through. But anyone who's ever used a computer search program like Altavista knows that the results it produces, often as many as 10,000 or 20,000 hits, are only the beginning. Sifting through those to find the good matches is difficult; the many mistaken conclusions drawn from such searches by those seeking to sensationalize pornography online are a testament to that. One of the more interesting experiments in early 1997 is HumanSearch, a search service set up by a Rhode Island college student and his father with about forty volunteers. You tell them what you want to know; they search for you using a variety of techniques.[15] The group hopes to build the new service into a profitable business.

Most of these new middlemen, especially those offering services with legal liability, such as key escrow agents, certifying authorities, and pseudonymous remailers, will be pressure points for regulators the way Internet service providers are now. The Net's diversity and freedom may well depend on encouraging as many of these services to develop as possible, so that users, both corporate and individual, have as much choice as possible.

In a technical environment, the best choice may be difficult to identify. Most people are not qualified themselves to check up on the strength of an encryption algorithm or the validity of certificates offered by a particular organization. This is again a question of trust, which builds up over time—by withstanding repeated attempts at cryptanalysis in the case of the algorithm, or by cross-checking in the case of certificates. In the real world, we make these checks all the time as part of developing a trust relationship, whether it's assessing the stories in our chosen newspaper by looking for errors in the areas we know about or examining our legislators' voting records.

An attempt to resolve this difficulty and restore the trust that is being lost as the Net grows and metamorphoses into a full-blown commercial medium is the Electronic Frontier Foundation's eTrust initiative.[16] The initiative was inspired by a lecture by author Francis Fukuyama, who claims that the greater the level of trust between the parties to a transaction, the less the transaction costs. A pilot program began with a hundred companies in late 1996, using licensed symbols that tell users what happens to data collected by the Web sites they visit. Coordinated by CommerceNet, eTrust is intended to build security and confidence into the public network by creating standards for the use and collection of personal data and for security. Understanding that in a new and unfamiliar environment familiar names are worth a great deal, the project is using well-known auditing firms KPMG and Coopers and Lybrand to develop a formal review process for Web sites. Some of the new middlemen, in other words, will be some of the same ones we've gotten used to in the physical world.

16

Dumping Tea in the
Virtual Harbor

As to government matters, it is not in the powers of Britain to do
this continent justice: The business of it will soon be too weighty,
and intricate, to be managed with any tolerable degree of convenience by a power, so distant from us, and so very ignorant of us;
for if they cannot conquer us, they cannot govern us.

— Thomas Paine, *Common Sense*

The day after the passage of the Communications Decency
Act (CDA), John Perry Barlow, Wyoming cattle rancher (retired), Grateful Dead lyricist, and Electronic Frontier Foundation co-founder, sent out
a proclamation he entitled "A Cyberspace Independence Declaration."

"They have declared war on Cyberspace," he wrote. "Let us show
them how cunning, baffling, and powerful we can be in our own defense." Addressing "Governments of the industrial world, you weary giants of flesh and steel," he went on,

On behalf of the future, I ask you of the past to leave us alone. You are not
welcome among us. You have no sovereignty where we gather.

We have no elected government, nor are we likely to have one, so I address you with no greater authority than that with which liberty itself always speaks. I declare the global social space we are building to be
naturally independent of the tyrannies you seek to impose on us. You have
no moral right to rule us nor do you possess any methods of enforcement
we have true reason to fear.

Governments derive their just powers from the consent of the governed.
You have neither solicited nor received ours. We did not invite you. You do
not know us, nor do you know our world. Cyberspace does not lie within

your borders. Do not think you can build it, as though it were a public construction project. You cannot. It is an act of nature and it grows itself through our collective actions.[1]

Barlow had started speaking about the natural sovereignty of cyberspace about a year earlier, but he had already planted the seeds in columns he wrote from 1990 onwards, in which he refers several times to a new, developing "social contract for cyberspace."[2]

Most of Barlow's writings over the years have captured important principles just coalescing on the Net. Not this time: he got a lot of heat even from friends, some of whom found the declaration embarrassing. Barlow himself was unfazed. "They were debugging my code," he said a couple of months later,[3] meaning that their arguments (such as that since the U.S. government funded the development of the early networks it wasn't right to say it had no part in building cyberspace) were small corrections like the ones you make to software to patch bugs.

Barlow's social contract may have been developing in the early 1990s, when the Net was relatively small and homogeneous, but the tumultuous years since 1994 have made it plain that not everyone coming onto the Net shares the same ideals. The 1960s-style vision of the Net as a new, virgin world in which the old world could be undone and remade entirely was dominant for a while, but although new groups coming onto the Net agree about remaking the world, each has a different image of what it should look like. Or not: successful multinational companies don't so much want to remake the world as find ways to exploit the Net as a new medium and assure themselves of continued dominance.

Barlow himself seems to think that the Net is spawning a new political future: "I think that the culture that lives on the net is much more infectious than anything that lives in a large industrial-period organisation," he said in April 1996. "You cannot convince me that there were 50 million screaming libertarians on the planet Earth 20 years ago."[4]

But do they exist now? The GVU surveys discussed in chapter 12 suggest that the political make-up of the Net (or at least, those users willing to sit on the Web and fill out surveys) is more centrist than anything else. Meanwhile, the particular brand of libertarianism that infuses at least some parts of the Net and is the predominant political color of *Wired*, the magazine of digital record, is being attacked as selfish, narrow-minded, and ungrateful. (In all fairness to Barlow, his own views as expressed in his writings are far more egalitarian than is sometimes realized.)

One of the most important critics is long-standing *Wired* contributor Paulina Borsook, who has described herself as the magazine's token "feminist/humanist/skeptic/Luddite."[5] In mid-1996, she published several scathing attacks on what she calls cyberlibertarianism, first in an essay in *Mother Jones*, and then in a two-part interview by writer David Hudson for the Web-based magazine *ReWired: Journal of a Strained Net*, a mixture of critique of and ballast for *Wired*'s occasional grandiosity. In both places Borsook argued that the residents of Silicon Valley failed to recognize the extent to which they were beneficiaries of government subsidies.

"Although the technologists I encountered there [on her arrival in Silicon Valley in 1981] were the liberals on social issues I would have expected (pro-choice, as far as abortion; pro-diversity, as far as domestic partner benefits; inclined to sanction the occasional use of recreational drugs), they were violently lacking in compassion, ravingly anti-government, and tremendously opposed to regulation," Borsook writes in her *Mother Jones* essay.[6] She continues:

> These are the inheritors of the greatest government subsidy of technology and expansion in technical education the planet has ever seen; and, like the ungrateful adolescent offspring of immigrants who have made it in the new country, they take for granted the richness of the environment in which they have flourished, and resent the hell out of the constraints that bind them. And, like privileged, spoiled teenagers everywhere, they haven't a clue what their existence would be like without the bounty showered on them. These high-tech libertarians believe the private sector can do everything—but of course, R&D is something that cannot by any short-term measurement meet the test of the marketplace, the libertarians' measure of all things. They decry regulation—except without it, there would be no mechanism to ensure profit from intellectual property, without which entrepreneurs would not get their payoffs, nor would there be equitable marketplaces in which to make their sales.

There is a strong strand of the kind of thinking she describes here, both on the Net and in many *Wired* articles. But it's far from universal. Barlow, for example, does worry that the Net will tend to create a meritocracy that rewards intelligence disproportionately, and he seems genuinely to care that the Net be opened to as much of the world's diverse population as possible. His one blind spot as a prophet for the future of a truly mass medium is that he hates television to the point of calling it toxic and saying there is no safe level of consumption. Of course, many intellectuals feel the same way and like to boast about how little television they and their children watch; but if you're going to make predictions about what people want, you'd better understand why they like what they like.

If you spend any time writing about technological development, you eventually come to notice that the people inventing this stuff often make assumptions about what people want that have nothing to do with reality. Barlow talks about the Net's leading to the death of the nation-state, a common idea in diplomatic circles, too. Is this likely to happen tomorrow? Will most people cheer if it does, if it means paying directly for schools, garbage collection, law enforcement, and emergency services and removes any safety net that might help people who, for reasons of poverty, unemployment, or disability, can't pay their way? MIT Media Lab director Nicholas Negroponte, on the other hand, dreams (or perhaps hallucinates) about a world in which my house recognizes my touch, news flows from the floor through my body to my glasses for me to read, and network communications are so fast and efficient that I can live alone on a Greek island with a telephone butler to block out all unwanted calls. How many Greek islands are there in the world? How many people can live on them before they get too crowded to be idyllic? Do I want to read news on my glasses? (Answer: No. I have enough trouble seeing as it is.)

At least some of these wild predictions may indeed come true. At the very least, technological hype-mongers have managed to convince the rest of the world that they could. Many old-time Net users believe that the Net may herald a new era of peace, instead of realizing that the more likely scenario is that the Net will let people misunderstand each and start fights faster. This is a medium in which flame wars are endemic. Fortunately, top-level diplomats understand this is not going to change because the participants work for the United Nations. Netizens should remember Douglas Adams's Babel Fish, which, when slipped inside your ear, could make you instantly understand anything said to you in any form of language and, "by effectively removing all barriers to communication between different races and cultures, has caused more and bloodier wars than anything else in the history of creation."[7]

If you wanted to inspire politicians and governments to look on you with fear as something that needed control, there could be no better way than to go around saying persuasively in every forum you could find that your new medium was going to remake the world, undermine the status quo, and kill off national governments and multinational corporations. If they believe you, what are they going to do? Impose controls.

All of these border wars really are about control. People in general, most of whom are not online, are not asking how or if the Net can be governed, but how it can be edited into their idea of something that's safe. Control is a one-way process. Government, at least of the kind we're used to, is supposed to be a two-way process. (This is apparently less obvious in the Western states, where people argue against the installation of traffic lights on the grounds that they're too damn much government interference.) If you accept that principle as a basis for reasoning, and also accept that the longer someone has been online and the more familiar they are with the Net the less they perceive it as frightening or dangerous, the way the Net reacts to threats to its sense of freedom starts to make sense.

From the point of view you begin to develop after many years on the Net, laws like the CDA impose restrictions but offer no benefits in return to the many Netizens who are confident of their ability to handle their kids' questions. After all, it's obvious to a lot of us that our kids are at much less risk disembodied over a phone line than they are on a street corner or even, in many cases, sadly, in their own homes, President Clinton's suggestion that a 7–11 store is safer notwithstanding.[8] Equally, restrictions on cryptography ban the equivalent of door locks and envelopes without fixing the security risks highlighted by hackers; pricing and bandwidth issues threaten ready access without perceptibly offering improved reliability or speed; and tougher laws on intellectual property wall off information and further restrict access without guaranteeing any improvement in the quality of that information. Is it any wonder that the Net feels under siege? Is it surprising that feeling threatened further bonds the community together, and that some elements unite in a determination to see that attempts at regulation fail?

Regulating cyberspace is a lot like shooting the messenger. The issue of how far a country or group of countries may go in imposing their standards on other countries is not new, and the flattering notion that we have only good motives for interfering, or that we even understand the consequences of doing so, is ludicrous. Most of the Irish Republican Army's funding for bombs comes from the United States and has for years. At the same time, we discourage cigarette smoking in our own country but demand that tobacco companies be allowed to open new markets for themselves in places like China and Africa. The Australia-based catalogue of mail-order brides from Russia and the Ukraine that University of Rhode Island professor Donna Hughes mentioned (see chapter 9) makes for surprising reading: many of the women are over thirty, with children and respectable-sounding jobs. If these details are accurate, whose right is it to decide if these adult women are capable of making choices?[9] If we ban Internet advertising, will that change the economic and social conditions that lie behind such choices?

It is nonsense to pretend that these are brand-new issues raised by the Internet, or to propose that there have never before been items that could be imported undetectably. By-passing national laws has always been an option for those rich, free, and leisured enough to travel, whether it was smuggling back banned books or pornography (or, in the case of Ireland in the 1970s, condoms), taking advantage of tax loopholes to store money in financial havens, or traveling to a liberal district or country to have an abortion. Abortion is one example of a banned purchase where there are no tangible goods to tax or confiscate; several thousand Irish women travel to England every year for just that purpose. Other intangible imports include exposure to cultural norms and media banned at home (films, plays, books, lectures) that may alter perceptibly someone's expectations of life (presumably one reason getting an exit visa was a sticky business in the former Soviet Union). If you're going to argue that some types of information must not be allowed to circulate, then you also have to ask whether, when cryptographic expert Matt Blaze leaves the country, he should be allowed to take his brain.

What the Internet *will* do is democratize, speed up, and extend these existing phenomena. Blaze can, undetectably, export at least some of the contents of his brain every day at low cost and high speed via email, just as someone from Britain might, Bandwidth willing, be able to view a copy of the film *A Clockwork Orange*, which is not available for public showing there. If you are going to seek to regulate the Net to eliminate those possibilities, you will have to deal with the fact that to a Netizen such a restriction on his freedom of mental movement feels like imprisonment. We no longer think the United States's McCarthy era refusal to issue passports to blacklisted musicians was a laudable policy, nor would we approve if Germany banned its citizens from visiting California because they might come in contact with Holocaust revisionists.

And yet, we are beginning to develop, even offline, a notion that a country's citizens might be responsible to their home country's legal system for their behavior abroad. Laws are beginning to pass in some countries against so-called "sex tourism," whereby (male) travelers take advantage of exotic locations to indulge sexual tastes that would be illegal or unacceptable at home, just as known "football hooligans," Britain's word for its violent soccer fans, may be banned from traveling to matches outside the country. Cyberspace has much in common with foreign countries, and people's behavior online has even more in common with people's behavior when they escape, however briefly, their real lives, where everything they do has consequences they have to live with. Cyberspace can give adults on a daily basis the kind of personal and intellectual experimentation that most of us only ever have for four years in college, if then. That's not all that's out there, of course, and those whose employers, spouses, and friends are all online with them don't experience that escape in the same way—I have always been conscious that anything I wrote online might be read later by someone I hoped to work for, and that's a strong motivator for me not to get into online fights or flame wars. If everyone gets online, eventually everyone will have those same real-life stakes, and that, more than any other change, may work to moderate at least some behavior.

Barlow, in dismissing the U.S. Congress from cyberspace's borders, did not think cyberspace could form any kind of government. But there certainly have been experiments within small online communities. The system of ballots on LambdaMOO is one such attempt, set up (like the U.S. government) as much to limit outside control (by the system's founder/ wizard) as to protect the residents. A different scheme was tried on MediaMOO, a project set up by MIT Media Lab researcher Amy Bruckman to investigate online interaction in a professional context.

Because she felt that the system on LambdaMOO was a non-stop "horrendous flame fest," Bruckman instituted a form of representative democracy that involved a council and a voting system that was updated once an hour. A council member whose actions were unpopular could therefore be voted out of office almost at once. What Bruckman found was that the design made it possible for the council's discussions to be dominated by the people who had the most time to write long postings. Worse, an early decision, demanded by one council member, to operate by consensus meant that even the smallest decision took endless amounts of time. "Shared values, patience, goodwill, mutual accountability," Bruckman told an April 1996 conference on Virtue and Virtuality, "all these things are what makes consensus process work. All of these things were one-hundred percent lacking in this experiment." After about ten months the experiment was dismantled.[10]

There is a significant difference between these communities and real life, and it's not the lack of bodies, but the verifiable existence of an ultimate, all-powerful god: the person who owns the machine can pull the plug. This is true whether you're talking about a bulletin board system in someone's bedroom, a commercial service answerable to its stockholders, the moderator of an online forum on a larger service, or, as is the case with these MOOs, an experiment set up by a researcher. This is why Usenet is in many ways the Net's bedrock: no one can pull the plug, and, at least on the *alt* hierarchy, there's no way to kill a newsgroup.

If there were ever to be a government of the Net, by the Net, and for the Net, it would have to be implemented in technology that worked universally, and it would have to be by consensus (as even one system administrator's refusal to adopt whatever was agreed upon would undermine any decision that was made). If Bruckman's MediaMOO, with a relatively homogeneous community of only a couple of hundred users, found consensus unworkable, the far more diverse, infinitely larger Net would have little chance.

There are few issues about which there is enough consensus to build on. Child pornography and junk email are probably the two subjects that attract the most widespread agreement. Even in those cases, some object to having junk email regulated or deleted for them, while others believe that removing the newsgroups to which child pornography is occasionally posted is a bad idea. The material, the argument goes, will simply find its way into some other, less obviously named area, where accidental contact with it, perhaps by a child, is far more likely; it will also go underground, raising the same kind of policing problems we're supposed to restrict cryptography to avoid.

This is one reason everyone has grumpily jumped on the ratings and filtering bandwagon. Using blocking software follows the Net's existing structure and its roots in decentralized, user choice, while ratings similarly distribute responsibility to the Net's millions of users. These systems will work, if by "work" you mean "give politicians something to point to that appears to show they've Done Something about the Net." They will not work, if what you expect is a cyberworld in which no one will ever see something they find offensive or distressing or a Net which will never be used for anything illegal. But neither will any other system, not because Netizens are uncontrollable but because the nature of a diverse world is to offend some of the people all of the time and all of the people some of the time. We see it every day in the real world.

Ratings have other problems, which few are talking about yet—Net users because they tend to figure ratings and filtering are the nearest they're going to get to a way out of all these regulatory threats, and politicians because they're not about to say there's nothing they can do. Ratings can be used to advertise, as well as block, salacious material—just look at all those "XXX" rated movies (there is no XXX rating, it just sounds more impressive) you see advertised in adult video catalogues. (The "Operation Clambake" home page displays yellow "Attacked by COS!" banners next to some of the page's links; a similar badge of pride.) In addition, if you can tell a software package to block all ratings above a certain level, you can probably tell the same software (or the inverse software that will doubtless be written) to go out and find only ratings above a certain level. Software is like that: it can be changed and emulated. If you're a teenager and someone tells you there are sex-10 rated sites out there that your school software won't show you, do you say, oh, yes, the grown-ups know best, or do you try to figure out a way to get a look at what you're not allowed to see?

For would-be regulators, focusing on the bogeymen—terrorists, drug dealers, spies, and pedophiles—is a clever strategy, because it puts those who would defend freedom of speech on the Net in a position where it looks like they're defending those crimes. The 1997 wave of European regulators is getting a lot of mileage out of the statement "The Internet is not a legal vacuum." If, their argument goes, something is illegal in the real world, it is illegal on the Internet or in any other medium. This sounds reasonable and logical, but it glosses over the fact that not everyone agrees the current laws are just, as well as the fact that there are massive legal differences between countries (and, in the case of the United States, individual states). Marijuana is legal in the Netherlands; depictions of explicit sex are legal in Sweden, which considers violence to be more harmful. Even where there is the most consensus—in the area of child pornography, which almost everyone agrees should be illegal—it's not clear how you define a standard when the age of consent varies from jurisdiction to jurisdiction.

At a conference on "Policing the Internet" held in London on February 13–14, 1997, Karl Heinz Moewes of the Munich police went for the maximum shock effect by showing a series of pictures (with the relevant genitalia blocked out) of adult and child pornography he said he had downloaded from the Net. On each page of photographs he had laid in the blue ribbon, the Net's symbol indicating support for free speech online. The conference chair, experienced BBC broadcaster Sue Cameron, regarded these pictures as so horrific that she passed on the request from staff at the venue, the Institute of Civil Engineers, to stop showing them.

There was no opportunity to ask Moewes the really important question: what was the original source of these photographs? Had they been scanned in from magazines? Were they photographs submitted in evidence from a particular case? And, most important, how old were they? An analysis along these lines of the small amount of material that shows up on the Net would be valuable and should be made; under British law, collecting the material to examine for such a study could land you in prison.

The pressure points everywhere are the Internet service providers, who are vulnerable because they're known, basically immoveable (unlike a Web site), and have businesses at stake as well as their owners' personal freedom. With less of a tradition of freedom of speech than the United States, it's extremely likely that the European Parliament's discussions, held in March and April 1997, will result in some form of regulation, and that the European Union will push heavily for joint international agreements about what may be placed on the Net.

If the Net is the inherently international medium John Perry Barlow has said it is, then let's also grant that its behavior, as recounted here, has generally been on the provocative side. The world's governments, accordingly, are likely to react as if they were confronting an alien invasion. If this happens, the net.wars of the 1990s may come to look like only minor skirmishes.

Notes

All the Web addresses included were checked when we went to press, but some, inevitably, may have moved or changed. Please check the *net.wars* Web site at http://www.nyupress.nyu.edu/netwars.html for updates.

NOTES TO CHAPTER I

1. "Beam Me Up, I'm Covered," at http://www.ufo2001.com. Partenia is at http://www.partenia.org. The McLibel trial is archived at http://www.mcspotlight.org. Zhu Ling's page is at http://www.radsci.ucla.edu/telemed/zhuling.

2. ASCII art is pictures made out of the simple characters an ordinary computer keyboard can produce. The original production of HamNet featured an elegant castle made out of characters like |, /, [, and ^.

3. Howard Rheingold, *The Virtual Community* (Secker and Warburg, 1994), 37.

4. In a confusion of abbreviations, there are two organizations calling themselves CIX. The better-known one in the United States is the Commercial Internet Exchange, a group set up in early 1991 by the then major regional Internet service providers to promote the commercial use of the Internet. As this organization only appears briefly in chapter 14, in general I will use CIX to mean the London conferencing system founded in 1987 whose full name is Compulink Information eXchange.

5. The reason this no longer works is that those joke conferences had no messages in them, since part of the joke was that the unwitting participants had no idea how they got into the conference or who had done it. Live online, you would see you had been joined to the conference, even if it was empty. And it wouldn't be for long, since someone would inevitably post something of scintillating brilliance like, "Hey! What am I doing in here?" Because offline readers only know how to pick up waiting messages, they don't see empty conferences, and while you could leave a few seed messages, your user name would be imprinted on them, spoiling the game.

6. The distinction between an online service like America Online and a direct-access ISP is an important one. Essentially, it's the difference between having your computer connected directly to the Internet and using someone else's connection by connecting to their computer and using it as an intermediary. There were no consumer-oriented ISPs until the mid-1990s, and services like CompuServe made a lot of money by being able to charge higher prices and sell access to even higher-priced databases of periodicals normally available only to businesses on subscription (the way a retailer buys a case of fruit and sells it to you in small

amounts). Dial-up online services had advantages over early Internet access: although they were more expensive, they were easier to set up and use, and they had search facilities when the Internet was still a jumbled mass of data. CompuServe now also sells direct Internet access, and version 3.0 of the information service integrates the service with standard Internet access.

7. Briefly, every Usenet newsgroup name is composed of a series of words or parts of words separated by dots, such as: *rec.sport.tennis*. The first part, *rec* in this case, is an abbreviation for "recreation" and gives a broad idea of the kind of newsgroup it is—a recreational topic, rather than a computer science one (*comp*). The second shows that the topic is a sport; the third identifies which sport. This style of naming newsgroups is easy both for computers to sort and humans to understand.

8. The "Usenet/Culture-FAQ," maintained by Tom Seidenberg, is reposted regularly to *alt.culture.usenet*. For more on "MAKE MONEY FAST" see chapter 2.

9. From Part 2 of "Net.Legends FAQ (Noticeable Phenomena of Usenet)," maintained by David DeLaney and archived at http://www.math.uiuc.edu/~tskirvin/faqs/legend.html.

10. WELL stands for Whole Earth 'Lectronic Link, and because it's based in the San Francisco area and was set up as early as 1985, a large percentage of those most responsible for defining the technology and ethos of cyberspace have at one time or another been members, who often style themselves "WELLperns" or, occasionally, "WELLbeings." Laurence Canter and Martha Siegel, the two lawyers who brought small-time marketing to Usenet (see chapter 2), speak of the WELL as if it were the headquarters of some kind of cabal or conspiracy. It's not, although significant discussions on the WELL have included much of the work of organizing the first and third Computers, Freedom, and Privacy conferences, the 1991 *Harper's* magazine forum on hacking, the dissection of *Time*'s 1995 cover story on "cyberporn" and the flawed study it was based on (see chapter 9), and many board members of the Electronic Frontier Foundation had or have accounts there. The WELL, which originally became known as the Net home for Grateful Dead fans, is an extremely quirky place, but its appeal has been limited in part by the technical demands of its eccentric, text-based interface, which tends to weed out a lot of casual users. If the Net has an online equivalent of the Algonquin Round Table, the WELL might be it.

11. "Freedom from a Strange, New Land," *Daily Telegraph*, April 16, 1996.

12. Personal interview conducted just after the 1995 Computers, Freedom, and Privacy Conference in early April; it eventually ran in the *Guardian* as "Hard Link to the Physical World," on January 11, 1996.

13. "Crime and Puzzlement" circulated widely on the Net. "Decrypting the Puzzle Palace" appeared in *Communications of the ACM*, July 1992. "Jackboots on the Infobahn" appeared in *Wired*, April 1994, 40–48. A complete archive of these and Barlow's other writings are available at http://www.eff.org/pub/Publications/John_Perry_Barlow/HTML.

14. Gilmore notes on his Web page that he is not actually sure when or where he said it, although he agrees, along with everyone else, that it probably was him.

15. Henry Hardy, "The History of the Net," (master's thesis, School of Communications, Grand Valley State University, 1993). Available on the Web at http://ginch.dial.umd.edu/users/cerberus.misc/history-net.html.

16. In "Email from Bill," originally published in the *New Yorker* and reprinted in *The New Science Journalists*, edited by Ted Anton and Rick McCourt (Ballantine, 1995).

17. As part of a profile of Dyson, "Esther Dyson: Pattern Recognizer," by agent and author John Brockman from his book *Digerati* (Wired Books, 1997), samples of which are archived on the Web at http://www.upside.com/texis/archive/search/article.html?UID=970301106. Dyson is also president of EDventure Holdings, organizer of the annual invitation-only conference PC Forum, and editor of the industry newsletter *Release 1.0*.

18. John Seabrook, *Deeper: My Two-Year Odyssey in Cyberspace* (Simon and Schuster, 1997), 234–35.

19. *Slate* is published weekly at http://www.slate.com and edited by former *New Yorker* writer and CNN *Cross-Fire* commentator Michael Kinsley. The only issue ever published of *Stale* is at http://www.stale.com. *Wired* publishes both new material commissioned just for the Net and articles from the magazine on its HotWired site at http://www.hotwired.com. This, too, had a parody site for a couple of years, HowTired, at http://www.howtired.com. *ReWired* is at http://www.rewired.com. Suck, begun by two *Wired* employees and sold to *Wired* in 1996, is at http://www.suck.com.

20. Todd Lappin, "Deja Vu all over Again," *Wired*, May 1995, 175.

NOTES TO CHAPTER 2

1. A personal prediction: Web-based home shopping will not kill off live shopping, although it may push retailers to make it more interesting, efficient, and fun. Grocery shopping over the Web has its limitations, at least in the early trial I joined in late November 1996. What you got was essentially a list of products from which you compiled a shopping list. You couldn't look up further information about unfamiliar items, or request labeling information such as ingredients, vital for people with allergies. However, the format is extremely promising, not least because this particular trial includes the facility for adding a note to each item to help the person who assembles your order. If you prefer underripe bananas, or want the labels checked on unfamiliar brands, you can note this. That human element seems most likely to make the project a success, although it raises the strange image of a half-empty store populated largely by staff shopping for other people. But the potential is clear for boring, unpleasant routine shopping for categories like groceries and office supplies, where you're typically ordering the same heavy or bulky items over and over again.

2. Laurence A. Canter and Martha S. Siegel, *How to Make a Fortune on the Information Superhighway* (HarperCollins 1994).

3. My comments are based on the version archived at http://www. urbanlegends.com/legal/green_card_spam.html. Other versions have slight differences (such as the more common originating email address cslaw@indirect.com).

4. A news server stores all the many news articles, or postings, that make up Usenet at each service provider; to get news, subscribers tap into this server and retrieve new articles from the groups they subscribe to.

5. To read news, you need a newsreader. On the university systems that most of the academic community (a very large percentage of those with access to Usenet at the time) would have been using, there were several in common usage, all of which have facilities to let you choose ("subscribe to") the newsgroups you want to read and display the messages on the same subject in such a way that you can see at a glance how they interrelate, a technique called "threading." As you read the messages in a given group (on Usenet, usually called articles, or postings), the newsreader marks them as "read" so that if you stop partway through you can come back and pick up where you left off.

6. An early version is archived at http://beacon-www.asa.utk.edu/archives/ iwriter/support/make-money-fast.html. The letter is followed by a list of names and addresses, which vary over time, along with a bunch of testimonials, allegedly from happy participants in the chain, and tells the story of "Dave Rhodes," who in 1988 was broke but within six months became "RICH!" following these simple instructions.

7. "Net.Legends FAQ (Noticeable Phenomena of Usenet)," maintained by David DeLaney and archived at http://www.math.uiuc.edu/~tskirvin/faqs/ legends.html.

8. More on Rhodes and other early spam is in "The Battle for Usenet," by Charles A. Gimon, at http://www.skypoint.com/members/gimonca/usewar.html.

9. The original message is archived at http://www.geog.mcgill.ca/other/ grassu/2859.html. Medical researchers generally are doubtful that this product can do what's claimed for it. For more on health claims and their regulation, see chapter 15. A run-down of the evidence (or lack thereof) is at http://www. kron.com/nc⁴/contact⁴/stories/thigh.html.

10. Stanton McCandlish, newsletter editor and program director/webmaster for the Electronic Frontier Foundation, noted in a posting dated October 3, 1995, that he believes the term "spam" was first used in 1993 or even earlier to describe loud, repetitive ranting on the role-playing services known as MUDs (or MOOs, MUSHes, or MUCKs). The posting is archived at http://www.eff.org/pub/ Social_responsibility/Spamming_and_net_abuse/archeology_of_spam.article.

11. Personal archive of contemporaneous messages posted by Internet Direct on its gopher server.

12. Canter and Siegel, *How to Make a Fortune*, 22, 27.

13. Ibid., 200. The rules for posting to Usenet were originally written by net.god Gene Spafford and are now part of the help system at Deja News (http://www.dejanews.com).

14. Mark Harrison, *The Usenet Handbook: A User's Guide to Netnews* (O'Reilly and Associates, 1995), 10.

15. Canter and Siegel, *How to Make a Fortune*, 17.

16. Ibid., 187, 204–5.

17. Ibid., 180.

18. Ibid., 217.

19. These IDs are a mix of letters and numbers that include the name of the machine on which the posting was written and a numerical identifier. The derivation of this varies from system to system, but is usually something like the number of seconds since the machine was turned on or some other non-duplicable number.

20. These appear in the "Better Living Through Forgery FAQ," posted regularly to *news.admin.policy* and *comp.security.misc.*

21. A binary file is any type of computer file that isn't plain text, such as a program, picture, video, or audio file. There are special newsgroups (*alt.binaries.**) just for these files, which are generally not welcome in the rest of Usenet because they tend to consume a lot of space. In addition, because Usenet was designed as a text-based system (like email), binary files must be split into small chunks and converted into text characters for transmission. The user then has to collect all the pieces and use special software to stitch them back together and decode them.

22. On the so-called Big Seven hierarchies of Usenet newsgroups—*comp*, *sci*, *talk*, *rec*, *news*, *soc*, and *misc*—starting a new newsgroup is a formal procedure that involves proposing the newsgroup, collecting comments, and finally taking a vote and posting the results. The intention is to keep the list of newsgroups orderly and populated with groups for which there is real demand. Other hierarchies work differently, notably the *alt* hierarchy, which was deliberately created to bypass these formal procedures and allow anyone to start a group on any subject; people are still encouraged to collect comments, but there is no voting procedure as such.

23. More information about how cancelers operate is in the "Cancel Message FAQ," maintained by Tim Skirvin and available at http://www.uiuc.edu/~tskirvin/faqs/cancel.html. This also includes useful information on how to proceed if you think one of your own postings was canceled by someone else or if you have reason to believe someone is sending out forged postings in your name.

24. In computing, the asterisk is a "wild card" character that stands for any number of letters. It's also a useful shorthand for quoting newsgroup names, where saying something like *alt.fan.** means any newsgroup whose name begins *alt.fan*— *alt.fan.letterman*, *alt.fan.jay-leno*, and so on. If you just say *alt.fan* you would be referring to just that newsgroup.

25. Source: "Cancelmoose[tm] Home Page," http://www.cm.org/.

26. A representative lengthy review appears in Wyn Hilty, "How the Web Was Lost: Business Conquers the Internet and Other Cyber Stories," *OC Weekly*, September 20–26, 1996, archived on the Web at http://www.pulpless.com/weblost.html.

27. The letter appeared in *Wired*, June 1996. For more of Martha Siegel's views on events, see K. K. Campbell, "A Net.Conspiracy So Immense: Chatting with Martha Siegel of the Internet's Infamous Canter and Siegel," dated October 1, 1994, and archived on the Web in *Computer Underground Digest* issue 6.89 at http://venus.soci.niu.edu/~cudigest/CUDS6/cud6.89.

28. The original Safety-Net proposals, archived on the Web at http://www.ispa.org.uk/safetypa.html.

29. Cyber Promotions has used, among others, cyberpromo.com, savetrees.com, pleaseread.com, cyberemag.com, and answerme.com.

30. The discussion can be retrieved from the Usenet archiving and search engine Deja News, at http://www.dejanews.com.

31. The Cyber Promotions Web site is at http://www.cyberpromo.com.

32. A killfile essentially filters out all mail (or Usenet postings) from a specific source, be it a whole site or an individual, according to rules set by the user.

NOTES TO CHAPTER 3

1. Josh Quittner, "The War between *alt.tasteless* and *rec.pets.cats*," *Wired*, May 1994, 46–53.

2. One of the things technology can do is create autoresponders. These are used widely on the Net—for example, if you follow the instructions to join an email discussion list, you'll get back an autoresponse telling you you've been joined to the list and enclosing a help file of information and instructions for using and posting to the list. Similarly, the *test* newsgroups are monitored by autoresponders that spot new messages and automatically spit out replies to their senders to confirm that their newsreaders are working correctly. Morons who send messages saying only "test" to other newsgroups deserve the flames they get. I mean, why pick *rec.sport.tennis* for these things?

3. "Net.Legends FAQ (Noticeable Phenomena of Usenet)," maintained by David DeLaney and archived at http://www.math.uiuc.edu/~tskirvin/faqs/legends.html.

4. The *alt.aol-sucks* home page is at http://www.aolsucks.org.

5. FTP stands for File Transfer Protocol, a method for transferring files, be they text, graphics, or computer programs, across the Internet. FTP sites function much like public libraries in the real world in that they maintain archives of files that users can download. When you get a file from a Web site, you're using FTP to retrieve it whether you know it or not; it's built into your browser. By 1996,

companies like Microsoft and Netscape used this sort of setup to sell software as well as give it away, but in 1994 pretty much all FTP sites were run by universities, and the expectation was that everyone would benefit more or less equally.

6. AOL's "easy-to-use interface" dubs these offline facilities "flash sessions," which may be why you never noticed their existence (if you're an AOLer). Look on the Mail menu.

7. Proxy servers are designed to minimize the duplication of traffic that's inevitable when millions of users all access the same popular sites. Instead of getting a new copy each time, your host site stores frequently accessed pages on a special machine (the proxy server). Users then pull down the copy, which is theoretically much faster. In practice, it seems to be rare for proxy servers to work out that way: searching through the cache of stored pages takes time. In addition, care has to be taken that the pages stored in the cache are up to date. If the page is stock quotes that are updated every fifteen minutes and the proxy server only requests a new copy of the page once a day, the information is frequently going to be out of date. When, late in 1996, Singapore instituted nationwide proxy servers to block citizens' access to pornography and other types of controversial material, reports came out very quickly of just this sort of problem.

8. A chat room looks like a small window on your computer screen. One piece of the window shows a list of the people in the discussion, another is a blank space into which you type your comments, and the main section shows the whole conversation scrolling by.

9. The story is archived on the Web at http://www.motley-focus.com/~timber/ccahist.html.

10. Jeff Goodell, "The Fevered Rise of America Online," *Rolling Stone*, October 3, 1996, 60–66.

11. "Demo of the AOL browser," at http://powered.cs.yale.edu:8000/~miller/aol/sim15.html. "AOL's Secret Dirty Word List," by Jordanne Holyoak, at http://www.motley-focus.com/~timber/dirtyword.html. "America Online Sucks" is at http://www.hooked.net/users/doorman/antiaol.html.

12. July 1, 1996, settlement announcement on AOL's Web site, archived at http://www.ag.ohio.gov/PressRel/aol2.htm, and contemporaneous coverage at http://cnnfn.com/news/9607/05/aol_settle/index.htm.

13. Used by permission. "The Now-official 'AOL is sucks!!!!!' Bisk Poetry Archive," at http://www.telepath.com/wma/aolbisk.shtml.

14. BOFH comes from a hilariously funny diary, written by *alt.sysadmin.recovery* poster Doug McLaren, of a supposedly fictional system administrator who spends his time doing everything he can to discombobulate his users, from rerouting all help desk calls to the off-duty librarian to telling users to type in commands to reformat their hard disks, erasing all their data. The full set of diaries is at http://www.ses.com/~joe/Bofh/bofh-toc.html.

NOTES TO CHAPTER 4

1. According to "Payne-O-the-Web's Cryptography Timeline" (http://www.ns. net/users/payne-o/timeline.html), which cites David Kahn's book *The Codebreakers* (Macmillan, 1972).

2. Herbert Zim, *Codes and Secret Writing* (William Morrow, 1948).

3. Quotes from personal interviews unless otherwise indicated.

4. W. Diffie and M. E. Hellman, "New Directions in Cryptography," *IEEE Transactions on Information Theory* IT-22, no. 6 (November 1976): 644–54; R. L. Rivest, A. Shamir and L. M. Adleman, "A Method for Obtaining Digital Signatures and Public-Key Cryptosystems," *Communications of the ACM* 21, no. 2 (February 1978): 120–26.

5. Unfortunately, computers don't speak English, so to tell them what to do you need a programming language that's designed for the purpose and a program called a compiler that takes the code you write and turns it into the ones and zeros that a machine can read. C is one of the most commonly used programming languages for commercial software for personal computers, though there are others such as BASIC, which is more like English and therefore somewhat easier to learn.

6. The legislation was introduced by Senators Joseph Biden (D-DE) and Dennis DeConcini (D-AZ) and Representative Tom Lantos (D-CA); after being removed from S. 266, the clause resurfaced in an omnibus anti-crime bill, from which it was also removed.

7. Email users do have some specific rights under the Electronic Communications Privacy Act; however, how private email and other communications are varies from system to system. Always read a system's terms of service before assuming your communications are private.

8. The WELL's *eff* conference, topic 206.

9. CIX's *crypto/general* #294.

10. An operating system is a vital layer between a software program and a computer that incorporates standard functions for controlling the machine. UNIX, because it is free and the source code was available for individual users to modify and improve, is extremely popular in the academic world. Since universities were among the earliest users of the Internet, UNIX is common on the Net, even though personal computers sold for home use typically come with the Microsoft proprietary operating systems DOS and/or Windows.

11. For a discussion of the issues surrounding software patenting, see Simon L. Garfinkel, Richard M. Stallman, and Mitchell Kapor, "Why Patents Are Bad for Software," and, arguing the case for patents, Paul Heckel, "Debunking the Software Patent Myths," both reprinted in *High Noon on the Electronic Frontier*, edited by Peter Ludlow (MIT Press, 1996), 35–107.

12. Notably James Love, director of the Washington-based Consumer Project on Technology, and University of California at Berkeley professor Pamela Samuelson.

13. RFC stands for "request for comments." These collaboratively written documents define the standards on which the Internet operates. The latest version of the RFC relevant to securing email is RFC1421. All RFCs can be retrieved via FTP from ftp.internic.net, as /rfc/rfcxxxx.txt replacing xxxx with the RFC's number.

14. From the PGP Web site, http://www.pgp.com. More information on where to find PGP is available in the "Where to find PGP" FAQ, which is posted regularly to *alt.answers*, *alt.2600*, *alt.security.pgp*, and *comp.security.pgp.resources*. It's also archived on the Web at http://www.well.com/user/ddt/crypto/where_is_ pgp.html. Within the United States, the primary site is PGP's own site, http:/ /www.pgp.com.

15. A personal prediction: when PGP Inc. gets really big and successful, a conspiracy theory will hatch on the Net to the effect that the government knows there is a fundamental weakness in PGP, and that it investigated Zimmerman precisely in order to make PGP look good so people would use it widely.

16. A switch is a single-letter command you type in when you start the program that toggles on or off some particular feature.

17. In a UNIX-based system, a signature is known as *.sig* because that's the name of the file. Most Usenet newsreader software lets you specify a signature that will be appended to all the messages you post. People post all kinds of things in their *.sigs*: their addresses and phone numbers, ASCII art, and favorite quotations. One *.sig* that was common in the early 1990s that expressed support for the free availability of encryption ran, "If encryption is outlawed, then only outlaws will have encryption." My favorite, though, has always been, "If you're not part of the solution, you're part of the precipitate."

18. See "Why Cryptography is Harder than it Looks," by Bruce Schneier (http:/ /www.counterpane.com), author of *Applied Cryptography*, and also the "Snake-Oil Warning Signs: Encryption Software to Avoid" FAQ, maintained by Matt Curtin at http://www.research.megasoft.com/people/cmcurtin/snake-oil-faq.html.

19. Unfortunately, this posting seems to have vanished and is not archived at Deja News. However, the letter from the Special Master, Beth Hamilton, was posted pseudonymously to *alt.religion.scientology* (message ID 4tb7hr$s4t @nyx10.cs.du.edu) on July 26, 1996, two days after it was written, and said in part, "The computer technicians were not able to decrypt any of the PGP files except the one that contained viruses." A copy of the Special Master's letter to the court explaining her failure to decrypt Ward's PGP-encrypted hard drive is archived on Ron Newman's Web site, at http://www2.thecia.net/ ~rnewman/scientology/home.html, and mirrored at http://www.xs4all.nl/ ~kspaink/rnewman/home.html.

NOTES TO CHAPTER 5

1. John Bamford, *The Puzzle Palace* (Houghton Mifflin, 1982).
2. "Don't Worry, Be Happy: Why Clipper is Good for You," *Wired*, June

1994, 100. Baker left the NSA in 1995, and became a partner in a Washington, DC, legal firm.

3. Prepared by the Committee to Study National Cryptography Policy, with support from the Computer Science and Telecommunications Board, the National Research Council, the National Academy of Sciences, and the National Academy of Engineering. A draft copy of the report dated May 30, 1996, is archived at http://www2.nas.edu/cstbweb/2646.html.

4. More worryingly, the report recommends that Congress "seriously consider legislation that would impose penalties on the use of encrypted communications in interstate commerce with the intent to commit a federal crime." In other words, using encryption on the email planning a kidnapping attempt would aggravate the crime the way using a gun aggravates the crime of robbery.

5. In personal conversation at CFP'94.

6. See "Why Cryptography is Harder than it Looks," by Bruce Schneier (http://www.counterpane.com), author of *Applied Cryptography*, and also the "Snake-Oil Warning Signs: Encryption Software to Avoid" FAQ, maintained by Matt Curtin at http://www.research.megasoft.com/people/cmcurtin/snake-oil-faq.html.

7. Personal interview.

8. On June 2, 1994, in an article by John Markoff.

9. The seven included Ronald L. Rivest (co-inventor of the RSA algorithm), Matt Blaze, Michael Wiener, Bruce Schneier, and Whitfield Diffie (co-inventor of public-key cryptography). The letter is archived at http://www.bsa.org/policy/encryption/cryptographers.html.

10. Leading John Perry Barlow to comment, "It does seem to me that if you're going to initiate a process that might end freedom in America, you probably need an argument that isn't classified." From "Jackboots on the Infobahn," which appeared in *Wired*, April, 1994, and is archived at http://www.hotwired.com/Lib/Privacy/privacy.barlow.html.

11. A complete collection of Denning's writings on the subject are on her "Cryptography Project" Web site at http://guru.cosc.georgetown.edu/~denning/crypto/index.html.

12. Froomkin's work, along with many useful links, is on his Web site at http://www.law.miami.edu/~froomkin.

13. Anderson's Web site is at http://www.cl.cam.ac.uk/users/rja14/.

14. The algorithms are, of course, already available electronically on the world's BBSs and FTP sites, though not always all together in one place.

15. A hash function is a process that takes a message of any size and computes a fixed-length digest; if it's hard to reverse this process the hash function can be used to verify that the attached message hasn't been tampered with.

16. All of the papers relating to the Bernstein case are available at http://www.mcglashan.com and also at the *eff*'s site (http://www.eff.org) by following the links to the cryptography archive. At the beginning of 1997, Bernstein's legal

team sought a ruling that the decision would stand in the face of the Clinton administration's announcement at the end of 1996 that jurisdiction over the export laws will shift to the Department of Commerce. Legal updates are at http://www. crypto.com.

17. These are S. 1726 (Burns) and S. 1587 (Leahy, with support from Burns and several others, including later presidential candidate Bob Dole). A good place to start for information on legislative measures is the Center for Democracy and Technology Web site, at http://www.cdt.org.

18. Matt Blaze, "My Life as an International Arms Courier," available via FTP from ftp://ftp.research.att.com/dist/mab/export.txt.

19. Chaum's seminal article on the subject, "Achieving Electronic Privacy," appeared in *Scientific American*, August 1992; it is archived on the Web on the Digicash site at http://www.digicash.com/publish/sciam.html. Chaum left Digicash in early 1997.

20. In September 1993, at the European Computers, Freedom, and Privacy Conference in London, a hostile questioner complained to Chaum and the rest of a panel on anonymity that all the smart card systems so far invented had been cracked. John Gilmore's reply: "It is my understanding that paper has also been cracked."

21. A. Michael Froomkin, "It Came from Planet Clipper: The Battle over Cryptographic Key 'Escrow'," his interpretation of "the Interagency Working Group's suggestion that access to the PKI might be denied to users of unescrowed cryptography." Published by University of Chicago Legal Forum, 1996, 15, or at http://www.law.miami.edu/~froomkin.

22. Draft paper available at ftp://ftp.research.att.com/dist/mab/policy.txt.

23. Timothy C. May, "Introduction to BlackNet," in *High Noon on the Electronic Frontier: Conceptual Issues in Cyberspace*, edited by Peter Ludlow (MIT Press, 1996), 241–43.

24. Timothy C. May, "BlackNet Worries," in Ludlow, ed., *High Noon on the Electronic Frontier*, 245–49.

25. From Gilmore's Web site, at http://www.cygnus.com/~gnu/swan.html.

26. "internet.l@w/europe.96, held February 13, 1996, at the Tropen Institute and hosted by the law firm Trenité Van Doorne.

NOTES TO CHAPTER 6

1. An important caveat here: after my article about Scientology versus the Net appeared in *Wired* (December 1995), CoS representative Leisa Goodman wrote to the magazine to complain that my article was "an indiscriminate skinful of innuendo and rumor, but highly selective about its facts." In 1987, I founded a magazine called *The Skeptic*, a British and Irish publication dedicated to rational examination of paranormal claims; its mission is similar to the much better known American journal *Skeptical Inquirer* (for which I have also written from

time to time) and its parent organization, the Committee for Scientific Investigation of Claims of the Paranormal (CSICOP). Goodman felt that this background inclined me to be biased against the CoS; you will have to judge this point for yourselves in the light of these criticisms (the magazine I founded is on the Web at http://www.cs.man.ac.uk/skeptic). When I called Helena Kobrin for comments on some of the court decisions for an update for *Wired* (November and December issues, 1996), she declined to comment unless *Wired* was willing to set up a full editorial board meeting with the CoS representatives to discuss matters, saying that they felt my reporting was unfair and one-sided, and that if she granted me an interview I would "just use that to give an aura of legitimacy to slanted reporting." For a highly critical discussion of the CoS and its practices, see Richard Behar, "The Thriving Cult of Greed and Power," *Time*, May 6, 1991. The group has tax-exempt status in the United States as a religion, as well as many celebrity supporters, including actors John Travolta, Kirstie Alley, Tom Cruise, and Mimi Rogers, jazz musician Chick Corea, and entertainer-turned-politician Sonny Bono. For more positive material on Scientology, see the group's own glossy promotional book *What Is Scientology?* or its Web site, at http://www.scientology.org.

2. *What Is Scientology?*, 359.

3. "Scientology in the News: Press Office," on the Web at http://www.scientology.org/p_jpg/scnnews/po1.htm.

4. As mentioned in chapter 2, the *alt.* * hierarchy was set up to by-pass the formal voting procedures required for the Big Seven hierarchies, so that, in the interests of freedom of speech, anyone could start a newsgroup at any time. This leads to some very silly newsgroup names and a minor amount of abuse, but it also gives Usenet a responsive, timely quality it would not have otherwise. Part of by-passing that formal structure is writing a message to form the new newsgroup, called a "newgroup" message, according to a specified format. More information about how to successfully start a new newsgroup is in the "So You Want to Create an *Alt* Newsgroup" FAQ, maintained by David Barr and available at http://www.cis.ohio-state.edu/~barr/alt-creation-guide.html, and the "How to Write a Good Newgroup Message" FAQ, maintained by Brian Edmonds and updated regularly on the Web at http://www.cs.ubc.ca/spider/edmonds/usenet/good-newgroup.html.

5. A copy of the original newgroup message is archived at http://remark-able.amazing.com/scientology/history-1.html.

6. Smith gets a brief mention in Part 3 of the "Net Legends FAQ (Noticeable Phenomena of Usenet)," maintained by David Delaney and archived at http://www.math.uiuc.edu/~tskirvin/faqs/legends.html.

7. A German organization, the Free Zone Association, has a Web page at http://www.freezone.org. The *alt.clearing.technology* home page is at http://www.clearing.org/doit.cgi.

8. Interview for *Wired*, March 1995.

9. The full text of Siegel's letter has been reproduced and circulated extensively on the Net and is archived on the Web at http://remarkable.amazing.com/scientology/history-1.html. However, this copy, like the others archived around the Net, is not dated. My personal copy was forwarded to me in an email message on June 3, 1994. At that time, the newsgroup had already been discussing Siegel's letter for a several weeks, so a best guess is that it was first posted to *alt.religion.scientology* in April or May 1994.

10. All quotes from personal interview, April 1995. An interesting sidelight: I read the newsgroup for a long time before picking Farmer to contact to find out what it was like to be an ordinary Scientologist confronting the newsgroup's anti-CoS atmosphere. Within twenty-four hours of our conversation, which took place on a Saturday evening, I received email from Leisa Goodman, then the CoS's chief PR person in LA, near where Farmer was based, to inquire about some of the questions I had asked and why.

11. In the "Cancel Messages FAQ," maintainer Tim Skirvin stresses the importance of accountability in issuing third-party cancels; the three-part FAQ is archived at http://www.uiuc.edu/~tskirvin/faqs/cancel.html. One of the other most important guidelines is that cancels should *not* be content- based, carefully delineating the difference between acting in the public net.interest and censorship.

12. The Church of the SubGenius predates the widespread use of the Net by a long way. For more on their beliefs, which focus on getting "Slack" from their deity, J. R. "Bob" Dobbs, see J. R. Dobbs, *The Book of the SubGenius* (McGraw-Hill, 1983), compiled by Reverend Ivan Stang, who is also the author of *High Weirdness by Mail* (Simon and Schuster, 1988).

13. This is very easy to do in Netscape, and other methods are detailed in the "Better Living Through Forgery" FAQ, on the Web at http://www.ccs.neu.edu/home/rogue/forge.html and posted regularly to *alt.censorship* and *news.admin.misc*, among others.

14. *alt.config* is the newsgroup in which the formation and withdrawal of newsgroups in the *alt* hierarchy is discussed. This message and the systems administrators' replies are archived at ftp://ftp.uu.net/usenet/control.

15. Newsgroup names of the formation xxx.yyy.aaa.aaa.aaa are an old Usenet joke that's only funny the first hundred times you see it. The original was *alt.swedish.chef.bork.bork.bork*, after the poster who signed himself the Swedish Chef.

16. All IDs on Helsingius's remailer took the form *anxxxx@anon.penet.fi*. One of the elegances of the system he wrote was that if you wanted to email an *anon.penet.fi* user but wanted to show your own identity all you had to do was reverse the "an" to "na."

17. By September 1996, when the remailer closed, its database had reached 716,000. Helsingius won the 1997 Electronic Frontier Foundation Pioneer Award for his work setting up and maintaining the remailer.

18. Contemporaneous statements, and press material available on the Web at http://www.scientology.org.

19. Personal interview, March 1995.

20. The most important archive belongs to Ron Newman, one of the most knowledgeable people about the inner workings of the Net and its technology, and is maintained on his Web site at http://www2.thecia.net/~rnewman/scientology/home.html. For comparison, the CoS's extensive official pages are at http:.//www.scientology.org. Newman's page is mirrored at http://www.xs4all.nl/~kspaink/rnewman/home.html.

21. *Biased Journalism*'s complete run of issues is archived on the Web at http://wpxx02.toxi.uni-wuerzburg.de/~krasel/CoS/biased/.

22. Personal interview, August 1996.

23. Settle made a name for himself in Net-related circles when, at the 1994 Computers, Freedom, and Privacy Conference, he mistakenly identified (and arrested) a young graduate student named Lee Nussbaum thinking he was the hacker Kevin Mitnick, then wanted on probation violations (see chapter 10).

24. Personal interview, March 1995, by email.

25. Daniel Davidson died in 1996.

26. Ed Regis, *Great Mambo Chicken and the Transhuman Condition* (Viking, 1990).

27. A FAQ for Los Angeles–area ISPs on the subject of ARSBOMB and its methods, called "The What is Scientology? (ARSBOMB) Spam Team FAQ for Los Angeles Area ISPs," is at http://www.panix.com/~tbetz/WIS_Spam_Team_FAQ.html.

28. On the Web at http://home.sol.no/~heldal/CoS/index2.html.

29. On the Web at http://www.dtek.chalmers.se/~d1dd/cgi-bin/nots-locator.cgi. However, the link was removed after CoS complaints that it encouraged copyright violations.

30. Spaink's home page is at http://www.xs4all.nl/~kspaink/.

31. Quoted in *ARS in Review*, January 5, 1997, a weekly digest of significant postings from the newsgroup archived on the Web at http://wpxx02.toxi.uni-wuerzburg.de/~krasel/CoS/ars-summary.html. More detail about Mante's claims is available on the main Scientology Web site at http://www.scientology.org/p_jpg/scnnews/holl1_1.htm.

NOTES TO CHAPTER 7

1. Paulsen's censorship speech is archived on the Web at http://www.amdest.com/Pat/PatTV.html. It also appeared in Paulsen's book *How to Wage a Successful Campaign for the Presidency* (Nash Publishing, 1972).

2. Estimates taken from the text of the court decision on the CDA, dated June 11, 1996. On the Web at http://www.ciec.org/victory.shtml.

3. See Barlow's January 1992 column for *Communications of the ACM*,

archived on the Web at http://www.eff.org/pub/Publications/John_Perry_ Barlow/HTML/complete_acm_columns.html. Andrew Brown's comment appeared in a posting to the WELL's *eff* conference in May 1995.

4. The CIEC home page is at http://www.ciec.org.

5. Archived on the Web at http://www.ciec.org/decision_PA/960612_Exon_ prs.html.

6. In "The Great Renaming FAQ," archived at http://www.vrx.net/usenet/ history/rename.html.

7. Reposting dated February 8, 1995, to *alt.culture.usenet, news.misc,* and *alt. folklore.computers,* of original message posted April 29, 1993, and headed "That's all, folks" from Gene Spafford.

8. Notes regarding the campaign can be reached from http://www.rt66.com/ ~nlopez/links.htm along with the "ASG Anti-FAQ," one of the funnier reads on the Net.

9. Contemporaneous information posted on the WELL (media.1108/eff.730).

10. A list of the banned newsgroups, purportedly obtained from a Compu-Serve staffer, was circulated on the Net. A copy is archived on the Web at http://www.well.com/user/abacard.

11. French's letter, to a CIX user and dated September 8, 1996, is about "illegal material" on the Net, and says, in part, "Unfortunately, one or more individuals, presumably from within ISP's, decided to publish the list. In my view a very irresponsible act, and perhaps an indication of the unfortunate attitude that exists in some parts of the industry, who wish to wrongly label this as a censorship debate." The letter is archived on CIX as message number 186 in *censorship/ chatter.*

12. Archived at gopher://gopher.igc.apc.org:5000/oo/int/hrw/general.

13. More detailed and up-to-date information about international censorship of the Net is available from the "Plague of Freedom" home page, maintained by Declan McCullagh at http://www.eff.org/~declan/global/.

14. A Web site tracking British censorship issues is http://www.liberty.org. uk/cacib/.

15. In a September 1995 survey I did of blocking software for Britain's *Personal Computer World* magazine, I tested Net Nanny, Cyber Patrol, CyberSurfer, and WinWatch, and all were easily defeated.

16. Proposals archived on the Web at http://www.ispa.org.uk/safetypa.html.

17. Media blackouts during criminal trials are common in Canada and Britain; the point is not to censor the information permanently but to avoid undue influence on these countries' unsequestered juries.

18. In a foreword to the 1964 republication of the book that sparked the debates, *The Tailor and Anstey,* by Eric Cross (Chapman and Hall, 1964).

19. "Intellectual property," used loosely to include not only software and literary works of all types but also movies, music, and some types of art—anything that can be digitized into a computer file, however large. Figure quoted in Nico-

las S. Gikkas, "International Licensing of Intellectual Property: The Promise and the Peril," *Journal of Law and Technology Policy*, Spring 1996, and archived at http://journal.law.ufl.edu/~techlaw/1/gikkas.html.

20. A. Michael Froomkin, "The Internet as a Source of Regulatory Arbitrage," presented January 29, 1996, at the Symposium on Information National Policies and International Infrastructure, held at Harvard Law School. Published in *Borders in Cyberspace*, edited by Brian Kahin and Charles Nesson (MIT Press, 1996). Archived on the Web at http://www.law.miami.edu/.

21. See http://www.eff.org/pub/Alerts/Foreign_and_local for updates.

22. Journalist Brock Meeks, writing for *HotWired*'s Muckraker Web site, estimated that the passage of the CDA and the subsequent court cases cost taxpayers roughly $2 million. The column is archived at http://wwww.muckraker.com/muckraker/archive. On January 14, the ACLU filed suit against the State of New York over its CDA-like statute, signed into law by Governor George Pataki in September 1996.

NOTES TO CHAPTER 8

1. Personal interview, 1993, and an official CompuServe survey published November 1995.

2. Dee Brown, *Wondrous Times on the Frontier* (Arrow, 1994), 271–72.

3. Philip Robinson and Nancy Tamosaitis, *The Joy of Cybersex* (Brady, 1993).

4. Women's Wire is at http://www.women.com and also runs a forum on CompuServe at GO WWFORUM. AmazonCity is at http://www.amazoncity.com. A search site specializing in women's topics is at http://www.wwwomen.com.

5. Deborah Tannen, *You Just Don't Understand* (William Morrow, 1990).

6. Susan Herring, "Gender Differences in Computer-Mediated Communication: Bringing Familiar Baggage to the New Frontier," keynote talk at panel entitled "Making the Net*Work*: Is There a Z39.50 in Gender Communication?" American Library Association Annual Convention, Miami, June 27, 1994. On the Web at http://www.women-online.com/women/women-tech.html.

7. Susan Herring, "Gender and Democracy in Computer-Mediated Communication" (Communication Institute for Online Scholarship, 1993).

8. Lee Sproull and Sara Kiesler, *Connections* (MIT Press, 1991), 61.

9. Judy Anderson, "Not for the Faint of Heart: Contemplations on Usenet," in *Wired Women*, edited by Lynn Cherny and Elizabeth Reba Weise (Seal Press, 1996), 138.

10. *Independent*, December 12, 1996, 11.

11. *Newsweek*, May 16, 1994.

12. Carol Tavris, *The Mismeasure of Woman* (Touchstone, 1992), 62.

13. Ibid., 290 (emphasis added). She goes on to cite Candace West and Don Zimmerman, "Doing Gender," (*Gender and Society*, vol. 1, 1987, 125–51) as well as linguist Robin Lakoff and psychologists Linda Carli and Laurence D. Cohn.

14. Tavris, *Mismeasure of Woman,* 299.

15. Ellen Spertus, "Social and Technical Means for Fighting On-Line Harassment," presented at the Virtue and Virtuality: Gender, Law, and Cyberspace Conference, on April 20–21, 1996, at MIT, archived at http://www.ai.mit.edu/people/ellens/Gender/glc.

16. *Time,* July 19, 1993.

17. The original topics are preserved on the WELL as part of the system archives, where they can be read by any WELL member. The women concerned never named the WELL user in the public conference; instead they offered to email his name/user ID privately to anyone who requested it. The "cybercad" is long gone from the WELL; the women are still around.

18. Cherny and Weise, *Wired Women,* 146.

19. Ellen Balka, "The Accessibility of Computers to Organizations Serving Women in the Province of Newfoundland: Preliminary Study Results," *Electronic Journal of Virtual Culture,* vol. 2, no. 3. On the Web at http://www.inform.umd.edu/EdRes/Topic/WomensStudies/computing/Articles+ResearchPapers/online-access-feminism.

20. Personal archive.

21. Leslie Regan Shade, "Gender Issues in Computer Networking," presented at the Community Networking: the International Free-Net Conference, August 17–19, 1993, at Carleton University, Ottawa, Ontario. Archived on the Web at http://www.cpsr.org/cpsr/gender/leslie_regan_shade.txt.

22. Amy Bruckman, "Finding One's Own in Cyberspace," January 1996, archived at http://web.mit.edu/afs/athena/org/t/techreview/www/articles/jan96/Bruckman.html.

23. Quoted in Shade, "Gender Issues in Computer Networking."

24. Judy Heim, *The Needlecrafter's Computer Companion* (No Starch Press, 1995), 218.

NOTES TO CHAPTER 9

1. Issue 3 of *The Media Poll,* by John Marcus, January 30, 1997. *The Media Poll* is available via email from xx609@prairienet.org and is on the Web at http://www.etext.org/Zines/ASCII/TheMediaPoll/.

2. Catharine MacKinnon, *Only Words* (Harvard University Press, 1993), 11–12.

3. The June 1995 dismissal was upheld by the Sixth U.S. Circuit Court of Appeals in Cincinnati on January 31, 1997. Details about the case are at http://www.eff.org/pub/Legal/Cases/Baker_UMich_case/.

4. Jeff Goodell, "The Fevered Rise of America Online," *Rolling Stone,* October 3, 1996, 60–66.

5. "Porn again," *Personal Computer World,* March 1995.

6. A binary file is any type of non-text computer file, such as a picture, audio, video, or program file.

7. Shortly after HTML, the Web page formatting language, was modified to allow Web page designers to choose their own background colors, in an effort to boost their page hits some people embedded sexually explicit words in their pages by using the same color for text and backgrounds. The page would get picked up by keyword searches on any of the search engines, but wouldn't actually contain any sexual material when you got there.

8. Published in the *Georgetown Law Journal* 83 (June 1995): 1849–1934.

9. These were broken down as follows: 450,620 items downloaded 6.4 million times from sixty-eight adult BBSs; 75,000 items with an unspecified number of downloads from six adult BBSs, 391,790 items with no download information from seven adult BBSs. Rimm looked at many fewer pictures than this, saying he "randomly downloaded" 10,000 "actual images" from adult BBSs, Usenet, or CD-ROM and used these to verify the accuracy of the descriptive listings he had collected.

10. *Time*, July 24, 1995. The WELL discussion is summarized with extracts on *HotWired* at http://www.hotwired.com/special/pornscare.

11. Donna Hoffman and Thomas P. Novak, "A Detailed Analysis of the Conceptual, Logical, and Methodological Flaws in the Article 'Marketing Pornography on the Information Superhighway,'" July 1, 1995. (Although the cover date of the *Time* cyberporn issue was July 2, 1995, the magazine actually hit the stands on June 26.) Archived on the Web at http://www2000.ogsm.vanderbilt.edu.

12. Archived at http://www2000.ogsm.vanderbilt.edu.

13. Meeks moved on to become chief correspondent for *HotWired* in December 1995; in November 1996, he resigned and was almost immediately hired by the relatively new MSNBC. His *Cyberwire Dispatch* e-letter continues to appear irregularly and is available from http://cyberwerks.com:70/cyberwire/.

14. More information on HomeNet is at http://homenet.andrew.cmu.edu/Progress.

15. GIF stands for Graphic Interchange Format, a popular format for picture files that was developed by CompuServe. The phrase "Beware of geeks bearing .GIFs" was coined by British hacker-turned-respectable journalist and security consultant Robert Schifreen.

16. *Today* newspaper, September 29, 1994.

17. McCullagh moved on to Time-Warner's *Netly News* in the fall of 1996.

18. "Jacking in from the 'Keys to the Kingdom' Port," *Cyberwire Dispatch*, July 1996, archived on the Web at http://www.eff.org/pub/Publications/Declan_McCullagh/.

19. According to McCullagh, the president of Solid Oak, the manufacturer of CyberSitter, threatened to sue Meeks and McCullagh for infringing his copyright by reverse-engineering his database. A high-school student who did some investi-

gating (apparently on his own) and posted a list of blocked CyberSitter sites on his Web pages was also reportedly threatened.

20. On December 20, 1996, at http://www.netlynews.com. *Netly News* is Time-Warner's Web-based news service.

21. At http://www.pathfinder.com/netly/spoofcentral/censored/.

NOTES TO CHAPTER 10

1. Robert Bickford, "Are YOU a Hacker?" in *MicroTimes*, January 1989, and also on the Web at http://www.well.com/user/rab/ayah.html. The article was also reprinted in *Tricks of the Internet Gurus*, edited by Philip Baczewski (SAMS, 1994).

2. *Takedown*, by *New York Times* reporter John Markoff and security expert Tsutomu Shimomura (Hyperion 1996); Jonathan Littman, *The Fugitive Game* (Little, Brown, 1996); Jeff Goodell, *The Cyberthief and the Samurai* (Dell, 1996). Mitnick also occupied about a third of Katie Hafner and John Markoff's *Cyberpunk* (Simon and Schuster, 1991); Writing in *2600*, Mitnick characterized the section about him as "20 percent fabricated and libelous."

3. Personal interview, July 1996.

4. At http://www.2600.com.

5. John Perry Barlow, "Crime and Puzzlement," 1990, archived on the Web at http://www.eff.org/Publications/John_Perry_Barlow/HTML.

6. EEPROM stands for Electrically Erasable Programmable Read-Only Memory and is a programmable memory chip that allows you to update a device's internal workings without having to take it apart and physically replace the chip.

7. On the Web at http://www.fish.com/satan/. The program runs only under UNIX and only tests UNIX networks.

8. Markoff and Shimomura, *Takedown*, 105–6.

9. A script is a small program that essentially automates a series of commands that would otherwise have to be typed manually.

10. Forging email addresses is ridiculously easy to do, but doing so doesn't mean the forger has access to your email box.

11. In 1996, Prince Philip became the third member of the Royal Family to get caught with his signals down in embarrassing circumstances.

12. The hacked versions of the pages are archived on the *2600* Web site, http://www.2600.com.

13. More details on this hoax are in the "AOL's 'Child Fun' UCE FAQ," posted at the time to *alt.aol-sucks* and *news.admin.net-abuse.misc*, among others. Retrievable through Deja News (http://www.dejanews.com).

14. Available on Usenet as *comp.risks*, or via email. To subscribe send email to risks-request@csl.sri.com with the word "subscribe" in the message body. Old issues are archived at http://www.CSL.sri/risksinfo.html.

15. In a March 1993 interview for *Personal Computer World,* reprinted in Wendy Grossman, *Remembering the Future* (Springer Verlag, 1997).

16. At Access All Areas Conference, July 1996, London.

17. "Information Security: Computer Attacks at Department of Defense Pose Increasing Risks," dated May 22, 1996, and designated GAO/AIMD-96-84. The report can be accessed on the Web at http://www.access.gpo.gov.

18. Paul A. Strassman and William Marlow, "Risk-Free Access into the Global Information Infrastructure via Anonymous Remailers," presented at the Symposium on the Global Information Infrastructure: Information Policy and International Infrastructure, January 28–30, 1996, Kennedy School of Government, Harvard University.

19. Interview for *Wired UK,* September 1996.

20. Ivars Peterson, *Fatal Defect* (Random House, 1995).

21. A write-up of how this works is at http://www.cs.princeton.edu/sip/.

NOTES TO CHAPTER 11

1. Banning someone from a CompuServe forum is a matter of assigning a software setting, known as a "flag," to that member's numbered user ID that tells the forum software not to let him or her in. Forum sysops have fairly wide discretion in these matters, but you are expected to consult with the product managers assigned to your forum, who can advise against it if they feel the member's behavior isn't egregious enough. Ultimately, though, it's up to the sysops: CompuServe seen close up is more like a collection of tiny kingdoms than it is the seamless monolith it appears to be at first.

2. "Net.Legends FAQ (Noticeable Phenomena of Usenet)," maintained by David DeLaney and archived at http://www.math.uiuc.edu/~tskirvin/faqs/legends.

3. There's a well-known sophisticated UNIX command called *grep* that allows you to search files for specific text strings; a couple of Usenet legends have used this to scan an entire Usenet feed and collect all the articles using a particular word. An entire religion, kibology, was created this way by a Usenet poster named James Kibo; he used to grep all of Usenet for his name, and then would answer postings unexpectedly. For more see *alt.religion.kibology.*

4. Maintained by M. Legare and archived at http://www.wetware.com/mlegare/kotm/.

5. At http://www.demon.co.uk/castle/helena/.

6. Deja News (http://www.dejanews.com) is a Usenet search service that holds archives of all of Usenet since early 1995. Many people are concerned about the loss of privacy involved in allowing permanent archiving of messages written in the expectation that they would be ephemeral. The X-no-archive header is easily inserted by typing in "X-no-archive:yes" at the top of Usenet postings before they're sent out, but too few people know about it and some new archiving services don't honor it.

7. Julian Dibbell, "A Rape in Cyberspace; or How an Evil Clown, a Haitian Trickster Spirit, Two Wizards, and a Cast of Dozens Turned a Database into a Society," *Village Voice*, December 21, 1993. Reprinted with other related material in *High Noon on the Electronic Frontier: Conceptual Issues in Cyberspace*, edited by Peter Ludlow (MIT Press, 1996), 376–95.

NOTES TO CHAPTER 12

1. Donna L. Hoffman and Thomas P. Novak, "Wanted: Net.Census," *Wired*, November 1994, 93–94.

2. All of Hoffman's and Novak's papers, plus a comprehensive set of links to other, related research and source material is at the Project 2000 Web site, http://www2000.ogsm.vanderbilt.edu.

3. Peter Lewis, "Doubts Are Raised on Actual Number of Internet Users," by *New York Times*, August 10, 1994, 1.

4. At http://www.nw.com/zone/WWW/top.html.

5. At gopher://gopher.tic.com:70/00/matrix/news/v4/faq.406.old.

6. The Executive Summary of the CommerceNet/Nielsen study is available on the Web at http://www.nielsenmedia.com.

7. Donna L. Hoffman, William D. Kalsbeek, and Thomas P. Novak, "Internet Use in the United States: 1995 Baseline Estimates and Preliminary Market Segments," *Communications of the ACM*, December 1996, special issue on "The Internet@Home." Draft dated April 12, 1996, available on the Web at http://www2000.ogsm.vanderbilt.edu.

8. Nielsen's rebuttal is on its Web site at http://www.nielsenmedia.com.

9. A comparative study of the various surveys is on Stanford Research International's Web site at http://www.sri.com.

10. Archived at http://future.sri.com/vals/trends.

11. Darrell Huff, *How to Lie with Statistics* (Penguin, 1954), 121.

12. Donna Hoffman and Tom Novak, "New Metrics for New Media: Toward the Development of Web Measurement Standards," *World Wide Web Journal* 2, no. 1 (winter 1997): 213–46, available on the Web at http://www2000.ogsm.vanderbilt.edu.

13. Estimates quoted by Hoffman and Novak from research organizations Bear Sterns and Jupiter.

14. According to market research specialist Jupiter; on the Web at http://www.jup.com.

15. The Anonymizer is at http://www.anonymizer.com. Internet Fast Forward belongs to Privnet, which in 1996 was bought up by PGP, Inc., and is available at http://www.pgp.com.

16. You, too, can become an alien abductee by signing up at http://www.slime.org/aliens.

17. GVU's Sixth WWW User Survey was conducted via a series of question-

naires available at their Web site from October 10 to November 10, 1996; the results were made available on December 10, 1996. The semiannual surveys began in January 1994, shortly after forms and scripts became available on the Web for the first time.

18. Cynthia Crossen, *Tainted Truth: The Manipulation of Fact in America* (Simon and Schuster, 1994), 112.

19. GVU's definitions of these terms came from the Advocates for Self-Government.

NOTES TO CHAPTER 13

1. Clifford Stoll, *Silicon Snake Oil* (Macmillan, 1995).

2. For an example of such an argument, see John Browning, "Universal Service (An Idea Whose Time Is Past)," *Wired*, September 1994, 102ff.

3. "Presidential Campaigning from 1960–1996: From Televised Debates to the Internet and Beyond," with The Honorable Edward M. Kennedy, John Perry Barlow, Kiki Moore, Sander Vanocur, Lisa McCormack, and John F. Kennedy, Jr. (Moderator), held at the John F. Kennedy School of Government at Harvard University on July 2, 1996. The panel discussion is archived on the Web at http://ksgwww.harvard.edu/~ksgpress/jfkforum.htm.

4. Robert W. McChesney, "Telecon! US Communications Law: Where We've Been and Where We're Headed," reprinted in the *Radio Resistor's Bulletin* 13 (winter 1996), archived on the Web at http://www.hear.com/rw/feature/rrb13.html.

5. Malamud's Town Hall site was at http://www.town.hall.org (it was taken down in April 1996).

6. As an example, a copy of the 1994 report on Computer Pornography cost £15.60 (about $23).

7. Personal interview for the *Guardian*, March 1993.

8. Department of Commerce, "Falling Through the Net: A Survey of the 'Have Nots' in Rural and Urban America," archived on the Web at http://www.ntia.doc.gov/ntiahome/fallingthru.html.

9. "Future Planning Document," at http://www/efi.org.ie/forfas/latestFPD.html (but currently unavailable).

10. Organization for Economic Cooperation and Development, "Information Infrastructure Convergence and Pricing the Internet," archived on the Web at http://www.oecd.org/dsti/gd_docs/s96_xxe.html.

11. At http://www2.echo.lu/archive/parliament/en/resoluti.html.

12. In fact, Pizza Hut (http://www.pizzahut.com) began accepting orders electronically in 1995 (orders are forwarded to your nearest franchise), and there is also a Pizza server (information is at http://www.ecst.csuchico.edu/~pizza), which given your instructions (in rather obscure command-line language) will email you a picture (or rather, a .GIF file) of a pizza built to specifications.

13. For some examples of this, see Pamela Samuelson, "The Copyright Grab," *Wired*, January 1996, 135ff.

14. *EFFector* 9, no. 14 (December 10, 1996), archived at http://www.eff.org/pub/EFF/Newsletters/EFFector/.

15. Further analysis of the treaty by the Digital Future Coalition, including comments from the EFF, is at http://www.dfc.org.

16. After press coverage raised questions about privacy, Nabil blocked off access to the plates database; in early 1997 the entire site was gone.

17. Survey.net is at http://www.survey.net.

18. At http://www.dejanews.com.

19. At http://www.reference.com.

20. GVU's sixth survey showed that as many as 25 percent of Web users browse at least some of the time without graphics; the percentage is higher in Europe, where connections are slower and more expensive.

21. The W3 Consortium's Disabilities page is at http://www.w3.org/pub/WWW/Disabilities/Activity.html. There is more information at the Yuri Rubinsky Insight Foundation's "Universal Access to the National Information Infrastructure" Web page at http://www.yuri.org/webable/univ-acc.html.

22. Nicolas S. Gikkas, "International Licensing of Intellectual Property: The Promise and the Peril," *Journal of Law and Technology Policy*, Spring 1996, archived at http://journal.law.ufl.edu/~techlaw/1/gikkas.html.

23. Zielinski moved on to the London-based Author's Licensing and Collection Society in mid-1996.

24. W. Wayt Gibbs, "Lost Science in the Third World," *Scientific American*, August 1995, 76–83.

25. Access to Africa Index Medicus is available via the WHO's Web site at http://www-pll.who.ch/programmes/pll/hlt/countrye.htm.

26. Andrew M. Odlyzko, "Tragic Loss or Good Riddance? The Impending Demise of Traditional Scholarly Journals" July 16, 1994, on the Web at http://mosaic.cecm.sfu.ca/projects/document_vault.html.

27. Christopher Zielinski, "The Electronic Age and the Information Poor: Threats and Opportunities," *Online Information Proceedings*, 1996, 507–21.

NOTES TO CHAPTER 14

1. Public letters to AOL members from CEO Steve Case (August 7, 1996) and U.K. managing director Jonathan Bulkeley (August 9, 1996).

2. Sharon Eisner Gillett and Mitchell Kapor, "The Self-Governing Internet: Coordination by Design," presented at the Coordination and Administration of the Internet Workshop, Kennedy School of Government, Harvard University, September 8–10, 1996. Archived on the Web at http://ccs.mit.edu/ccswp197.html.

3. Ibid.

4. Transcription of the FCC Bandwidth Forum, held January 23, 1997, in

Washington, D.C. Both the transcript and the audio broadcast of the day's proceedings are archived on the FCC's Web site at http://www.fcc.gov.

5. Shabbir Safdar, "Is the Phone System Broken?" *VTW Billwatch*, Issue 72, January 25, 1997. Archived on the Web at http://www.vtw.org/archive/970125_090725.html.

6. Personal interview, March 1996, which appeared in the *Independent* as "Father to the Ethernet," June 10, 1996.

7. "The Economics of the Internet: Too Cheap to Meter?" *Economist*, October 19, 1996.

8. Ibid.

9. Neal Stephenson, "Mother Earth Mother Board," *Wired*, December 1996, 95–161.

10. There have already been cases where poorly designed spiders and Web crawlers—automated indexing agents—have caused problems by hogging resources. See David Eichmann, "Ethical Web Agents," at http://rbse.jsc.nasa.gov/eichmann/www-f94/ethics/ethics.html; Martin Koster, "Guidelines for Robot Writers," at http://info.webcrawler.com/mak/projects/robots/guidelines.html; and Koster, "WWW Robot FAQ," at http://info.webcrawler.com/mak/projects/robots/faq.html.

11. For a fuller discussion of the players in providing broadband access, see Steven E. Miller, *Civilizing Cyberspace* (ACM Press, 1996).

12. Derneval, "The Brazilian Phone System," *2600 Magazine*, autumn 1996, 11–13.

13. In a presentation to the Internet Economics Workshop held at MIT, March 9 and 10, 1995. Notes from the workshop are archived on the Web at http://rpcp.mit.edu/Workshops/cfp.html.

14. Personal interview, November 1996.

15. Stephenson, "Mother Earth Mother Board," 103.

NOTES TO CHAPTER 15

1. Personal interview, July 1996.

2. A. Michael Froomkin, "The Essential Role of Trusted Third Parties in Electronic Commerce," *Oregon Law Review* 75, no. 1 (Spring 1996): 75–115. Archived on Froomkin's Web site, at http://www.law.miami.edu/~froomkin.

3. The development of Java, a programming language created at Sun Microsystems in which programs may be written once but run on any computer using special emulator software inside a Web browser, is expected to open up precisely this type of "out-sourced" application. Instead of buying a big, fat word processor with every feature under the sun, you might instead pay for special features only when you need them, running them by accessing the appropriate Web site.

4. Archived at http://www.forrester.com.

5. The draft proposal is at http://www.w3.org/pub/WWW/TR/WD-mptp.

6. A summary of proposed electronic payment mechanisms with links to the relevant organizations is at http://www2.echo.lu./oii/en/payment.html.

7. VeriSign's Web site is at http://www.verisign.com.

8. At http://www.doubleclick.net.

9. In November 1996, Privnet was bought by PGP, Inc.

10. An explanation of cookies and what they do is available at Donna Hoffman and Tom Novak's Project 2000 site, http://www2000.ogsm.vanderbilt.edu. In fact, they're more easily defeated than most Net users realize. Instead of setting your browser to alert you every time a site asks to write a cookie, which turns browsing into a continually interrupted experience, open an empty file in a text editor and save it as cookies.txt in the same directory as your existing file and set it to read-only.

11. Personal interview, September 1996.

12. Burst! Media is at http://www.burstmedia.com.

13. The Advertising Standards Authority passed its first judgment against a claim made on a Web site in 1996; the records of its judgments are at http://www.asa.org.uk.

14. The FDA held a forum on October 16–17, 1996, "FDA and the Internet: Advertising and Promotion of Medical Products." Transcripts and audio recordings of the sessions are at http://www.fda.gov/opacom/morechoices/transcript1096/fdainet.html.

15. HumanSearch is at http://www.humansearch.w1.com; a write-up of the service appeared in the *Netly News* on February 7, 1997.

16. From the eTrust Web site, at http://etrust.org.

NOTES TO CHAPTER 16

1. Archived on Barlow's Web site, at http://www.eff.org/~barlow.

2. John Perry Barlow, "Coming into the Country," *Communications of the ACM*, January 1991; and Barlow, "Bill o' Rights Lite," *Communications of the ACM*, March 1993. The complete set of Barlow's Electronic Frontier columns through March 1995 is on the Web at http://www.eff.org/pub/Publications/John_Perry_Barlow/HTML/complete_acm_columns.html.

3. Personal interview for "Freedom from a Strange, New Land," *Daily Telegraph*, April 16, 1996.

4. Ibid.

5. Paulina Borsook, "The Memoirs of a Token: An Aging Berkeley Feminist Examines *Wired*," in *Wired Women: Gender and New Realities in Cyberspace*, edited by Elizabeth Reba Weise and Lynn Cherny (Seal Press, 1996), 40.

6. Paulina Borsook, "Cyberselfish," *Mother Jones*, July 1996. Archived on the Web at http://www.mojones.com/.

7. Douglas Adams, *Hitchhiker's Guide to the Galaxy*, the book (Harmony Books, 1979), the BBC Radio series, the BBC TV series, and the record set.

8. In a spring 1995, speech to the American Society of Newspaper Editors, quoted in Edwin Diamond and Stephen Bates, "Law and Order Comes to Cyberspace," *Tech Review*, October 1995. Archived on the Web at http://web.mit.edu/afs/athena/org/t/techreview/www/articles/oct95/Diamond.html.

9. Based on examples from the Australia-based Lantana International Agency catalogue at http://www.kineticmedia.com.au/lantana.

10. Amy Bruckman, "'Democracy' in Cyberspace: Lessons from a Failed Political Experiment," presented at the Virtue and Virtuality Conference, MIT, April 20–21, 1996. Archived on the Web at http://web.mit.edu/womens-studies/www/bruckman.html.

Additional References

Alderman, Ellen, and Caroline Kennedy. *The Right to Privacy*. Alfred A. Knopf, 1995.

Cornwall, Hugo, and Steve Gold. *New Hacker's Handbook*. Century, 1989.

Davies, Simon. *Big Brother: Britain's Web of Surveillance and the New Technological Order*. Pan, 1996.

Garfinkel, Simson. *PGP: Pretty Good Privacy*. O'Reilly and Associates, 1995.

Hafner, Katie, and Matthew Lyon. *Where Wizards Stay Up Late: The Origins of the Internet*. Simon and Schuster, 1996.

Hardin, Garrett. "The Tragedy of the Commons." *Science*, December 13, 1968. Archived on the Web at http://www.dac.neu.edu/DACHomePage/common.html.

Harrison, Mark. *The Usenet Handbook*. O'Reilly and Associates, 1995.

Kling, Rob. *Computerization and Controversy*. Second Edition, Academic Press, 1996.

Miller, Steven E. *Civilizing Cyberspace*. ACM Press (Addison Wesley), 1996.

Ronfeldt, David. *Cyberocracy Is Coming*. Taylor and Francis, 1992.

Rose, Lance. *Netlaw: Your Rights in the Online World*. Osborne/McGraw-Hill, 1995.

Schneier, Bruce. *Applied Cryptography*. Second Edition. Wiley, 1996.

Sterling, Bruce. *The Hacker Crackdown*. Bantam, 1992.

Turkle, Sherry. *Life on the Screen*. Simon and Schuster, 1995.

Wallace, Jonathan, and Mark Mangan. *Sex, Laws, and Cyberspace: Freedom and Censorship on the Frontiers of the Online Revolution*. Henry Holt, 1996.

Zimmermann, Philip R. *The Official PGP User's Guide*. MIT Press, 1995.

Index

About the Author

Wendy M. Grossman is an American writer based in London since 1990 and a graduate of Cornell University (1975). She writes primarily about science and technology for publications such as *New Scientist* and the national newspaper *The Daily Telegraph* and has also written for *Wired*. Her collection of interviews with leading computer industry figures, *Remembering the Future: Interviews from Personal Computer World*, was released in January 1997 by Springer Verlag.

She was founder of Britain's *The Skeptic* (http://www.cs.man.ac.uk/skeptic) magazine in 1987; it is a publication dedicated to scientific examination of paranormal claims. Before that, she was an internationally obscure folksinger travelling the United States, Canada, and various European countries with a banjo, guitar, and concertina. She made one record, *Roseville Fair*, which was released on Lincoln House Records in 1980.

Her personal Web page is at http://www.well.com/~wendyg, and she is best emailed at wendyg@skeptic.demon.co.uk. We warn, however, that she can be a shade on the irritable side, so before emailing that address you might want to check the mood button on the Web page for a prediction as to what kind of response you're likely to get.